THE DIVE SITES OF
THE CAYMAN ISLANDS

LAWSON WOOD

Series Consultant: Nick Hanna

PASSPORT BOOKS
NTC/Contemporary Publishing Group

Lawson Wood is a highly experienced diver and is considered one of the world's leading underwater photographers.

This edition first published in 1997 by
Passport Books
A division of NTC/Contemporary Publishing Group, Inc.
4255 West Touhy Avenue, Lincolnwood (Chicago), Illinois, 60646-1975
U.S.A.

Updated in 1998

International Standard Book Number: 0-8442-4864-9
Library of Congress Catalog Card Number: on file

First published in the UK in 1995 by
New Holland Publishers (UK) Ltd
London • Cape Town • Sydney • Auckland

Project development: Charlotte Parry-Crooke
Series editors: Charlotte Fox, Lynn Bresler, Pete Duncan
Design concept: Philip Mann, ACE Ltd
Design/cartography: ML Design
Cover design: Peter Bosman
Index: Alex Corrin

Typeset by ML Design, London
Reproduction by Hirt and Carter, South Africa
Printed and bound in Malaysia by Times Offset (m) Sdn Bdh

All the photographs in this book were taken by Lawson Wood with the exception of the following: Department of Tourism 63; Footprints (Nick Hanna) 9, 47 bottom right, 126; Paul Kay 7, 49, 85, 122, 123, 150.

PHOTOGRAPHY

The author's photographs were taken using Nikonos III, Nikonos IVA, Nikonos V, Nikon F–801, Nikon F–90 and the Pentax LX. Lenses used on the amphibious Nikonos system were 35mm; 15mm; 12mm and various extension tubes. The lenses for the housed Nikons' and Pentax were 14mm; 50mm; 60mm; 105mm; 28–200mm zoom and 70–300mm zoom; housing manufacture by Subal in Austria and Hugyphot in Switzerland.

Electronic flash, supplied by Sea & Sea Ltd, was used in virtually all of the underwater photographs: YS20, YS50, YS200 and YS300. For the land cameras, the Nikon SB24 and SB26 were used. Film stock used was Fujichrome Velvia, Fujichrome Provia and Fujichrome RDP.

Title page: *Juvenile Queen Angelfish, Holacanthus ciliaris.*
Contents page: *Diver at Stingray City.*

AUTHOR'S ACKNOWLEDGEMENTS

Writing and compiling information for this style of dive guide book has required a great amount of support and help from many local experts. Of the many people who have provided time, effort and assistance in the Cayman Islands, I would like to express my sincere appreciation to:

- Judith Greeven, Judy McCluskey and Bronwen Griffiths of Sugden McCluskey Associates who provided the logistical support in all my endeavours in and out of the Cayman Islands
- Catherine Leech, Regional Manager and Vicky from the Cayman Islands Department of Tourism in London who were unflappable, committed and enthusiastic for the project from its inception
- Barbara Currie Dailey who was the hands–on expert with the necessary statistical information and Mrs L. Angela Martins, the Director of Tourism whose encouragement and support was vital
- Gina Ebanks–Petrie, the Assistant Director of the Protection and Conservation Unit of the Cayman Islands Department of Environment along with Phil Bush and Mike Grundy who spearhead marine conservation in Cayman waters and install the mooring buoys
- Michael Greenberg and Cayman Island Divers – Branch #360 of the British Sub–Aqua Club who man and operate the Islands' only Hyperbaric recompression chamber – our safety net
- David Feinberg and Ruth Purwin at Little Cayman Beach Resort; Gladys Howard and Gay Morse at Pirates Point; Stevo Schwartz at Divi Resorts; Cornell Burke from Brac Aquatics – an absolute mine of information
- Ronnie and Burnley (Bunny) Foster, owners of Indies Suites, without whose help I would have struggled even more
- Penny Williams, Janice Monk, Tim 'Bradley' and Barry Poppleton of Indies Divers who showed me the way
- Wayne Hasson and the many and varied crew and guests of the Cayman Aggressor who introduced me to Bloody Bay
- Peter Millburn of Dive Cayman, staunch and active conservationist; Keith Neale at the Morritts Tortuga Club for East End dive sites
- Frank at Eden Rock
- Dennis Denton, Al and Steve at the Atlantis Submarine
- Cathy Church and Adrien Briggs at Sunset House
- Atlee Ebanks at the Cayman Turtle Farm
- The Cayman Islands National Museum
- Northwest Airlines
- Caledonian operated by British Airways
- Cayman Airways and Island Air who provided the aerial support
- Last but not least my wife Lesley who helps in more ways than I care to admit

PUBLISHERS' ACKNOWLEDGEMENTS

The publishers gratefully acknowledge the generous assistance during the compilation of this book of Nick Hanna for his involvement in developing the series and consulting throughout and Dr Elizabeth M. Wood for acting as Marine Biological Consultant on the series.

CONTENTS

FEATURES

How to use this Book

THE REGIONS
The dive sites included in the book are divided into the three islands: Grand Cayman, Cayman Brac and Little Cayman. Regional introductions describe the key characteristics and features of these areas and provide background information on climate, the environment, points of interest, and advantages and disadvantages of diving in the locality.

THE MAPS
A map is included near the front of each regional or subregional section. The prime purpose of the maps is to identify the location of the dive sites described and to provide other useful information for divers and snorkellers. Though reefs are indicated, the maps do not set out to provide detailed nautical information such as exact reef contours or water depths. In general the maps show: the locations of the dive sites, indicated by white numbers in red boxes corresponding to those placed at the start of the individual dive site descriptions; the locations of key access points to the sites (ports, marinas, beach resorts and so on); reefs and wrecks. (Note: the border around the maps is not a scale bar.)

MAP LEGEND

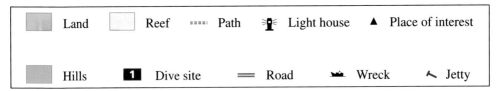

| Land | Reef | ::::: Path | Light house | ▲ Place of interest |
| Hills | **1** Dive site | = Road | Wreck | Jetty |

THE DIVE SITE DESCRIPTIONS
Placed within the geographical sections are the descriptions of each region's premier dive sites. Each site description starts with a number (to enable the site to be located on the relevant map), a star rating (see below), and a selection of key symbols (see below). Crucial practical details (on location, access, conditions, typical visibility and minimum and maximum depths) precede the description of the site, its marine life and special points of interest. In these entries, 'typical visibility' assumes good conditions.

THE STAR RATING SYSTEM

Each site has been awarded a star rating, with a maximum of five red stars for diving and five blue stars for snorkelling.

Diving		*Snorkelling*	
★★★★★	first class	★★★★★	first class
★★★★	highly recommended	★★★★	highly recommended
★★★	good	★★★	good
★★	average	★★	average
★	poor	★	poor

THE SYMBOLS

The symbols placed at the start of each site description provide a quick reference to crucial information pertinent to individual sites.

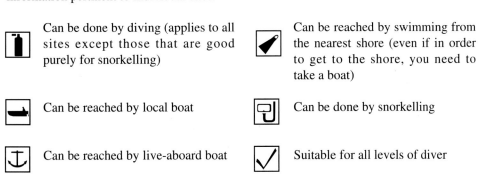

Can be done by diving (applies to all sites except those that are good purely for snorkelling)

Can be reached by swimming from the nearest shore (even if in order to get to the shore, you need to take a boat)

Can be reached by local boat

Can be done by snorkelling

Can be reached by live-aboard boat

Suitable for all levels of diver

THE REGIONAL DIRECTORIES

A 'regional directory', which will help you plan and make the most of your trip, is included at the end of each regional or sub-regional section. Here you will find, where relevant, practical information on how to get to an area, where to stay and eat and available dive facilities. Local 'non-diving' highlights are also described, with suggestions for sightseeing and excursions.

OTHER FEATURES

At the start of the book you will find practical details and tips about travelling to and in The Caymans, as well as a general introduction to the islands. Also provided is a wealth of information about the general principles and conditions of diving in the area. Throughout the book, features and small fact panels on topics of interest to divers and snorkellers are included. As the end of the book are sections on the marine environment (including coverage of marine life, conservation and codes of practice) and underwater photography and video. Also to be found here is information on health, safety and first aid as well as a guide to marine creatures to look out for when diving in The Cayman Islands.

INTRODUCTION TO THE CAYMAN ISLANDS

The Cayman Islands are a British Crown Colony, one of six remaining in the South Atlantic/Caribbean region. Situated 240km (150m) south of Cuba and 288km (180m) west of Jamaica in the central Caribbean, the largest of the three Cayman Islands is Grand Cayman. Her smaller sisters, Cayman Brac and Little Cayman, are located some 144km (90m) northeast of Grand Cayman. The three islands are situated on the edge of the Cayman Trench, a 7500m (25000ft) trough which is the deepest part of Caribbean waters.

Above sea level the vegetation on the islands is rather scrub-like and there is little break in the topography. However, the beaches are superb and Seven Mile Beach – which is actually only 5.6m (9km) long – on the west coast of Grand Caymans is justifiably world famous. The diving to be found here is world class and the Caymans are quite rightly listed as one of the top diving destinations in the world.

A Brief History of the Caymans

Christopher Columbus discovered the Cayman Islands on 10 May 1503, after crossing the Atlantic and the Caribbean in his fourth and last attempt to find the alternative route to Cathay (China). The ships were en route from Panama to Hispaniola (the Dominican Republic) when they were blown well off their course. With little food left on board, the crew decided to tack north in a last desperate attempt to reach land – and came across Cayman Brac and Little Cayman. The log entry written by Ferdinand Columbus, the Admiral's son, records '...we were in sight of two very small islands, full of tortoise (turtle), as was the sea about, in so much as they looked like little rocks'. They named the islands 'Las Tortugas' – which is Spanish for tortoise. A 1523 map named the islands 'Lagartos' which means large lizard, and by 1530 the name had changed yet again to 'Caymanas' which is the Carib Indian word for the marine crocodile. By the time Sir Francis Drake arrived on the islands in 1586, the name 'Caymans' had stuck.

Cayman crocodiles were once prolific on the islands and – like the turtles – were also an important source of food. The many years that ships were provisioned on the islands had a

---

Opposite: *East end beach, one of the many beautiful beaches on Grand Cayman.*
Above: *Yachts and paddle boats on Seven Mile Beach, Grand Cayman.*

drastic effect on the turtle population and it is only in the last decade that serious attempts have been made to breed and protect the turtles. The last of the Cayman crocodiles had vanished off Little Cayman by the beginning of this century, but the Cayman blue iguana, though an endangered species, is still fairly prolific to this day.

In 1654, Oliver Cromwell sought to oust the Spanish from the Caribbean; Admiral Sir William Penn and General Robert Venebles launched an attack on Hispaniola with 7000 men. After their defeat at St Domingo, the army then went on successfully to attack Jamaica. Cromwell had entered the Caribbean not only to rid himself of the Royalist sympathisers, he had already thought to colonise both Jamaica and the Cayman Islands – and it was from these early volunteers that the first colonisation of the Cayman Islands took place. The first recorded settlement was of Little Cayman and Cayman Brac between 1666 and 1671 whilst Sir Thomas Modyford was installed as Governor of Jamaica.

On 14 April 1670 the Spanish successfully attacked the turtle station at Hudson's Hole (South Hole) on Little Cayman. However, their glory was short-lived because the Treaty of Madrid in 1670 stated that Jamaica, and their dependency the Cayman Islands, were ceded by Spain to the British Crown. During the lawless years that followed, Grand Cayman became renowned as a pirate stronghold and the infamous Blackbeard (Edward Teach) stopped regularly for fresh water and provisions, as did other notorious pirates of that era such as Neal Walker and Henry Morgan. They would have anchored their ships off Hogsty Bay on Grand Cayman or Stake Bay on Cayman Brac.

By 1713, peace reigned once more and by 1730 the last of the pirates and privateers were finally wiped out. Stories of hidden treasure on the islands attracted even more settlers and adventurers who, by bringing their slaves and servants with them, contributed further to the already increasing population.

The first royal land grant, signalling a permanent settlement on Grand Cayman, was recorded in 1734, covering land between Prospect and North Sound. By the early 1770s there were 175 settlers registered on Grand Cayman – though none at all on Cayman Brac and Little Cayman. A population census in 1802 stated that there were 545 slaves in a total population of 933. The population gradually increased and, when slavery was outlawed in Britain in 1835, many of the slave ships were intercepted in Cayman waters and their human cargo released on to Grand Cayman. Assimilation and inter-marriage soon followed with the end result of a happy mixture of people living in harmony.

The Cayman Islands became a Crown Colony under the jurisdiction of the Governor of Jamaica. When Jamaica gained her independence in 1962 the Cayman Islands opted to remain a British Crown Colony and have remained so ever since and there is a still a sense of British tradition on the islands.

THE CAYMAN ISLANDS TODAY

The history of the Caymans' tax free status dates back to 8 February 1794 when the lead ship of a group of ten merchant traders was blown onto the treacherous reefs and shoals at Gun Bay off the east end of Grand Cayman. All ten ships were wrecked but the Caymanians rallied together and managed to save every single passenger and crew member. King George III of England was so grateful to the islanders, and so impressed by their bravery, that he granted them freedom from taxation in perpetuity.

> **RELIGION**
>
> There are around 90 places of worship on Grand Cayman, including Anglican, Church of God, Wesleyan, Catholic, United Church of Jamaica, Baptist, Seventh Day Adventists, Moravian, Bahai, Hindu, Muslim and Jehovah Witness. English is spoken everywhere and all the local publications are written in English.

Above: *The shoreline on the east coast of Grand Cayman is marked by the spiky rock, ironstone.*
Below: *There is seldom a footprint to be found on the unspoilt beaches of Little Cayman.*

The Cayman Islands still enjoy this tax free status and have become one of the world's leading offshore financial centres and the world's largest island banking location boasting 560 licensed A and B class banks, 380 insurance companies and 31,612 registered corporations (making it the fifth largest financial centre worldwide). This successful offshore financial industry dates back to 1966 when the first banking and trust laws were passed. At one time the number of registered companies and corporations outnumbered the population. The financial gain from these institutions has helped fund the construction of hotels, condominiums, tourism infrastructure and diving facilities.

The Caymans' central position in the Caribbean has also been instrumental in their popularity as a stop-over point for travellers, particularly those attracted by the tax free shopping. Several cruise ships dock each week just outside the capital of George Town and disgorge tourists by the hundreds to snap up luxury duty-free items and other goods.

Most of the tourism and financial activity is centred around the capital George Town. Seven Mile Beach along West Side has the largest concentration of hotels, restaurants and condominiums. There are also many smaller guest houses situated all over Grand Cayman as well as on her sister islands.

Bottom: *Dive boats in the sunset near Cayman Brac.*

WRECK OF THE TEN SAILS

Through detailed research by Dr Margaret Leshikar Denton and the Cayman Islands National Museum, more of the story about the Wreck of the Ten Sails has come to light.

On 8 February 1794, and not November 1788 as originally thought, ten merchant vessels ran aground off the treacherous reefs in Grand Cayman's East End. Led by HMS Convert and captained by William Martin, the lead ship hit the reef and fired a cannon as a signal to warn the others following. Unfortunately the other vessels mistook this signal as a warning that they were being attacked by pirates and hastily sped to their impending doom. En route to England via Jamaica with 58 ships in all, six of the ships were wrecked but four were eventually able to be salvaged and continued on their way to England. Most of the cannon from the remaining wrecked ships were eventually salvaged and sent to England as scrap. The area is now known as Gun Bay.

Not all of the ships' names were discovered but the ten included HMS Convert, the Cordelia, Dean, Romanoff, Skudland, El Rica, Florence and HMS Caradosa. Contrary to enduring belief and popular legend, the convoy of ships did not carry Prince William, the future King William IV, or in fact any member of the royal family.

The daring rescue and salvage by the local Caymanians so impressed King George III, that he granted the Islands ' freedom from taxation, in perpetuity '. At the time, America and England were still estranged after America declared independence on 4 July 1766. George Washington became America's first President in 1789 and he was still in office when the ten unfortunate ships hit the reef off Grand Cayman. Smarting from the loss of the 'colonies', when Britain was ousted in 1783, it is more than likely that King George was still 'hedging his bets' in the Caribbean. Once America became the 'United States' after the Treaty of Paris was drawn up establishing the US boundaries, he was making certain that the central Caribbean Islands would remain loyal to the throne.

TOURISM OFFICES AND TOURISM

Tourism in the Cayman Islands has grown beyond all expectations since 1966, when the Islands' Department of Tourism was formed. That year, arrivals totalled 8,054. Ten years later the figure had risen to 64,875, by 1986 it had reached 166,100, and, with more cruise ships arriving, it rose to 940,878 in 1994, with 341,491 people arriving by air. Now, about 79 per cent of tourists are from the USA In terms of diving and other water sports, these numbers have represented over $16,250,000 input into the islands' economy. It is estimated that one–third of all air arrivals come to dive. With direct flights from the UK, the market saw a dramatic rise of 81 per cent in 1994 over the previous year.

The Department of Tourism maintains offices at home and abroad to assist those wishing to visit the Cayman Islands.

CAYMAN ISLANDS
The Pavilion, Cricket Square, PO Box 67, George Town, Grand Cayman Island.
tel toll free (from USA): 800–346–3313
tel: 949–0623
fax: 949–4053

UNITED STATES OF AMERICA
Chicago: 9525 West Bryn Mawr, 160, Rosemount, IL 60018.

tel: 708–678–6446
fax: 708–678–6675
Houston: Two Memorial City Plaza, 820 Gessner, Suite 170, Houston, TX.
tel: 713–461–1317
fax: 713–461–1829
Los Angeles: 3440 Wiltshire Boulevard, Suite 1202, Los Angeles, CA 90010.
tel: 213–738–1968
fax: 213–738–1829
Miami: 6100 Blue Lagoon Drive, Suite 150, Miami, FL 33126–2085.
tel: 305–266–2300
fax: 305–267–2932
New York: 420 Lexington Avenue, Suite 2733, New York, NY 10170.
tel: 212–682–5582
fax: 212–986–5123

CANADA
Toronto: Earl B Smith, Travel Marketing Consultants, 234 Eglington Avenue, Suite 306, Toronto, Ontario, M4P 1K5.
tel: 416–485–1550
fax: 416–485–7578

JAPAN
Tokyo: International Travel Produce Inc., 4-3-12-201-Tsukji, Chuo–ku, Tokyo 104.
tel: 03–3546–1754
fax: 03–3545–8756

UNITED KINGDOM
London: 6 Arlington Street, London SW1A 1RE.
tel: 0171–491–7771
fax: 0171–409–7773
email <infocayman@demon.co.uk>

FRANCE/SCANDINAVIA/BENELUX
Paris: KPMG Axe Consultants, 12 rue de Madrid, 75005 Paris, France.
tel: (1)-53–424136
fax: (1)-43–873285

GERMANY/AUSTRIA/SWITZERLAND
Frankfurt: Marketing Services International, Walter Stohrer and Partner, Johanna Melber Weg 12, D–60599 Frankfurt, Germany.
tel: 069–60–320–94
fax: 069–62–92–64

ITALY
Milan: G & A Martinego, Via Fratelli, Ruffini 9, 20123 Milano.
tel: 02–4801–2068
fax: 02–4635–32

SPAIN
Barcelona: Sergat Espana SL, Pau Casals 4, 08021 Barcelona.
tel: 93–414–0210
fax: 93–201–8657

TOURIST BOOKING AGENCIES

US REPRESENTATIVES
Divi Hotels, Inc., 2401 N.W. 34th Avenue, Miami, FL 33142.
tel toll free: 800–367–3484
tel: 305–633–3484
fax: 305–633–1621
Holiday Inn, 648 W. Brook Have Circle, 2nd Floor, Memphis, TN 38117.
tel toll free: 800–421–9999
tel: 901–767–8050
fax: 901–682–7502
International Travel and Resorts, 4 Park Avenue, New York, NY 10016.
tel: 212–251–1737
fax: 212–251–1767
Robert Reid Associates, 500 Plaza Drive, Secaucus, NJ 07096.
tel toll free: 800–223–6510
tel: 201–902–7878
fax: 201–902–7738

CAYMAN ISLANDS REPRESENTATIVES
Cayman Villas, PO Box 681, George Town, Grand Cayman.
tel toll free (from USA): 800–235–5888

tel: 947–4144
tel: 949–7471
Hospitality World Ltd, PO Box 30123, George Town, Grand Cayman.
tel toll free (from USA): 800–232–1034
tel: 949–8098
fax: 949–7054
Tradewinds Property Management, PO Box 107, Bodden Town, Grand Cayman.
tel: 947–3029
fax: 947–2338
Tropical Real Estate and Property Management, PO Box 1540, George Town, Grand Cayman.
tel: 947–4787/5023
fax: 947–5399

TRAVEL AGENCIES IN GRAND CAYMAN (IATA APPROVED)
Action Travel, PO Box 1233, Robert Bodden Building, Elgin Avenue, George Town, Grand Cayman.
tel: 949–8082
fax: 949–8790

Cayman Tours and Travel Ltd,
PO Box 89, The Village, Grand Cayman.
tel: 949–2355
fax: 949–2464
Cayman Travel Services, Ltd., PO Box 1759, Elizabethan Square, Grand Cayman.
tel: 949–5400/5790
fax: 949–0487
International Travel, PO Box 925, Fort Street, Grand Cayman.
tel: 949–2923
fax: 949–0455

INCENTIVE, CORPORATE AND GROUP TRAVEL
Destination Management Services, Ltd, PO Box 1960, George Town, Grand Cayman.
tel: 947–4025
fax: 947–5408

TRAVELLING TO AND IN THE CAYMAN ISLANDS

This section provides a summary of useful travel details to help you plan your trip; for more specific information check the Regional Directory at the end of each of the three regional sections in the book.

ACCOMMODATION

Currently there are approximately 20 hotels and 50 condominiums, cottages and guest houses registered with the Cayman Islands Department of Tourism. Hotel rooms are charged per person, per night; condominiums are generally on a self-catering basis and are hired by the apartment. There are also around 70 villas available for hire, all registered with the Cayman Islands Department of Tourism and bookable through a central booking office on Grand Cayman Island. Ninety per cent of all the accommodation is located along Seven Mile Beach: this beautiful beach is not just for diving – there are also superb facilities for sailing, windsurfing, swimming and just enjoying yourself in the sun.

It is always easier to select your preferred accommodation once you are acquainted with the islands, but for first-timers the Department of Tourism has a comprehensive list of everything to suit most pockets. There is, however, a 10 per cent Government Tax on all hotel accommodation and hotels will also add a 10 per cent service charge to your bill.

HEALTH

No vaccinations are required when visiting the islands. The drinking water is safe, but it is best to enquire in more remote areas, because the water will be from either cisterns or through desalination. The food is always prepared to a very high standard. The sun is a problem, however and you must protect yourself with a high factor sun block and tan gradually: many a holiday is ruined by sunburn. It is recommended that you take out full medical and holiday insurance before you visit the Cayman Islands. If for some reason there is a medical emergency, for instance the bends, it may cost a great deal to obtain the full medical attention required including emergency air travel.

Opposite: *Yacht moored in George Town Harbour on the west side of Grand Cayman.*
Above: *Cayman Brac is only a half hour flight from Grand Cayman.*

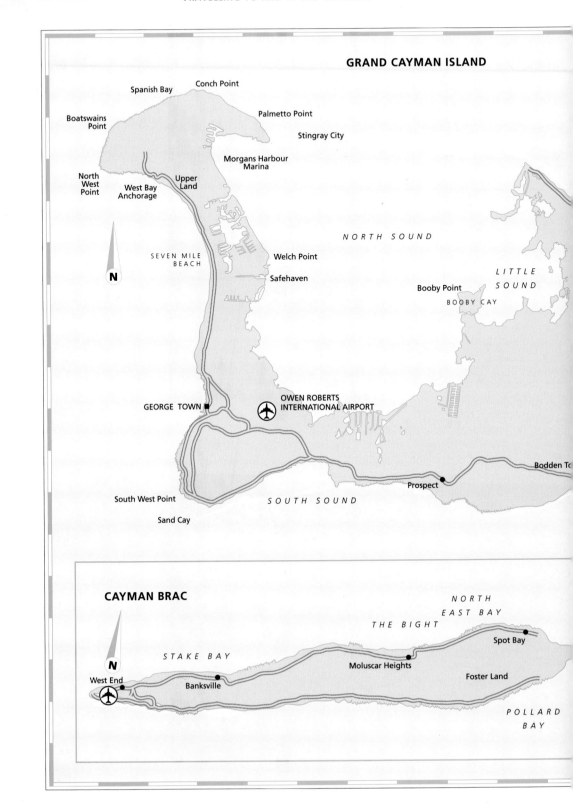

GRAND CAYMAN ISLAND

Spanish Bay

Conch Point

Palmetto Point

Boatswains Point

Stingray City

North West Point

West Bay Anchorage

Upper Land

Morgans Harbour Marina

NORTH SOUND

LITTLE SOUND

SEVEN MILE BEACH

N

Welch Point

Safehaven

Booby Point

BOOBY CAY

GEORGE TOWN

OWEN ROBERTS INTERNATIONAL AIRPORT

Bodden To

Prospect

South West Point

SOUTH SOUND

Sand Cay

CAYMAN BRAC

NORTH EAST BAY

THE BIGHT

Spot Bay

N

STAKE BAY

Moluscar Heights

Foster Land

West End

Banksville

POLLARD BAY

THE CAYMAN ISLANDS

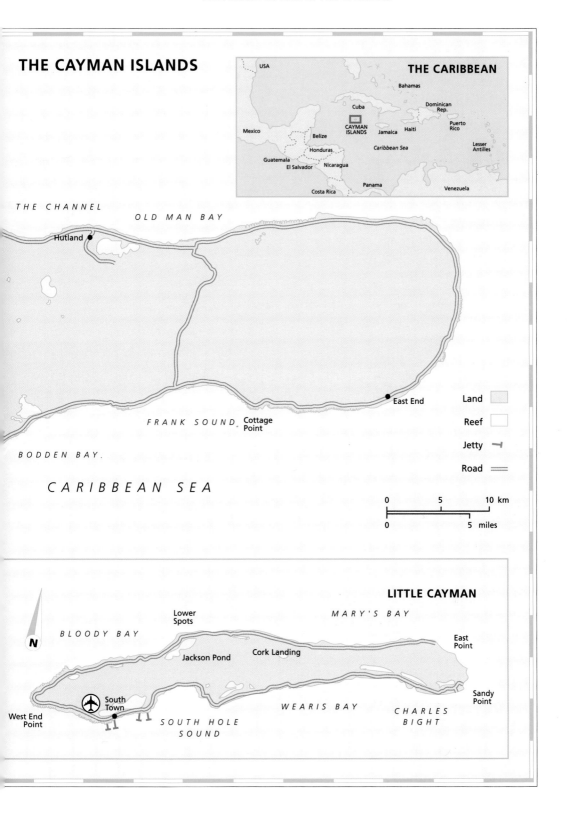

THE CARIBBEAN

USA

Bahamas

Cuba

Dominican
Rep.

Mexico

CAYMAN
ISLANDS

Puerto
Rico

Belize

Jamaica

Haiti

Honduras

Caribbean Sea

Lesser
Antilles

Guatemala

El Salvador

Nicaragua

Panama

Venezuela

Costa Rica

THE CHANNEL

OLD MAN BAY

Hutland

FRANK SOUND Cottage
Point

East End

BODDEN BAY.

CARIBBEAN SEA

Land

Reef

Jetty

Road

0	5	10 km
0		5 miles

LITTLE CAYMAN

Lower
Spots

MARY'S BAY

BLOODY BAY

East
Point

N

Jackson Pond

Cork Landing

West End
Point

South
Town

Sandy
Point

*SOUTH HOLE
SOUND*

WEARIS BAY

*CHARLES
BIGHT*

Climate

The Cayman Islands are fortunate in having fine weather virtually all year round because of their geographical location away from any major land mass and the influence of the sea around them. The islands lie between latitudes 19 and 20 north and are generally untroubled by hurricanes thanks to the bulk of the island of Cuba in the north and of Jamaica to the east.

There is very little change in the water and air temperature during the year. In the winter months the water temperature drops to around 27°C (77°F) and rises to about 28°C (82°F) in the summer. The summer air temperature averages between 30–40°C (80–90°F) and only drops to the low 20s°C (70s°F) during the short winter season. During the summer months, the high humidity can be a problem, rising to above 92 per cent.

The rainy season starts in May and the heaviest rainfall is usually in October. During the summer months there can be short, sharp falls of rain, but these months also boast the highest number of sunshine hours. The annual rainfall is estimated at 115cm (46in).

Money

The official currency was first issued in 1972 and is the Cayman dollar, worth approximately US$1.25, which has a fixed exchange rate. Cayman dollars are issued in denominations of CI$100, 50, 25, 10, 5 and 1; the coins are valued at 25 cents, 10, 5 and 1 cents. When dining out be sure to ask whether the prices are in US or CI dollars. Most restaurants will automatically charge you a 10–15 per cent service charge – check before adding gratuities. American dollars are probably more widely used, but you may get CI dollars in your change.

Credit cards are used most of all and the dive stores, hotels and restaurants accept them (some may charge a small commission). The dive shops will also run up a tab during the length of your stay. Traveller's cheques are perhaps the safest, because everyone uses them, but make sure they are in dollars and not sterling.

Customs and Immigration

A full passport is required for everyone visiting the Cayman Islands, except for American and Canadian citizens. The law requires proof of identity, a completed immigration form and a return air ticket, and you will be required to complete an immigration card on entry. A full driver's licence is required for car rental, but is not deemed proper proof of identity; always use your passport or your birth certificate for identification.

Customs officers are required to search your bags and diving gear, and this may therefore take some time if you are carrying a lot of camera equipment. It is advisable to compile a list of your equipment and serial numbers. Be advised that the Cayman Islands have the most severe anti-drug laws in the Caribbean. Anyone found in possession will be jailed

---

ELECTRICITY

The Cayman Islands power supply is 110 volts AC at 60 cycles and is suited to American-style electrical appliances, with two flat pins. When travelling from Europe you must use a compatible electrical adapter.

KEY TELEPHONE NUMBERS

- Police emergency — 911
- Police Headquarters — 948–8331
- Fire emergency — 500/911
- Hospital emergency — 555 or 948–2243/5
- Divers decompression chamber emergency — 555
- Electricity — 948–4252
- Tourism hotline — 949–8989
- Sister Islands Tourism Association — 949–1385
- Government offices — 948–4252
- Chamber of Commerce — 949–8090
- Hotel & Condominium Association — 945–4057
- CIWOA — 949–8522
- Taxi services — 947–4491/1718/1173, 949–4811
- Telephone enquiries — 949–7800
- Overseas operator assistance — 010

Opposite: *The Edward Bodden Field airport is situated at the west end of Little Cayman.*

immediately and can face massive fines and up to ten years in jail. No exceptions are made – you have been warned.

GETTING THERE

There are more than 35 weekly direct non-stop flights between Miami and Grand Cayman. The islands are serviced from Miami by United Airlines, North West Airlines, Cayman Airways and American Airlines. Cayman Airways also offer flights from Tampa, Orlando and Houston. Cayman Airways and Air Jamaica fly regularly to Montego Bay and Kingston, Jamaica.

American Airlines fly between Raleigh Durham and Cayman; US Air fly directly from Charlotte, North Carolina, to Cayman and from Tampa, Florida; Islena fly directly between Honduras and Cayman, and American Trans Air has a weekly service from Indianapolis via Cincinnati.

Until only recently all flights from Europe were routed through Miami. The flight time to Miami from the UK is about nine hours and then 70 minutes to Grand Cayman once you have changed carrier at Miami. With the introduction of direct British Airways flights there has been a substantial increase in numbers flying into the Caymans from the UK.

> ### TELEPHONE SERVICES
>
> Direct dialling is available from all the islands worldwide – dial the Cayman Islands international code, 1-345, followed by the seven digit number. For local Cayman calls you use only the last five digits of the telephone number. Note that Europeans cannot use the toll free telephone service outside the USA.

> ### NATIONAL TRUST FOR THE CAYMAN ISLANDS
>
> This non-governmental conservation organization is working to protect and maintain the biological diversity of the Caymans. It has bought many locations, including the 263-hectare (650-acre) Salina Reserve on Grand Cayman and the 40.5-hectare (100-acre) Brac Parrot reserve on Cayman Brac.
> Tel: 949–0121, fax: 949–7494.

Owen Roberts International Airport on Grand Cayman lies about 3km (2m) east of George Town. The airstrip was opened in 1953. Gerrard Smith International Airport is on Cayman Brac and the Edward Bodden Field is a grass strip runway on Little Cayman.

Little Cayman and Cayman Brac are serviced regularly by Cayman Airways and Island Air, and a private charter can be obtained from Executive Air. There are very few trolleys at the airport for your gear and you may find you have to use the services of an American-style 'skycap' service.

You are reminded always to confirm your return flight at least 72 hours before take-off. You will have to pay CI$10.00 (US$12.00) departure tax when you leave the islands.

GETTING AROUND

Cayman law dictates that the only vehicles allowed to make commercial passenger pick-ups are licensed taxis, but taxis are readily available on Grand Cayman and the charges are Government regulated. The West Side hotels along Seven Mile Beach and around George Town are not therefore allowed to use their courtesy coaches to pick up passengers at the airport – the only exception to the rule is the hotels on the far East End and North Shore who are allowed to provide a courtesy coach due to the greater distances involved. However, the ride by taxi is inexpensive and the drivers are all used to divers and their equipment.

> **TIME**
>
> The Cayman Islands are in the Eastern Standard Time zone, five hours behind Greenwich Mean Time (six hours behind British Summer Time), the same as New York, Toronto and Miami. However, the islands do not change over to Daylight Saving Time during the summer months, consequently they will then be one hour behind Miami time.

There is a very efficient and cheap local mini-bus service from George Town along Seven Mile Beach and the other main routes around Grand Cayman. There are 15 car hire companies registered with the Tourist Authority and a few of these are located at the Owen Roberts International Airport. Driving is on the left and open-top jeeps seem to be the most popular made of transport for visitors. More upmarket saloon cars, motorbikes, scooters and bicycles are also available, and some of these services are offered on Little Cayman and Cayman Brac. All visitors must obtain a temporary Cayman Islands driving permit for the duration of their stay, costing CI$7.50. This can be obtained by presenting your valid driver's licence to the police station or any car rental agency.

CRUISE LINES

There is no cruise ship dock in the Cayman Islands and until recently there were no permanent moorings for cruise ships. They were required to anchor offshore and passengers were transferred by tender to the passenger terminals at North and South Dock in George Town. These terminals are directly on the waterfront of downtown George Town and opposite the main shopping precincts. A taxi rank is located at the terminals and the average fare for an island tour is approximately US$25.00 per person for four persons, per hour. In the event of inclement weather on West Side, the cruise ships will anchor off Spotts on the south coast, which is about a ten-minute taxi ride from the town. Seven Mile Beach is only a ten-minute ride by taxi from George Town.

The Cayman Islands limit the number of cruise passengers per day to 5500, which means that only three or four cruise ships can visit at any one time, depending on their capacity. Tuesday, Wednesday and Thursday are the busiest days all year round.

Cruise lines calling on a regular basis include Carnival, Celebrity Cruise Lines, Chandris Fantasy, Costa, Crown Commodore Cruises, Crystal Cruises, Cunard, Epirotiki Lines, Hapah Lloyd Cruises, Holland America, Kloster Cruise Line, Majestic, Norwegian Caribbean (NCL), Premier Cruise Line, Princess Cruises, Radisson Cruise, Renaissance Cruises, Regency, Royal Caribbean, Royal, Starlite Cruises, Sun Line Cruises and Ulysses Cruises.

> **RADIO**
>
> There are three radio stations in the Cayman Islands. Radio Cayman started in 1977 and is a revenue–earning department of the Government. ICCI–FM is based at the International College and run by students and volunteers studying journalism and broadcasting. Z–99 FM broadcasts 24–hour–a–day popular music.

As you can appreciate, there was extreme concern over the environmental impact that this number of cruise ships had on the seabed and finally all the efforts being made to install a permanent mooring system to prevent further damage being done have been answered.

Unfortunately in some areas it is already too late. The

last study done off George Town indicated an area of 2.3km of reef had been reduced to coral rubble. This continues down the spur and groove slope to over 106 metres (350ft). Even when the weather is calm, cruise ships continue to swing at anchor and their chain links weighing at over 60kg each (132lbs) wreck havoc on the sea bed.

The entire area off George Town where the cruise ships anchor is now off limits to all sport divers and the ecology of the reef is near collapse. You can imagine the damage done by an anchor weighing over 4500kg (4.5 tons). Broken and damaged coral quickly becomes overgrown and smothered by algae, further hampering any regrowth.

It is not just the environmental impact which is causing concern. Many local residents are also up in arms over the physical number of tourists which are being off-loaded onto Cayman soil. Arguments range from the taxi drivers who are in favour of the business to those who feel that they now cause too much congestion. Some shopkeepers complain noisily about the effects on their livelihood by the increased percentage of shoplifters and lack of spending by the cruise ship tourists, while others applaud the numbers coming ashore and look forward to being able to serve them to the very best of their ability.

ANNUAL EVENTS	
January	• Windsurfing Regatta
March/April	• Easter Regatta
End April	• Annual Batabano Carnival
June	• Annual Million Dollar Month Fishing Tournament
	• Cayman Islands International Aviation Week
	• Queen's Birthday Celebration
July	• Taste of Cayman Food Festival
August	• Cayman Islands Club Light Tackle Fishing Tournament
October	• Tourism Awareness Week
	• Annual Pirates Week Festival
November	• All Tackle Fishing Tournament

There will always be problems over the economic impact from cruise ships and their passengers, however I am happy to say that three permanent moorings have recently been installed in West Bay, saving further destruction to the Cayman reef ecology.

SHOPPING

Shopping on the Cayman Islands is unique in the Caribbean. The main interest for shop-aholics is the range of imported gifts from Europe and Asia – expensive perfumes, camera and electronic equipment, linen, leather work, crystal, china and spirits – all duty free! Another attraction is crafts made by local artisans who work with from black coral, ancient doubloons and Caymanite, the Island's own semi-precious stone.

As well as the downtown shops the major hotels each have boutiques and speciality stores and there are a number of small plazas on West Bay Road including Seven Mile Shops, Westshore Plaza, Galleria Plaza and Queen's Court Mall. There are around seven local galleries which feature local art and craftwork. Beautiful underwater photographs by Cathy Church are available from Sunset House Underwater Photo Centre at the Sunset House Resort.

PUBLIC HOLIDAYS	
1 January	New Year's Day
February/March	Ash Wednesday
March/April	Good Friday
	Easter Monday
15 May	Discovery Day
12 June	Queen's Birthday
1st Monday of July	Constitution Day
2nd Monday of November	Remembrance Day
25 December	Christmas Day
26 December	Boxing Day

DINING OUT IN THE CAYMANS

The cuisine tends to be distinctly fishy with shrimp, lobster and local fish always on the menu. There are over 60 restaurants catering for almost every taste. You will also find farmed turtle meat and the Caribbean conch (pronounced 'conk'). This large marine mollusc is rubbery in texture and is prepared in endless ways. There is a distinct Jamaican influence in jerk beef or chicken, with side dishes of yams, breadfruit, cassava, rice or peas.

All hotels offer international cuisine, but with an obvious American influence. Apart from the Caribbean style there are also a variety of excellent restaurants including European, Indian, Italian, Greek, Mexican, Japanese, Thai, German and Chinese restaurants. Fast-food eateries are spaced along Seven Mile Beach for those who are after ribs, burgers, pizza or chicken. When dining out, it is advisable to book well in advance – eating out in the Caymans is regarded as a hobby by many people and the restaurants get very crowded.

There are six small local restaurants on Cayman Brac in addition to the buffet-style restaurants in the local hotels. Little Cayman has one restaurant, the Hungry Iguana, situated next to the airport. Dining is available for non-residents at the Southern Cross Club, Little Cayman Beach Resort, Pirates Point and Sam McCoy's Lodge, but must be booked well in advance to avoid disappointment.

Casual lightweight clothes are the norm for day-wear in the Caymans but many restaurants require more formal dress in the evenings. Men should take a lightweight jacket with them just in case. Smart shorts are still acceptable attire for dinner.

SPORTS AND SIGHTSEEING
The islands offer many other sporting opportunities for non-divers, so for those accompanying their diving partners there is no need to despair!

Aerial tours
Aerial tours are available of Grand Cayman through Island Air (see Directory page 93) and Cayman Helicopters Ltd; tel 949–4400. Seaborn Flightseeing Adventures is a narrated tour using Island Air which lasts 25 minutes; tel 949–6029.

Golf courses
There are two golf courses: December 1993 saw the opening of a championship 18-hole golf course at the Links, Safe Haven at a cost of US$8.6 million. The more established course (designed by Jack Nicklaus for the Britannia resort at the Hyatt,) is an immaculate, and challenging, three-in-one course. It was here that the Cayman Ball was introduced – the ball has a much shorter flight, to keep it out of the sea! These two courses can more than cater for your golfing needs at every level: The Links, Safe Haven; tel 949–5988/fax 949–5457 or the Britannia Golf Club; tel 949–8020/fax 949–8528.

Windsurfing
The islands are rapidly gaining an international reputation as a great windsurfing location. Both of the areas used are protected by a reef and enjoy good on-shore winds and the latest equipment. These centres are at the Tortuga Club on the northeast of the Island and at Safe Haven, in the North Sound; tel 949–1068.

Sport fishing
Sport fishing has advanced tremendously over the last few years. The year-round season for big game fish such as blue marlin, tuna and wahoo is serviced by 12 registered companies with a large fleet of boats run by competent local seamen. Over 100 boats take part in an international fishing tournament held every June, known as 'Million Dollar Month'. Sport fisherman should contact the Cayman Islands Department of Tourism for a full list of boat

captains and details of events such as the Million Dollar Month. For information from the relevant marinas contact Cayman Islands Yacht Club; tel 945–4322/fax 945–4432, Kaibo; tel 945–9064 or Morgan's Harbour Marina; tel 949–3099/fax 949–3822.

Other water sports
In addition to swimming, diving and snorkelling, there are jet-skiing, pedalo rides, glass-bottom boat rides, parasailing and water-skiing. Simply lying on the beach, soaking up the sun, is a great way to spend a day but please remember that topless sunbathing is not allowed.

The water sports areas around Grand Cayman are:
- Seven Mile Beach, for about 800m (^{1}/2 mile) north of Public Beach and 160m (600ft) out to sea.
- South Sound, for about 800 m (^{1}/2 mile) west from Red Bay and out to the reef.
- Duck Pond Bight, in North Sound, out to a line between the western points of Head Sound Barcadere.
- Duck Pond Cay; an area 800m (^{1}/2 mile) long south of the public beach.
- Water Point, Cayman Kai; an area just under 800m (^{1}/2 mile) east of the Frank Sound Road, out to the reef.
- East Point, an area westward from Gorling Bluff Lighthouse for about 800m (^{1}/2mile), out to the reef.
- Colliers Bay, between Colliers Cay and Colliers Point, out to the reef.

Opposite: *Foster's Marina, on Grand Cayman (see page 96 for further details).*

DIVING AND SNORKELLING IN CAYMAN WATERS

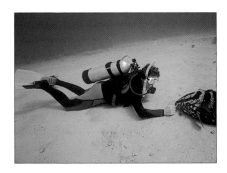

Many divers and snorkellers regard the aquamarine waters of the Cayman Islands as the crème de la crème of the Caribbean. The offer of unlimited diving and an unrivalled abundance of marine life has brought divers back year after year. The conservation policies enforced on all three islands have helped to ensure that the reefs, walls and shoals are protected to the highest level, with a great degree of understanding and empathy towards marine life.

Virtually all diving in the Cayman Islands comes under the direct supervision of the Cayman Islands Watersports Operators Association, the CIWOA (see feature page 27). This body is also responsible for the training of all the dive masters and instructors used in their member dive organisations. The training includes conservation information as well as health and safety aspects, and every visiting tourist is presented with the same information, no matter which dive centre they are using.

Although the on-board dive masters will plan your dive and dive time, it is also very important to do your own pre-dive planning and stick to that plan. If you are diving from a shore location during the day or at night, it is advisable to leave a message at your hotel, or with someone reliable, to inform them of your dive plan and approximate time of your exit from the water.

A usual day's diving consists of a morning deep dive to approximately 30m (100ft), followed by a shallow dive to 18m (60ft) for 60 minutes, on the same reef or on another suitable shallow reef or wreck, usually within two hours of your first dive. Night diving is always a bonus and there are a number of popular locations such as the wreck of the Balboa and Eden Rock.

Virtually all of the major hotels either operate their own dive centre or have a concession with one of the larger diving operators. All the dive centres offer instruction courses, snorkelling, shore diving, boat diving, reef, wreck and wall dives to any level of diving expertise. The islands are indeed a diver's paradise and the choice of accommodation and diving available allow you to quickly decide what is best for you.

Opposite: *Snorkellers and stingrays at the Sandbar, Grand Cayman (see feature on page 100).*
Above: *Diver strokes a tame Nassau grouper near the Oro Verde wreck (Site 30, page 50).*

WATER VISIBILITY

The water visibility is excellent and very rarely influenced by tide and current, although the visibility along the north wall of Grand Cayman can alter slightly during high and low tide due to the large shallow lagoon closer to the shore. (Like all island locations the Cayman waters suffer from the spring and autumn plankton bloom when all of the many animals and plants of the reef cast their eggs and sperm into the water. This primordial soup is the lifeblood of the oceans.)

After particularly heavy rainfall, the islands' water table reaches its capacity and the islands seem to 'flush' themselves clean. A period of murky water follows but this soon passes. The Cayman dive operators boast that you can dive every day of the year and because of the size of the islands, you will always find a lee shore, even during the worst weather, and always be able to dive safely.

DIVE SITES AND BUOYS

All the dive sites listed in this book are currently dived and registered with the Cayman Islands Department of Environment Natural Resources Unit, the Cayman Islands Watersports Operators Association and individual diving and snorkelling operators. Wherever possible, each site has a mooring buoy to avoid coral damage and it is hoped that all sites in the future will be protected by this system. The dive sites which have no mooring buoy are rarely dived but

WATER WEAR

You only require a swimsuit when in the sea due to the almost constant water temperature all year round, even at depth. However, it is recommended that you wear either a lycra skin-suit or thin wet suit for diving and snorkelling. These will protect you against coral abrasions and stings from those unseen planktonic beasties in the water as well as the fierce sun whilst on the surface. Topless bathing is not permitted.

NAVIGATIONAL CHANNELS

There are 21 designated navigational channels around the islands and no one may swim, dive or anchor in such channels without being specially authorised. Also, diving or swimming is restricted within 180m (600ft) of the shoreline unless a 'divers down' flag or other marker is displayed; at night, lights must be displayed.

Below: *The experience of being in the midst of silversides is not to be missed.*

The CIWOA was set up in 1980 by a number of local dive operators who were concerned about safety, standards and instruction. There are now over 60 participating members and these have around 200 individual diving instructors as part of the permanent staff. The dive leaders and instructors are particularly conservation-minded and the CIWOA has standardized the dive briefing details so that there is a consistency among dive operators. Over 95 per cent of watersports operators are affiliated to the CIWOA.

The CIWOA also produces a number of leaflets designed to help visiting divers and have also been instrumental in influencing local government over conservation laws, mooring buoys and tourism policies. They also produce a free magazine, *Splash! Cayman*.

The CIWOA have put a safe depth maximum limit of 33m (110ft) on all dives and insist that everyone entering the water is not only qualified, but that they are accompanied by a competent dive instructor or dive leader and that everyone is aware of the conservation policies in force. Local dive operators tend to set the safe limit at 30m (100ft) and, as an additional safety precaution, all divers are required to do a safety stop on the way to the surface on the completion of every dive. This is generally for 3 minutes at 3m (10ft).

During required pre-dive and snorkelling briefings, everyone (including underwater photographers, who are often cited as offenders by coming in contact with corals to stabilize themselves) is advised to observe CIWOA rules of safe diving including the CIWOA's strict 'hands-and fins-off ' policy for all forms of marine life.

The organization is very proud of the way its conservation policies are starting to have a long-term effect on the islands, but it is also very conscious of the fact that conservation measures need funding, and is looking at ways to be able to fund full-time marine wardens and provide different moorings for cruise ships.

The CIWOA is in step with the needs of today's divers by catering to everyone's specific needs. It is committed to providing customers with the best service possible, by maintaining a positive professional attitude. The commitment and cooperative efforts of the CIWOA will ensure that the Cayman Islands remain a world-class destination for many years.

If you would like further information about CIWOA contact: The Executive Director's Office, PO Box 31495 SMB, Grand Cayman; tel 949–8522/fax 949–0220. Or call at the Cayman Islands Chamber of Commerce office, 1st Floor, Harbour Centre, North Church Street, George Town, Grand Cayman.

CIWOA MEMBERSHIP LIST – MARCH 1995

Ambassador Divers: tel 949–8839/fax 949–7577; Aquanauts: tel 945–1990/fax 945–1991; Atlantis Submarines Ltd: tel 949–7700/fax 949–8574; Beach Club Divers: tel 949–8100/fax 945–5167; Bob Soto's Diving Ltd: tel 949–2022/fax 949–8731; Brac Aquatics: tel 948–1429/fax 948–1207; Brac Reef Beach Resort: tel 948–0133/fax 948–1040; Cayman Aggressor: tel 949–5551/fax 949–8729; Cayman Dive College: tel 949–4125/fax 949–1983; Cayman Diving Lodge: tel 947–7555/fax 947–7560; Cayman Mama: tel 916–1847/fax 945–5114;

Cayman Marine Lab: tel 916–0849/fax 945–5586, Dive Cayman Ltd: tel 945–4341/fax 945–5786; Dive Inn: tel 949–0321/fax 949–8729; Dive N' Stuff: tel 947–1314/fax 947–2095; Divers Supply/Parrots Landing: tel 949–7621/fax 949–0294; Divers World: tel 949–8128/fax 949–7178; Don Fosters Dive: tel 949–5679/fax 945–5133; Eden Rock Divers: tel 949–7243/fax 949–7243; Fisheye: tel 945–4209/fax 945–4208; Indies Suites/Divers: tel 945–5025/fax 945–5024; Little Cayman Beach Resort: tel 948–1033/fax 948–1040; Off The Wall

Divers: tel 947–7790/fax 947–7790; Paradise Divers: tel 948–0004/fax 948–0004; Peter Hughs' Dive Tiara: tel 948–1553/fax 948–1316; Pirates Point: tel 948–1010/fax 948–1011; Quabbin Divers: tel 949–5597/fax 949–4781; Quabo Divers: tel 945–4769/fax 945–4978; Red Sail Sports: tel 945–5965/fax 945–5808; Sunset Divers: tel 949–7111/fax 949–7101; Surfside Watersports: tel 947–6031/fax 947–9102; Tortuga Surfside Divers: tel 947–2097/fax 947–9486; Treasure Island Divers: tel 949–7777/fax 949–7125.

when diving does occur, the diving operators are careful to let their anchors down onto a sandy area or they stay stationery above the divers with no anchor drop at all.

The mooring buoys are placed by the Natural Resources Unit and are of two types: a single pin buoy, which is lighter in weight for the day boats and small cruisers and the double pin mooring buoys which are of much heavier construction and strength for the live-aboard dive boats such as the *Aggressor*.

I have listed as many of the diving and snorkelling sites as possible within the confines of the book. It would be impossible to include every site in the Caymans as there are over 1000 recorded dive sites around all three of the islands. (There are also a further 600 or so sites which have been dived by various people at some time but which are not recorded.) Some of the sites listed in this book are a slightly different section of another named site and in these instances the dives are cross referred to the other parts of the reef.

I have used the site names which are most commonly used. The names in brackets are secondary or older names previously used by some operators. (Wherever a name starts with a specific species name such as Wahoo Wall or Hammerhead Hill, this does not mean that you will definitely encounter these species on every, or indeed any dive at that site. However you may be lucky! The only site name where you are guaranteed to see the actual species is Stingray City.) All this can be confusing so, if in doubt, refer to the individual operator for the site names they use.

DIVE GUIDE DESCRIPTIONS

Canyon: a slice in the coral reef; **Chimney:** generally a narrow tunnel running vertically up through the edge of the reef; **Groove:** a sand channel; **Pinnacle:** a large coral head, tower–shaped; **Sand chute:** a deep gulley which connects the sand plane above the reef to the depths below and will cut the wall vertically; **Shelf:** where the deep water begins; **Spur:** narrow ridges of coral separated by a sand channel; **Tunnel:** a hole running through the reef, sometimes known as a swim-through, ravine or crevice; **Wall** or **Drop-off:** the reef which forms the shelf.

DIVERS DOWN LIGHTS

Used when divers are diving at night, this is a series of three lights, red over white over red, displayed vertically, with a 360° visibility at a maximum of 180m (600ft). It is an offence to show such lights if diving is not in progress.

DIVE BOATS

When diving off the West Bay area of Seven Mile Beach, the majority of the dive boats are the flat bed type with twin outboard motors. These twin-hulled boats are robust, but probably more suited to the inland waterways of Florida than the exposed open water dive sites of the Cayman Islands. They have a very shallow draft and most come directly into the beach to on-load passengers and after the dive to off-load air cylinders (with which you will generally be expected to lend a hand). Travel time along the west side is generally 15-20 minutes. The second dive (if you are on a two tank dive) will probably involve a journey time of no more than ten minutes. Diving is usually over by lunch-time unless otherwise arranged or unless you are a student attending one of the many on-going classes.

South Side diving is also generally a short journey-time to the dive sites. These boats have a deeper single 'V' hull with a much faster engine attached to extend your diving range. Pick up is more commonly from the number of jetties attached to the dive operations. Again, unless exploratory long range diving is being planned, it will only take 15-20 minutes to the dive site.

East Side boats are also of the fast launch type and accommodate up to 16 passengers. Travel time may take a little longer due to the distance from the shore to the outer reef and dive sites.

When diving the North Wall, there is generally a 35-45 minute boat ride on one of the faster day boats. The slower flat bed types also make the journey with snorkellers and the time may be as much as one hour. The area of the outer reef is generally much more choppy with a large surface swell. This makes entry back onto the boats rather difficult and the time between dives may make you sea-sick so precautions should be taken. If there is a longer time-gap between dives on the North Wall, most operators will seek shelter from the swell inside the barrier reef.

Little Cayman boats are fast and well equipped to get you round the Island to Bloody Bay. This can be rather rough at times and you may get wet. Travel time is around 30 minutes. These boats have a 'V' shaped hull and are well equipped for handling ten to twenty divers.

On Cayman Brac, the boats are also 'V' shaped hulled and are designed for speed, not for comfort. These boats regularly make the crossing to Little Cayman and this trip can be rather arduous at times. Journey time can be over 1 hour to your destination point.

Live-aboard boats are a different matter. The *Aggressor* has bunk-style rooms for eighteen guests and absolutely everything is included (except alcoholic drinks). Trips are for six days, seven nights. The *Little Cayman Diver II* takes less passengers and all rooms are ensuite, which some people prefer. Her range is not as far as the *Aggressor*.

DEEP DIVING TIPS

- Attend deep diving course
- Increase depth slowly
- Dive only with experienced deep divers
- Do not put yourself or others at risk
- Be safe
- Plan your dive and Dive your plan
- Recognise symptoms of Nitrogen Narcosis
- When symptoms appear, ascend immediately until symptoms are relieved.

Divers often inadvertently cause serious damage to coral reefs. Listed on page 69 are a few golden rules for diving in Cayman Islands waters.

TIDE TABLES

Tide tables are calculated by the Civil Aviation Meteorological Service, located at Owen Roberts International Airport. They are produced monthly and published on a daily basis through local radio and newspapers.

DIVE FLAGS

The most used flag in Caribbean waters is the 'divers down' flag and is a red flag with a white diagonal stripe running top left to bottom right. The other flag used is the International Code 'A' flag, a white rectangular box on the inside and a blue box on the outside with an inverted 'v' shape cut out. It is an offence to show such flags if diving is not in progress.

Divers preparing to dive from an Indies dive boat (see page 96).

DIVE PRICES

The vast majority of diving is done through the many and varied diving and snorkelling operators. This diving is done by boat, for which you have to pay a premium. A two tank dive will generally cost in the region of $45-$65 depending on the operation and the distance you are travelling.

Many of these operators will not even tell you that there is shore diving in the Cayman Islands and this costs considerably less. Assuming that you already have all of your own diving equipment, you will only to hire weights and a tank full of air. This will cost approximately $10.00.

Open Water Certification courses with PADI cost around $450 with a Discover Scuba course around the $100. For those who only dive from one holiday vacation to the next, then a PADI refresher course will cost in the region of $35. Specialist diving instruction courses are also readily available and each resort will be able to keep you advised of any costs to be incurred.

Snorkelling costs considerably less, bearing in mind that the only equipment you may need to hire is mask, fins and snorkel ($10). Most snorkellers already own their own equipment and to join a boat for snorkelling with the stingrays out at the Sand Bar, you will pay in the region of $20-$45 depending on the length of time and whether or not ground transportation is required as well as lunch on the boat.

Live-aboard trips are at the top end of the scale, offering unlimited diving, excellent food; some are even completely en-suite. You are paying full hotel suite prices around $1500 for the week's package. Alcoholic drinks (after diving only) cost extra.

Most of the resorts offer all inclusive packages with food and diving at approximately $140–$240. These do not include air flights, however a number of resorts on the sister islands offer two and three day packages with snorkelling and transportation and air flights included. Again, check with your local tourist office or contact the resorts directly to find out exactly what is included in the price. Operators also sell all inclusive weeks including air fares from the 'States at around $1000 per week.

LEARNING TO DIVE IN THE CAYMAN ISLANDS

The inter island network of dive shops has an enviable reputation of instruction to the highest level and their safety record is the best in the Caribbean.

Clear, warm water all year round and above average safety requirements make the Cayman Islands a perfect location for learning to dive. When first choosing a dive operation, make sure that they are affiliated to the CIWOA. Also be certain that the instructors used are qualified by PADI, NAUI or BSAC – the world's leading diver training organisations and all trained to the very highest standards. PADI (Professional Association of Diving Instructors) is probably the top rated association in use in the Cayman Islands, although most of the larger dive operators have instructors qualified with at least two or three different organisations. PADI certifies 85 per cent of all scuba divers in the world and is represented in 87 countries.

NAUI (National Association of Underwater Instructors) is not as widely known, but they are also very competent. The BSAC (British Sub-Aqua Club) is very strong in Europe and Japan. There is a BSAC Branch on the island, which caters for many of the ex-pat workers who are resident in the Caymans.

Once you have chosen your dive organisation, you must gain certification before you are allowed to rent equipment and you and your 'buddy' go off to dive independently. The most popular way to start is to enrol in a resort course, also known as the Discover Scuba Programme.

The resort course crams a lot into two to four hours of instruction and is designed to give you a taste of diving, fire your enthusiasm and teach you basic water safety and conservation (not only of your own life, but those people and creatures around you). A resort course is also highly recommended if you only have a few days' vacation. If you decide to take your training further and invest in several hundred dollars and a lot more time, you can go onto a five day open water certification course. This will give you the chance to dive on several of the fabulous Cayman Island dive sites with a fully qualified dive instructor to a maximum depth of 18m (60ft).

Resort courses are aimed at age 12 and over (teenagers up to age 18 must have full parental consent). There is no upper age limit. Cost is minimal and includes full rental equipment. Approximately 25 per cent of all first timers go on to sit the open water certification course in the same location.

Upon passing the open water course you can continue your scuba diving education by enrolling in many other speciality courses including wreck diving, underwater photography or becoming an instructor and teaching others this fascinating and rewarding sport. All of these courses are available in the Cayman Islands.

Once fully qualified, your certification or 'C' card is actually your diving passport and is recognised world-wide. It is valid for life, but if for some reason you are unable to dive from one year to the next vacation, it is recommended that you enrol in a refresher course at any dive centre.

SNORKEL TIPS, TECHNIQUE AND EQUIPMENT

Snorkelling is a sport for all ages and is best enjoyed with at least one partner or 'buddy', although it can be a complete family sport. There is absolutely no age limit to snorkelling and as long as you are in safe protected waters, many hours of enjoyment can be had. Sharing the experience of snorkelling and the opportunity to view the wonders of our underwater world at a safe distance is thrilling.

As a beginner, entering the water for the first time wearing a mask, snorkel and fins can be quite daunting, but

---

CAYMAN MARINE LABORATORY

Personalised tours are offered for groups of 2–10 divers on two boats, to learn about the ecology of the reefs with a qualified Marine Biologist. Mini-lectures are given between each dive as well as special topics such as fish, invertebrates, symbiosis, bioluminescence, mangroves and coral reef structures. College credits are offered and the lectures are supplemented by informative video and slide shows.

The programme starts off with a description about the fragility of the reef and how your buoyancy in the water is extremely important to minimise diver damage. Two other points recommended are that gloves are never worn, nor is a knife. A similar programme is also offered by Kirk's Sea Tours (see page 97 for contact details).

Many divers come to the Caymans for the impressive wreck diving. This tugboat wreck is near Cayman Brac.

BSAC BRANCH #360

Cayman Islands Divers Branch #360 of the British Sub-Aqua Club is a non profit organisation, founded in 1969 by a group of local divers when diving was still in its infancy in the Cayman Islands. In 1974 the branch were awarded the Heinke Trophy for their achievements in furthering the aims of the British Sub-Aqua Club and promoting the sport. In 1972 and again in 1994 the Club was the recipient of the Cayman Islands Hotel and Condominium Association's Tourism Award for their outstanding contribution towards the advancement of tourism in the Cayman Islands.

First and foremost, they are an active diving club and have a lively membership with 17 instructors who train their members to the highest standards, all on a voluntary basis. They encourage Caymanians to train in the sport and offer sponsorship. They also foster friendship and companionship with a very hefty social schedule which includes beach barbecues and formal dinners as well as offering diving each weekend on their dive boat.

Their main goal is to make diving as safe and secure as possible in the Cayman Islands. With this in mind, they were instrumental in the setting up of the islands' only hyperbaric recompression chamber, see box page 33.

with the correct techniques you will quickly discover that snorkelling requires little physical effort. Although the ability to swim is essential, there is no need to have Olympic abilities.

Always consult your doctor before snorkelling – this is especially important for those who have a known medical condition. Asthma and epilepsy can be a problem so it is important to get medical advice.

The sport combines active swimming by use of the legs and fins as well as breath-hold diving to explore a little way below the surface. With correct instruction you may soon be able to visit the splendours of a coral reef, such as those found very close to shore around Eden Rock and the Devil's Grotto, just south of George Town harbour.

Snorkelling is not an expensive hobby and all of the member organisations of the Cayman Islands Watersports Operators Association will have all the equipment that you and your family will need to take a first peek beneath the waves. Instruction is always offered and this may take place in the centre's swimming pool.

Once you are hooked (and you will be!) you will be able to go off on your own and, once competent, will feel confident enough to purchase your own equipment. There are a number of retail outfits in the Caymans who will be able to cater to all your snorkelling and diving needs. If the dive centre you are renting from does not have equipment for sale, they will be able to offer the best advice on where to get the equipment you need.

The equipment consists of a mask with adjustable strap and toughened glass. The mask must also have an area around the nose to enable you to adjust the air pressure inside. Several types of mask also have the provision for optical lenses to be installed. For those people who wear contact lenses, a close fitting, low volume mask should be adequate, but it is important to remember to close your eyes if you have to clear your mask.

The snorkel must not be too long or too wide as you may have to be able to clear the water out of it in a single breath if you submerge yourself too far. More modern snorkels have a self-draining device which will remove any excess water. The snorkel must fit snugly in the mouth and be able to be attached to the outside of the mask strap and must not have any type of restriction to impair breathing.

Fins, or flippers, come in two different styles. There is a slip-on type with an adjustable ankle strap, which is often worn over a pair of waterproof pumps or a diving bootee. The smaller, softer kind is a type of shoe fitting, which fits snugly around the foot.

Buoyancy vests may also be worn as an additional safety measure, but for shallow water snorkelling, they are rarely used. Again, just check with your dive shop whether the area you are planning to snorkel is safe enough for you and your family. If in any doubt, do not enter the water and always seek local advice first.

The CIWOA has a full list of all the dive shops which offer snorkel instruction and special trips, including snorkelling with the world-famous stingrays out at Stingray City and at the Sandbar along North Shore.

In addition to your basic equipment you can also choose to wear a Lycra swimskin or a thin, full wetsuit. These will not only protect you against the sun's rays but also from stings from microscopic planktonic creatures. However, if you have no other protection, at least wear a T-shirt of some type against the sun's rays.

DIVING EQUIPMENT
In addition to the basic snorkelling equipment, the diving equipment you require will consist of the following:
- an air tank and air;
- a regulator or demand valve, to breath through;
- a contents gauge to be able to indicate how much air you have left in your tank;
- an easily read depth gauge to indicate your current depth and maximum depth reached;
- a watch with an adjustable bezel or timer device to let you know how long you have been at a specific depth and the duration of your dive;
- a buoyancy compensator or lifejacket of some description to enable you to adjust your buoyancy at depth and so keep off the corals, and to support you on the surface, as the need arises;
- a protective suit to guard against abrasions;
- a weight belt and weights to keep you neutrally buoyant at depth;
- a full wet suit rather than a 'skin' or a Lycra protective suit, as the water temperature drops as low as 24°C (74°F) during the winter months.

DISABLED DIVERS

Red Sail Sports, who have four dive operations round the world, are specialists in instructing and catering for disabled divers. The two boats they use on Grand Cayman are specially adapted for wheelchairs. The dive centre can certify people with any disability, provided they are medically capable of diving. Any prospective student must see a physician prior to taking a certification course.

The centre can cater for paraplegics and quadriplegics, and for students with hearing loss or reduced vision. Anyone requiring information on disability diving should contact Red Sail Sports directly, (see Grand Cayman Regional Directory page 97).

For advice on diving for the disabled in advance of your visit, contact:

BSAC
Telford's Quay,
Ellesmere Port, South Wirral,
Cheshire, L65 4FY, England.
tel: 0151–357–1951
fax: 0151–357–1250

Handicapped Scuba Association (HSA)
116 West El Portal, Suite 104,
San Clemente, CA 92672, USA
tel: 1–714–498–6128

RECOMPRESSION FACILITIES

One of the most important aspects of safe diving in the Cayman Islands is the recompression chamber. The hyperbaric chamber is run by the Cayman Islands Government and all the chamber operators are volunteers, including the nurses and paramedics. There are 62 on the team, 10 of whom are on call on beepers for instant response to a decompression incident. There are 11 senior operators and at least 15 members of staff are required during any incident. The chamber is on-line 24 hours a day and there is a 24-hour medi-vac service from Little Cayman and Cayman Brac to Grand Cayman to assure prompt treatment for any diving-related emergency; tel 949–2989 or 555.

Since the chamber opened in 1972 there have been approximately 600 treatments. There were 27 in 1992, 16 in 1993 and 47 in 1994. Statistically these figures are very low, considering the high level of diving taking place, and that on most two-tank dives your first dive is to 30m (100ft) for 20 minutes and your second is to 18m (60ft) for 60 minutes. All

divers are recommended to make a safety stop of 3 minutes at 3m (10ft) when approaching the surface after every dive.

Most decompression incidents dealt with were caused by a gradual accumulation of nitrogen over a one- or two-week vacation period, when people are diving three, four or more dives per day. Gradually the residual nitrogen in the bloodstream will tip them over the safety margin.

It is important to avoid the temptation to snorkel and do deep breath-held dives between sorties underwater. All divers know they must take time surfacing from a dive to avoid the bends. During a deep breath-held dive, however, you recompress the nitrogen, and if you rush back up to the surface, the same nitrogen bubbles expand rapidly and cause a 'bend' or decompression sickness (see page 167).

The chamber crew refer to DAN, the Divers Alert Network, whenever necessary.

Water temperatures in the Cayman Islands do not necessitate dry suits, hoods or gloves, although some people like to wear a hood whilst diving at night. A small knife may also be worn. However, this is not to be used to stab at or kill any marine life. You just may happen to venture into an area that has fishing line loose in the water, and the knife should be able to cut you free from that line.

A computer is recommended for those more experienced divers who are on an unlimited dive package. Diving three or more times each day over a sustained period is not only exhausting, it is also dangerous and can lead to residual nitrogen problems in the bloodstream and may contribute towards the 'bends'.

It is always advisable to dive with another competent partner or 'buddy' and to dive with a registered member of CIWOA. This is not just for your own safety. The resident dive guides and instructors invariably know the dive location much better than you do and will guide you to the best scenic and safe area of any particular dive you are on.

> **DIVE BOAT SAFETY**
>
> All dive boats registered with the CIWOA carry emergency and safety equipment. This will include VHF radio, first aid kit, oxygen supply, tilt board, dive tables, float line, dive flag and at least one flotation device per person on board.

Below: *Divers at Green House reef, Cayman Brac (Site 2, page 105).*

Above: *Atlantis Submarine and submersible dive submarine (Site 2, page 105).*
Below: *Front dome of Atlantis submarine at a depth of 18m (60ft).*

GRAND CAYMAN

The Cayman Islands – limestone outcroppings – sit atop a huge subterranean massif called the Cayman Ridge. The southern slopes of this submarine mountain range – the Cayman Trench – are actually the deepest in the Caribbean, reaching depths of over 6km (4 miles). This has been instrumental, along with the lack of rivers, in combining to produce an area of clear, clean water quite unrivalled in the Americas, with a climate of 'perpetual summer'. The islands do suffer from seasonal winds, but conditions here are such that you are always able to get in the water and enjoy some of the best diving in the Caribbean.

Grand Cayman is the largest of the three islands and is 35km (22miles) in length, and between 6-12km wide (4-8m), with an area of 197sq km (122sq miles), and lies some 800km (490 miles) southwest of Miami. Grand Cayman only rises above the waters some 12m (40ft) at its highest point and was virtually destroyed in a terrible hurricane back in 1932. More recently, Hurricane Gilbert in 1988 also took its toll. There is no direct run-off, so any rain drains in towards its centre and filters through the old coral limestone before eventually seeping back out into the sea.

The total Cayman population was estimated in 1993 at 31,200, with the population of Grand Cayman accounting for more than 90 per cent of the total. Of these, expatriates numbered about 8600, less than a third of the total population. George Town is the most heavily populated district in Grand Cayman, with approximately 13,500 residents. For the Cayman Island as a whole, West Bay, Bodden Town, Cayman Brac, East End, North Side and Little Cayman rank in that order by population.

There are around 20 hotels and 50 condominiums and guest houses servicing Grand Cayman, providing enough of a choice to suit all tastes and pocket. There are over 30 professional dive organisations registered with the Cayman islands Watersports Operators Association (CIWOA) running over 60 boats, see page 27 for further details.

The diving can be split up into four areas for convenience: West Side (which has the highest concentration of dive sites), South Shore, East End and North Wall.

Opposite: *Snorkellers congregate at the Sandbar where the water is only 1m (3ft) deep (page 100).*
Above: *Situated on Seven Mile Beach, these cottages have breathtaking sea-views.*

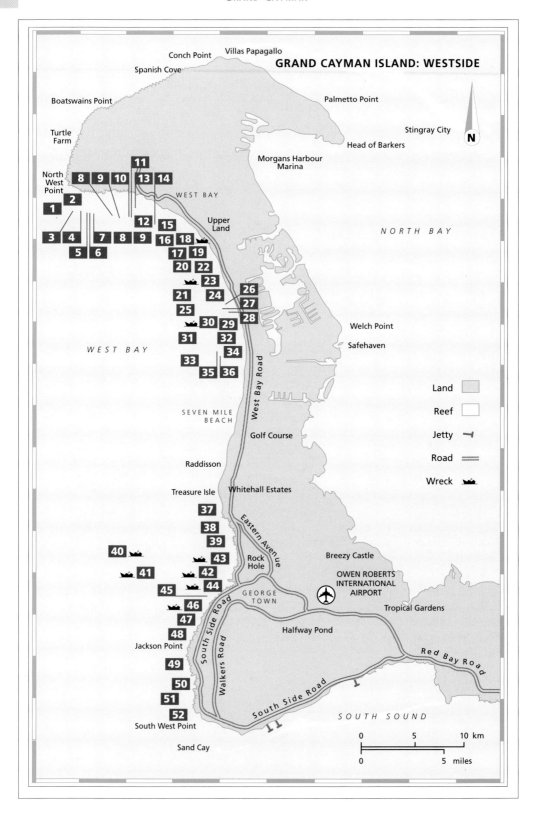

GRAND CAYMAN ISLAND: WESTSIDE

West Side

The majority of the dive centres are located along Seven Mile Beach where, subsequently, most of the diving takes place. Some dive centres are located in the larger hotels as concessions, but many operate independently and some may also have a range of small apartments or condominiums. Seven Mile Beach is also the base for the majority of the other watersports on Grand Cayman.

Most dive boats leave between 7:30-8:00 and tend not to travel long distances to the dive sites. Although the largest concentration of dive sites is along West Side, this does not ensure that you will dive your chosen location. Many dive operators have their favourite locations for training purposes, photography or whatever, and it is still a first-come-first served system. If an operator leaves for his chosen site early enough in the morning he may reserve it for whatever he plans to do that day. There are certain 'favourite' sites which now show signs of diver pollution and damage due to the sheer force of numbers who choose to dive there.

The dive operators run several dive instruction courses to all levels and these trainees will be visiting the reefs later on in the day. Most dive trips actually consist of a two tank dive, the first on the wall to about 30m (100ft) and the second a short time after to 12-18m (40-60ft). This will get all the dive boats back to base by around lunch time. For die-hards, a number of boats run in the afternoon and, in fact, some of the dive sites are best seen in the afternoon to get the most out of the sun's position and the quantity of the light.

1 NORTH WEST POINT DROP-OFF
★★★★

Location: Southwest from North West Point. Single pin mooring buoy. See map page 38.
Access: Boat dive.
Conditions: Exposed site, may be current. Visibility over 20m (66ft).
Minimum depth: 20m (66ft)
Maximum depth: Beyond 30m (100ft)
This is a deep dive, with the wall starting at 18m (60ft) and dropping rapidly to over 30m (100ft). From the mooring line, follow the edge of the reef crest to the wall through a series of spur and groove reefs.

Large yellow and orange sponges (*Pseudoceratina crassa*) abound as well as barrel and rope sponges. Gorgonian sea fans as well as plumes house a number of species of fish including trumpet fish (*Aulostomus maculatus*) and numerous species of small grouper.

Steeply sloping wall, deeply indented with good coral growths on the crest. Always look out into the open water in this area as there is a good chance of seeing the green turtle (*Chelonia mydas*).

To counteract the serious depletion of turtles, especially the Green turtle, a Turtle Farm was set up on Grand Cayman in 1968. The programme has been very successful, while achieving its conservation aims, has become a major tourist attraction. See feature page 46.

2 BONNIES ARCH
★★★★★★★★

Location: Shallow dive. A surface marker buoy indicates the start of the dive above the sand chute. Double pin mooring buoy. See map page 38.
Access: The shoreline here is hard 'ironstone' and care should be taken when entering the water. The buoy can be reached by strong swimmers from Bonnies Arch Condominiums and Dolphin Point Condominiums. Although popular with snorkellers, much of the reef is a little too deep.
Conditions: The spur and groove reef starts around 6m (20ft) and it is best to start at the mooring buoy to determine which way the current is flowing, if any. The surface can be choppy, underwater visibility in the 18m (60ft) region.
Minimum depth: 12m (40ft)
Maximum depth: 21m (70ft)
The spectacular Bonnies Arch is definitely worth seeing. It actually forms the entrance to a wide amphitheatre-type formation and is very fragile, even though it is heavily encrusted in corals and sponges. Avoid exhaling when diving under any underwater archways as the air bubbles can get trapped and kill coral encrustations. There is a school of tarpon in this area and some very large 3m (10ft) specimens of barrel sponge (*Xestospongia muta*): please resist the temptation to

climb inside them. You will also find quite friendly angelfish as well as filefish species, parrotfish and the ubiquitous yellowtail snappers (*Ocyurus chrysurus*).

3 ORANGE CANYON
★★★★

Location: Close to the beach and to the south of Bonnies Arch in front of Dolphin Point Condominiums. Mooring buoy marks the location to the top of the reef crest at around 15m (50ft). Single pin mooring buoy. See map page 38.

Access: The mooring buoy can be reached by strong swimmers, but again this is best done from a boat. Most dive operators will come here.

Conditions: May be a strong current. Visibility variable, better on the outer wall.

Minimum depth: 18m (60ft)

Maximum depth: Beyond 30m (100ft)

This superb location is named after the concentration of large orange sponges (*Pseudoceratina crassa*) which form one side of the canyon. This deep dive is concentrated around the largest of the coral pinnacles and the narrow cave at its base, which you can swim through with caution.

Orange Canyon has been known in the past for the large school of silversides which inhabit the area during the summer months.

If they are there, watch out for the tarpon (*Megalops atlanticus*) and the several species of jacks which also feed on them.

4 SENTINEL ROCK
★★★★

Location: Deep dive. Almost due east of Orange Canyon (site 3). Double pin mooring buoy. See map page 38.

Access: From the mooring buoy down to large coral pinnacle.

Conditions: This is quite an exposed site and should not be tackled lightly since it is a deep dive. Visibility normally over 30m (100ft)

Minimum depth: 20m (66ft)

Maximum depth: Beyond 30m (100ft)

This large coral pinnacle adjoins the spur and groove reef system which continues all the way along here parallel to the coast, and is part of Big Tunnel (Site 5). These coral pinnacles are very typical of West End diving: some are completely separated from the reef system, others appear as enlarged mounds stretching up and out from the reef crest. Overall there is reasonable coral growth, with some damage showing on the crests.

5 BIG TUNNEL
★★★★

Location: Deep dive. South of North West Point, close to Orange Canyon (Site 3) and part of the Western Wall. Single pin mooring buoy. See map page 38.

Access: Boat.

Conditions: Very little to moderate current, but no problem for experienced divers. The reeftop crest here is at 15m (50ft) and drops rapidly through a complicated array of tunnels, canyons, gulleys and caves. Visibility beyond 30m (100ft).

Minimum depth: 25m (80ft)

Maximum depth: Beyond 37m (120ft)

The main feature is a pair of large tunnels first discovered in 1970, which slice down through the reef system and then open out on to the wall, the first of the tunnels at 33m (110ft). These really are spectacular tunnels, adorned by sponges of every hue, making this a highly memorable dive. Divers are accompanied by curious grey angelfish (*Pomacanthus arcuatus*) and French angelfish (*Pomacanthus paru*). This is one of those dives to remember. At least three species of black coral are to be found in the archway.

6 EASY STREET
★★★★

Location: Deep dive. West Bay Wall, further southeast. Single pin mooring buoy. See map page 38.

Access: Boat.

Conditions: Slight to moderate current. Visibility around 30m (100ft)

Minimum depth: 15m (50ft)

Maximum depth: Beyond 30m (100ft)

Easy Street lies some 25m (80ft) from Big Dipper (Site 8) and is located very close to the mooring buoy. The tunnels twist and wind through the reef and will lead you out onto the wall which features large barrel sponges and gorgonian fan corals.

7 DRAGON'S HOLE
★★★★

Location: Deep dive. Single pin mooring buoy. See map page 38.

Access: Boat.

Conditions: Slight to moderate current, visibility not as good as outer wall.

Minimum depth: 20m (66ft)

Maximum depth: Beyond 30m (100ft)

Dragon's Hole is a narrow tunnel which cuts through Big

Dipper (Site 8). It can be dived to 30m (100ft) and 40m (132ft), but you should be accompanied by a knowledgeable dive master or dive guide. The hole or tunnel is approximately 10m (33ft) long and is entered at a depth of 20m (66ft) from the narrow chute which leads to the tunnel. It is very dark when you first enter it from the chimney, due to its bends. This hole is quite spectacular and has many different types of sponge and coral growth. You can also find silverside minnows here during the summer months.

8 BIG DIPPER (BLACK HOLE) (TEXAS HOLE)

★★★★

Location: Deep dive. West Bay Wall, continuing southeast parallel to the shore. Single pin mooring buoy. See map page 38.
Access: Boat.
Conditions: Slight to moderate current. Good visibility on outer wall.
Minimum depth: 15m (50ft)
Maximum depth: Beyond 30m (100ft)
This large coral pinnacle is an extension of the reef crest and is similar in many respects to most of the other coral pinnacles along this stretch of reef. However, it does have the Dragon's Hole (Site 7) which winds its way down through the reef. Numerous sea fans and black corals are to be found on the lower slopes of the reef, plus a myriad of fish.

9 LITTLE DIPPER (LITTLE TUNNELS)

★★★★

Location: Deep dive continuing along West Bay Wall. Single pin mooring buoy. See map page 38.
Access: Boat, down mooring buoy line to a sand chute and gulley system.
Conditions: Moderate current in exposed areas, none on canyons. Visibility 25m (80ft).
Minimum depth: 20m (66ft)
Maximum depth: Beyond 30m (100ft)
Although all of the West Bay Wall is similar in nature and topography, there are always surprises when you dive along it. Each site is individual even though it may only be a few metres from the next one – there is just so much to see. Here there are a number of small ravines and a little tunnel. Reef dwellers here include yellow snapper, sergeant majors, coney, margate, Creole wrasse, parrotfish, box fish and pufferfish.

Below: *The stunning Golden zoanthid, Parazoanthus swiftii, colonises sponge.*

10 ROUND ROCK CAVE
★★★★

Location: Deep dive. West Bay Wall, continuing southeast and near to Trinity Caves, (Site 12). Double and single pin mooring buoys. See map page 38.

Access: Boat. The set route is to enter on the north exit of the horseshoe-shaped reef.

Conditions: Slight to moderate current. Visibility normally over 25m (80ft)

Minimum depth: 18m (60ft)

Maximum depth: Beyond 30m (100ft)

This single coral pinnacle is a delight to swim around. The walls are covered in sea plumes, black coral trees and sponges, with lots of very nice crinoids and feather stars amongst the fan corals. There is a large elephant's ear sponge (*Agelas clathrodes*) which has broken off, but is still alive. Numerous shrimps and hermit crabs can also be found.

11 FISHEYE FANTASY
★★★★★

Location: Between Trinity Caves (Site 12) and the Sand Chute site 17. See map page 38.

Access: Boat.

Conditions: Deep dive. Can be current and exposed further out from the reef. Excellent visibility.

Minimum depth: 18m (60ft)

Maximum depth: Beyond 30m (100ft)

Fisheye Fantasy consists of three large coral pinnacles close together and easily dived at the same time. This site is very colourful with large sea fans and plenty of fish and invertebrates. It seems odd sometimes to concentrate on close up photography when faced with a wide angle vista such as there is here, but there are an awful lot of little creatures amongst the pinnacles: coral banded shrimp, peppermint shrimp, fairy basslet, Creole wrasse, cowfish and anemones.

12 TRINITY CAVES
★★★★

Location: Moving southeast along West Bay Wall. Single pin mooring buoy. See map page 38.

Access: Boat.

Conditions: Deep dive. Average current. Visibility is dependent on the number of divers who are able to control their buoyancy on the sand plain.

Minimum depth: 14m (45ft)

Maximum depth: Beyond 30m (100ft)

The coral mass starts at 14m (45ft) and slopes down steeply through a number of chimneys and gulleys, most

Opposite: *Visibility is generally excellent and rarely influenced by tide or current.*
Below: *The Peppermint Goby, Coryphopterus lipernes, is one of around 1500 species of goby.*

of which are almost completely overgrown. Large gorgonian fan corals and black coral can be found as well as a myriad of fish and invertebrates. A superb dive location: look closely under the overhangs for the waving antennae of lobster and various shrimp.

13 CEMETERY REEF
★★★☆☆☆

Location: North side of the Slaughterhouse Reef and opposite Cemetery Road off West Bay Road. See map page 38.
Access: Boat. Over reef crest into a steep spur and groove reef system.
Conditions: Shallow dive. Moderate current, but sheltered in grooves. Visibility 15m (50ft).
Minimum depth: 15m (50ft)
Maximum depth: 18m (60ft)
This is a nice steep wall, well cut with fissures and ravines featuring large barrel sponges, rope sponges, black corals and gorgonian sea fans. Moray eels and lobster of several types can also be found. The top of the reef crest looks sparse at first but, on closer examination, there are large numbers of blennies, gobies and juvenile wrasse all over the harder coral surfaces.

14 NEPTUNE'S WALL
★★★★

Location: South of Trinity Caves (Site 12) and further out from Slaughterhouse Reef. On a continuation of the West Bay Wall, running southeast parallel to the shore. Double pin mooring buoy. See map page 38.
Access: Boat.
Conditions: Deep dive. Slight to moderate current. Visibility usually over 20m (66ft).
Minimum depth: 20m (66ft)
Maximum depth: Beyond 30m (100ft)
This is a spur and groove reef more gently sloping than Trinity. There is a large coral pinnacle and a cave gulley system with black coral and large sponges. Fairly tame French angelfish may follow you around. Yellow snapper plus barred hamlet (*Hypoplectrus puella*) and yellowtail reeffish (*Chromis enchrysura*). Many juvenile wrasse.

15 SLAUGHTERHOUSE WALL
★★★

Location: Further south from Cemetery Reef (Site 13) – really just an extension of the same inner fringing reef. Single pin mooring buoy. See map page 38.

Access: From the shore beach or day boat.
Conditions: Shallow dive. Little or no current. Visibility not as clear as outer reef. Coral rubble in shallows.
Minimum depth: 12m (40ft)
Maximum depth: 14m (50ft)
This is a fairly popular site as a second dive. Lots of fish life with giant anemones (*Condylactis gigantea*) and Pederson cleaning shrimp (*Periclimenes pedersoni*) in the crevices. Some turtle grass (*Thalassia testiudinum*). The coral rubble, although on first appearance quite boring, actually has some very interesting marine organisms such as brittle starfish, marine worms, tiny hydroids, small snails and sea urchins.

16 WALL STREET
★★★★

Location: Deep dive before the Sand Chute (Site 17). Single pin mooring buoy. See map p.38.
Access: Boat, follow mooring line down to steeply cut spur and groove reef and work along wall.
Conditions: Moderate to strong current. Visibility over 30m (100ft)
Minimum depth: 20m (66ft)
Maximum depth: Beyond 30m (100ft)
Wall Street features very good quality corals on the walls plus large barrel sponges, yellow tube sponges and bright pink vase sponges (*Niphates digitalis*). There are many juvenile wrasse and curious grouper and coney, with smooth trunkfish (*Lactophrys triqueter*) and scrawled filefish (*Aluterus scriptus*) to be found amongst the sea fans. The sea fans are numerous and fairly evenly spaced all over the reef tops of the spurs.

17 SAND CHUTE
★★★★

Location: Deep dive, southeast of Neptune's Wall (Site 14). Single pin mooring buoy. See map page 38.
Access: Boat.
Conditions: Variable due to the increased level of sand particles in suspension. Generally little current and it is easy to dive too deep here. Visibility over 25m (80ft).

Above and below: *Christmas tree worms, Spirobranchus giganteus, are commonly found embedded in the upper sunlit parts of coral heads. The feathery radioles appear in stunning colour variations.*

The Cayman Island's flag, official seal and currency all depict the Turtle. Originally called Las Tortugas by the explorer Christopher Columbus, the islands were named after the large numbers of turtles found on land and in the water and it was the turtle which brought back sailors to these enchanting islands. The turtle was an important food supplement to the mariners' diet, because the animals could be kept alive as an important additional source of food to stave off the ravages of scurvy.

Over the centuries the world's oceans have been depleted of many species of turtle and all are on the international endangered species list. The Cayman Islands' population suffered greatly, but fortunately the tide has now turned for these aquatic giants. The Turtle Farm on Grand Cayman was originally set up in 1968 by a private company, Mariculture Ltd, in a tidal creek along North Sound. The venture was somewhat of a gamble because there was no statistical information on breeding turtles in captivity. By trial and error and refining techniques, the project has enjoyed amazing success.

In the very early stages breeding stock and eggs had to be collected from the wild. It was agreed by the conservation authorities of several countries that eggs could only be collected from nests found below the tide line, where the eggs would have no chance of hatching. Gradually, the collection grew from sources as far away as Surinam, Costa Rica and Ascension Island.

The farm moved to its present location in West Bay in 1971 and by 1978 had achieved its objective of having sufficient breeding stock to make the farm self-sufficient and financially viable. There are now approximately 350 turtles in the breeding stock selected from creatures caught in the wild, eggs collected in the wild and raised on the farm and, increasingly, from eggs laid, incubated and hatched from the farm's own stock.

When the eggs are laid in the farm's enclosure, about 30 days after mating, they are collected and placed in an incubator. At 28°C (82°F) there will be an equal proportion of male and females hatched. Any cooler and only males would emerge, any higher and only females would be born. The baby turtles hatch after 60 days and are transferred to special tanks and fed on a specially formulated diet.

This is the only commercial turtle farm in the world and 8000 turtles are reared each year for its commercial commitments and products. A number are specially selected from wild egg stock to enhance the breeding programme. So far, around 30,000 have been released into the wild. All of these animals have been tagged for scientific and recognition purposes. Constant monitoring of the turtles has found that some of the Cayman-released turtles have been found in Mexico, Honduras, Cuba and Venezuela.

The turtle most favoured in the commercial programme is the green turtle (*Chelonia mydas*). There are also hawksbill and loggerhead turtles at the farm, but one of their breeding successes is of the Kemp's Ridley turtle (*Lepidochelys kempi*) which is the smallest of the turtles in their programme and they are the world's most endangered sea turtle. The first hatchlings were born in 1968. They are raised to be released into the wild and as the nucleus for a future captive breeding programme to ensure that they do not become extinct.

The Cayman Turtle Farm has been owned and operated by the Cayman Government since 1983. They also support post-graduate research and their researchers now supply the international community with scientific information. Although the farm is one of the Cayman's major tourist attractions, it is also a scientific research station with a very high reputation concentrating on research and breeding programmes to cast more light on and to help re-colonise our oceans with the once common sea turtle.

This shift in the farm's emphasis from breeding stock for commercial uses to scientific work was forced upon them by the decision of the USA in 1978 to adhere to the CITES convention and ban all turtle products. This included the banning of any turtle products being shipped through US ports resulted in the farm losing 80% of its markets overnight.

The farm is still hoping for a change in the regulations, based on their argument that the interests of the green sea turtle are best served if the commercial markets are catered for by farmed animals, as this would relinquish the need to hunt them in the wild.

As part of the farm's other tourist attractions, you can find representatives of most of the Island's indigenous flora and fauna including butterflies, the rare Cayman parrot, Cayman crocodile and iguanas. The Turtle Farm is open seven days a week, 8:30-17:00; tel 949-3893/4/fax 949-1387

Below: *View of Turtle Farm.*
Bottom left: *Visitors handling turtles.*
Bottom right: *Young turtles are placed in tanks and fed a special diet.*

TURTLE PRODUCTS

Although farmed turtle meat is sold in local restaurants, turtle products are NOT sold in any of the islands' souvenir shops. Due to the CITES law (Convention on International Trade for Endangered Species) enacted in 1978 by the US Government, visitors from the US and Europe are prohibited from taking home any sea turtle products, nor will the US Customs authorities permit the shipment of any turtle products through any type of US port.

Turtle meat has been eaten traditionally by Caymanians ever since the islands were first settled and this cultural traditional fishery is allowed under CITES. If you can get over any emotional feelings about eating turtle meat, then the Cayman Islands can be justified in selling the product.

Until the CITES review over the question of farmed turtle meat and products can be answered, there is a rising stockpile of turtle shell waiting for a commercial market. It has already been indicated that there may not be a market for the products due to the length of time that they have not been available worldwide. Governments are concerned that if turtle products are re-introduced into the commercial market, there may also be an increase in poaching worldwide.

However, as a side issue to righting the world's wrongs, the Cayman Turtle Farm is undeniably an enormously popular tourist attraction earning millions of dollars. Much needed research is being obtained and vast numbers of the animals are being released into the wild.

Minimum depth: 20m (66ft)
Maximum depth: Beyond 30m (100ft)
This is a large river of sand which bisects the wall. The Sand Chute is around 90m (300ft) wide: you cannot miss it! The best area is down the edge of the reef wall which can tower 20m (66ft) above you. Lots of interesting small caves filled with all manner of marine life. Watch out for stingrays (*Dasyatis americana*), garden eels (*Heteroconger halis*) and spotted eaglerays (*Aetobatus narinari*). There are a number of types of large sponges also as well as black coral.

18 DOC POULSON WRECK
★★★

Location: In a sand patch surrounded by good coral growth. Single pin mooring buoy. See map page 38.
Access: Boat. Mooring buoy is attached to wreck.
Conditions: Slight current. Visibility 15m (50ft)
Minimum depth: 12m (40ft)
Maximum depth: 15m (50ft)
Named after Dr Poulson in honour of his work with the hyperbaric recompression chamber at the hospital, this anchor barge was sunk deliberately in March 1991 as an addition to the existing reef system. The reef is a better dive than the wreck, but it will improve in time.

19 MITCH MILLER'S REEF
★★★☆☆☆☆

Location: Shallow dive. Named after the famous 1960s band leader who used to own a house on the shore. South of Cemetery Road, towards Timms Point. Single pin mooring buoy. See map page 38.
Access: From the shore or boat.
Conditions: Slight to no current. Visibility cloudy.
Minimum depth: 15m (50ft)
Maximum depth: 18m (60ft)
The reef here comprises lots of large coral heads divided by gulleys and canyons, the walls of which are covered in marine life. Watch out for flamingo tongue shells (*Cyphoma gibbosum*) on the sea fans. Reef dwellers here include small schools of snapper and grunts as well as parrotfish and wrasse.

20 MARTY'S WALL
★★★★

Location: Deep dive. Single pin mooring buoy. See map page 38.
Access: Boat

Conditions: Moderate current.
Minimum depth: 20m (66ft)
Maximum depth: Beyond 30m (100ft)
Similar to Site 21.

21 KNIFE
★★★★☆

Location: To the south of the Sand Chute (Site 17). Single pin mooring buoy. See map page 38.
Access: Boat
Conditions: Moderate current.
Minimum depth: 20m (66ft)
Maximum depth: Beyond 30m (100ft)
This is the next stretch of West Bay Wall, although the angle is less steep here.

The reef is still cut dramatically by fissures and tunnels, with lots of sponges and invertebrates. You will also find a number of varieties of moray eels and small grouper, with parrotfish and small schools of juvenile wrasse continually moving over the reef.

22 LOST TREASURE REEF
★★★☆☆☆

Location: Shallow dive. Single pin mooring buoy. See map page 38.
Access: Shore and small boat. Mooring buoy clearly locates position.
Conditions: Slight current. Visibility not as good as outer reef.
Minimum depth: 13m (40ft)
Maximum depth: 15m (50ft)
Similar to Site 23.

23 SPANISH ANCHOR
★★★☆☆☆

Location: Shallow dive. Further southeast from Mitch Miller's Reef (Site 19) about 1km (0.75 mile) from the public beach. Single pin mooring buoy. See map page 38.
Access: Shore and small boat. Mooring buoy clearly locates position.
Conditions: Slight current. Visibility not as good as outer reef.
Minimum depth: 13m (40ft)
Maximum depth: 15m (50ft)
This is generally done as a second dive by the various dive operators on this stretch of coast. This is a spur and groove reef with what is said to be an old Spanish

anchor embedded in the reef. Although heavily encrusted, there is no evidence of any wreck and the anchor is probably much more modern than indicated, due to its shape. A high proportion of anchors which have been dropped on these reefs in the past are never recovered (hence one of the reasons for the introduction of mooring buoys for dive boats), which is another reason for doubting the authenticity of this one.

24 ANGELFISH REEF
★★★☆☆☆

Location: Shallow dive. Continuing southeast along inner fringing reef. Double pin mooring buoy. See map page 38.
Access: Boat. Down mooring line onto reef crest.
Conditions: Light to moderate current. Visibility good.
Minimum depth: 10m (33ft)
Maximum depth: 15m (50ft)
As the name implies, you can find a number of species of angelfish here including the queen angelfish (*Holacanthus ciliaris*), while the French angelfish are particularly inquisitive and make for superb photographic subjects. This is a very colourful dive with sea fans and plumes.

You will also find coronetfish (*Fistularia tabacaria*) and tiger grouper (*Mycteroperca tigris*) waiting at the cleaning stations along this reef. Octopus can be located at night.

25 EAGLE'S NEST
★★★☆☆☆

Location: Deep dive. Further out from Angelfish Reef (Site 24). Single pin mooring buoy. See map page 38.
Access: Boat.
Conditions: Moderate current. Visibility good.
Minimum depth: 15m (50ft)
Maximum depth: 25m (83ft)
Eagle's Nest has a lovely reef structure interspaced with sand patches. Spotted eaglerays are often seen here as well as turtles cruising past the outer wall. The walls are covered in encrusting sponges, with lobster and shrimps all over them as well as the measled cowrie shell (*Cyprae zebra*). There are good quality corals and big barrel sponges at the top of the reef crest. This is a very good dive to explore each spur and groove in turn, and is a popular dive with day boat operators.

Green turtles, Chelonia mydas, are not scared of divers but touching them causes distress.

26 AQUARIUM (KILLER PUFFER)
★★★★

Location: Shallow dive. Due west from Harbour Heights Condominiums. Two single pin mooring buoys to the north and south of the reef. See map page 38.
Access: Boat. Down either mooring line.
Conditions: No current, quite sheltered. Visibility around 15m (50ft).
Minimum depth: 10m (33ft)
Maximum depth: 13m (43ft)
This well-known reef is aptly named, but I feel that all of the islands' reefs could be called the 'Aquarium' due to the profusion of life and colour to be found: 'Killer Puffer' refers to a previous name. Large pillar corals (*Dendrogyra cylindrus*) and staghorn coral (*Acropora cervicornis*) are much in evidence, and barrel sponges and yellow sponges can also be found. Very tame fish, such as Sergeant majors (*Abudefduf saxatilis*), snapper and sharpnosed pufferfish (*Canthigaster rostrata*), are joined by lots of parrotfish and wrasse. Blennies and gobies are all over the stony coral surfaces. Excellent for photography due to the physical amount and diversity of marine life to be found.

27 PETER'S REEF (GOVERNOR'S) (JAX DAX)
★★★★★★★★

Location: Shallow dive. Continuation of Aquarium (Site 26), south towards the Governor's home. Single pin mooring buoy. See map page 38.
Access: Boat. Too far from shore to swim, although shallow enough to see when snorkelling from a boat.
Conditions: No current. Calm, sheltered location. Visibility 15m (50ft).
Minimum depth: 8m (30ft)
Maximum depth: 13m (43ft)
Named after Peter Milburn, a local conservationist who has been feeding fish and entertaining divers on this reef for many years. This reef is directly inshore from the wreck of the *Oro Verde*, and consists of shallow sand gulleys and coral ridges very similar to the Aquarium – a large and scattered patch reef which eventually descends towards the outer reef crest and the wall. Reef alive with tame French angelfish and parrotfish.

28 THREE TREES
★★★★★★★★

Location: Shallow dive. Further south on same fringing reef. Other side of Governor's home. See map page 38.

Access: Boat. Although the reef is relatively shallow, this is still inaccessible from the shore.
Conditions: Little or no current, good light and visibility, sheltered and calm.
Minimum depth: 8m (30ft)
Maximum depth: 13m (43ft)
Very similar to Sites 26 and 27, this low-lying spur and groove reef features barrel sponges, gorgonian fan corals, staghorn coral and large brain corals with a variety of coloured Christmas tree worms (*Spirobranchus giganteus*).

29 PARADISE REEF
★★★

Location: Shallow dive. Further south, reef system joins on to the reef in front of the Oro Verde. Single pin mooring buoy. See map page 38.
Access: Boat. Mooring line to patch reef and spur and groove reef.
Conditions: Little or no current. Visibility 20m (66ft).
Minimum depth: 12m (40ft)
Maximum depth: 15m (50ft)
Coral life not as good as Three Trees (Site 28), but lots of sea fans (*Gorgonia flabellum*) and sea plumes (*Pseodopterogorgia sp.*). Lima file clams (*Lima scabra*) in crevices as well as cleaner shrimps including the coral banded shrimp (*Stenopus hispidus*). Reef has plenty of tame fish including a very large, tame dog snapper (*Lutjanus joco*) called 'Fang'.

30 ORO VERDE WRECK
★★★★

Location: Deep dive. Directly opposite the Holiday Inn. Double pin mooring buoy on the bow and a single pin mooring buoy on the stern. See map page 38.
Access: Boat. Down either mooring line onto wreck.
Conditions: Calm, good light for photography. Visibility over 20m (66ft).
Minimum depth: 13m (40ft)
Maximum depth: 17m (56ft)
The *Oro Verde* was bought by a group of dive operators and became the Cayman Islands first man-made dive site when she was sunk on 31 May 1980. This 55-m (181-ft) wreck is now well broken up by winter storms and actually moved 90m (300ft) during its first winter season. The wreck now lies on its port side with the bow facing north. Although the wreck has only been submerged since 1980, it is now home to an amazing array of marine life including a variety of species of

Opposite: *Unusual rock formations make diving in the Caymans endlessly fascinating.*

snapper and arrow crabs (*Stenorhynchus seticornis*). There is a very tame Nassau grouper (*Epinephelus striatus*) and there is even a small colony of garden eels (*Heteroconger halis*). A very comfortable introduction for beginners to wreck diving and photography.

31 SHARK HOLE (HAMMERHEAD HOLE)
★★★★

Location: Shallow dive. Single pin mooring buoy. See map page 38.
Access: Boat. Down mooring line, onto reef crest, then over into chute.
Conditions: Similar to Sand Chute (Site 17). Very easy to go beyond your dive profile. Visibility 15m (50 feet).
Minimum depth: 20m (66ft)
Maximum depth: Beyond 30m (100ft)
Similar to Site 33. (Named after the chance encounter of a hammerhead shark at some time.)

32 WILDLIFE REEF
★★★★

Location: Shallow dive. Single pin mooring buoy. See map page 38.
Access: Boat. Down mooring line, onto reef crest, then over into chute.

Conditions: Similar to Sand Chute (Site 17). Very easy to go beyond your dive profile. Visibility 15m (50 feet).
Minimum depth: 20m (66ft)
Maximum depth: Beyond 30m (100ft)
Similar to Site 33.

33 CARIBBEAN CLUB SAND CHUTE
★★★★

Location: Deep dive. Opposite the Caribbean Club. Single pin mooring buoy. See map page 38.
Access: Boat. Down mooring line, onto reef crest, then over into chute.
Conditions: Similar to Sand Chute (Site 17). Very easy to go beyond your dive profile. Visibility 15m (50 feet).
Minimum depth: 20m (66ft)
Maximum depth: Beyond 30m (100ft)
This river of sand cuts through the inner fringing spur and groove reef until it reaches the outer reef crest and the wall. It has a very gradual incline and you will find stingrays and the occasional spotted eagleray foraging for molluscs and worms. There is a small section of coral which cuts the chute in half at the apex of the reef crest where there is a large black coral (*Antipathes sp.*). Nearby is a large barrel sponge which was pulled apart by Hurricane Gilbert in 1988.

Above: *Star horseshoe worm, Pomatostegus stellatus.*

LONE STAR REEF
★★★★★

Location: Shallow dive. Single pin mooring buoy. See map page 38.
Access: Boat.
Conditions: Coral growth and fish life is above average as this is still a relatively new site. Little or no current and no sedimentation.
Minimum depth: 15m (50ft)
Maximum depth: 18m (60ft)
Similar to Site 35.

35 MESA (FISH REEF) (RHAPSODY)
★★★★★

Location: Shallow dive. Close to the Marriott along Seven Mile Beach to the north of George Town. Single pin mooring buoy. See map page 38.
Access: Boat.
Conditions: Coral growth and fish life is above average as this is still a relatively new site. Little or no current and no sedimentation.
Minimum depth: 15m (50ft)
Maximum depth: 18m (60ft)
Very nice coral plateau with fine brain and other stony

ORO VERDE

Oro Verde is Spanish for 'green gold'. She was a sister ship of the SS *Pueblo* and SS *Navaho* , famous for their spying missions during the Korean and Vietnam wars. After the *Oro Verde* was decommissioned she was bought by the Green Banana Trader. Because the *Oro Verde* is so popular as a dive site (Site 30, page 50), the two mooring buoys are often taken. When this happens, dive charter boats tend to attach onto the Paradise mooring (Site 29, page 50).

---

corals. Sea fans some overgrown with fire coral (*Millepora alcicornis*), are perfect for filefish (*Monacanthus tuckeri*) and flamingo tongues (*Cyphoma gibbosum*). Barracuda, snappers and grunts are all over as well as parrotfish and trunkfish. The overhang seems to be scooped out of the coral and makes an oval-like formation which hosts several species of grunts and snapper.

This site has the most fish I have ever seen in one small area in the Caymans; large tiger grouper being cleaned by small gobies and golden hamlet (*Hypoplectrus gummingatta*) with their distinctive blue and black face markings were all over. An absolutely superb site for photography. Octopus, squid, shrimp and lobster are seen on night dives as well as the bearded fireworm (*Hermodice carunculata*).

Below: *Blackedge triplefin, Enneanectes atrorus*

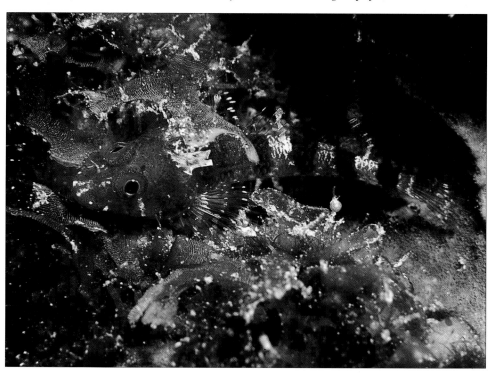

36 ROYAL PALMS LEDGE
★★★☆☆☆

Location: Opposite the Marriott. Single pin mooring buoy. See map page 38.

Access: Always by boat because it is the furthest out of the shallow reefs.

Conditions: Safe, easy shallow dive, little or no current. Visibility 15m (50ft).

Minimum depth: 14m (46ft)

Maximum depth: 17m (56ft)

Whereas the normal spur and groove formations lead away from the shore, this large 'groove' with its sandy base actually curves around towards the shore and forms a giant horseshoe-shaped reef formation. There is a deeply defined overhang as it forms around the bend and the whole area is teeming with life. This is a very popular night dive location with lots of shrimp and squid in the shallower water.

37 PAGEANT BEACH REEF (THE WHARF)
★★★☆☆☆

Location: Shallow dive. Further south along West Bay. Single pin mooring buoy. See map page 38.

Access: Boat and shore, but is a lengthy swim. Eight metres (25ft) to the bottom of the mooring pin.

Conditions: Little or no current, fair visibility.

Minimum depth: 13m (42ft)

Maximum depth: 15m (50ft)

Very similar to the other spur and groove sites, with number of tight valleys and overhangs framed by all manner of corals. There is some coral damage. The fish are very tame and well used to divers all along this reef system. Lots of sandy areas and small tunnels with occasional tarpon and silversides during the summer months. For photography, the fish can be a nuisance, because they are constantly searching for food. It is **not** recommended that you feed them.

38 SOTO'S (CHEESEBURGER)
★★☆☆☆

Location: Shallow dive. Directly opposite Bob Soto's and the Lobster Pot. Marked by two single pin mooring buoys in the north and central parts of the reef. See map page 38.

Access: Boat. Follow each of the mooring lines down to the reef platform.

Conditions: Excellent light for photography.

Minimum depth: 2m (6ft)

STINGING CELLS

Anemones, corals and jellyfish are armed with a battery of stinging cells called nematocysts. These cells are actually a tiny barbed harpoon tipped with a paralysing poison which the creature will fire into its prey should they happen to brush against them. These microscopic cells are particularly effective in the case of the Portuguese Man-of-War, whose tentacles can trail underneath over 10m (33ft). During late spring and early summer large aggregations of thimble jellyfish (*Linuche unguiculata*) can be found in the waters, which can cause irritation to the softer parts of the skin. Local remedies are known for these conditions.

Maximum depth: 16m (53ft)

Very popular dive for beginners and 'class room' work. Consequently it is dived a great deal and there is some coral damage. Large colonies of elkhorn and staghorn coral rise to 2m (6ft) from the surface. There are lots of narrow passageways through the coral heads and the fish are well used to divers invading their realm. Very busy site with many snorkellers, but not that special for divers, considering some of the other amazing sites a short distance away.

39 FISH POT REEF
★★★☆☆

Location: Shallow dive. Adjoining Soto's on the southern end. Single pin mooring buoy. See map page 38.

Access: Boat or lengthy swim from shore.

Conditions: A safe, shallow dive with no current. Be careful of boat traffic as this area of the fringing reef is very busy. Visibility 10m (33ft).

Minimum depth: 8m (26ft)

Maximum depth: 14m (46ft)

Very similar to Soto's (Site 38), with lots of coral heads topped with sea fans and plumes, small gorgonians in the fissures and plenty of tame fish. Yellowtail snapper and grunts are very common, as are sergeant majors and numerous damselfish as well as juvenile wrasse and parrotfish. Crabs and lobsters abound at night.

40 KIRK PRIDE WRECK
★★★★★

Location: North of George Town harbour over the edge of the drop-off. See map page 38.

Access: By Atlantis Research Submersible, (see p. 23).

Opposite: *A vast array of soft corals stretch out to catch nutrients.*

Conditions: Awesome!
Maximum depth: 242m (800ft)
The *Kirk Pride* was presumed lost until rediscovered accidentally by the Atlantis Research Submersible whilst carrying her two passengers along the deeper edge of the wall. At 54m (180ft) long and grossing 506 tonnes (498 tons), she is 'hooked' on an ancient coral outcrop. The *Kirk Pride* sank at 9:30 on 9 January 1976.

The journey down the reef wall is spectacular with giant elephant's ear sponges over 5m (18ft) across. Huge arrow crabs and delicate deep water sea lilies inhabit the rocky outcrops. In this cooler water below the thermocline, the underwater visibility is in excess of 130m (429ft).

You can only begin to appreciate the scale of all this when the submersible hangs off the stern of the *Kirk Pride*, switches off the 600 watt quartz halogen lamps and you can see the entire shipwreck by the filtered light from above. This dive is not to be missed.

41 CARRIE LEE WRECK
★★★★

Location: North of George Town harbour. See map page 38.
Access: Boat and scenic view from the Atlantis XI submarine, (see box page 23).
Conditions: Very deep dive, beyond the recommended safe range of the CIWOA.
Minimum depth: 40m (130ft)
Maximum depth: 60m (200ft)
The *Carrie Lee* was a 30-m (100-ft) freighter. She had originally sunk on the north side of Grand Cayman, but she had 'turned turtle' and in an effort to save her she was towed around to George Town. Sadly, she flipped over once more and sank. She now rests upright in very deep water.

42 BALBOA
★★★★★

Location: Shallow dive. Directly out from George Town harbour in main shipping lane. Single pin mooring buoy. See map page 38.
Access: Boat. Now generally dived only at night due to the movement of cruise ships.
Conditions: Excellent night dive. No current, but poor visibility due to ship movements.
Minimum depth: 8m (26ft)
Maximum depth: 10m (33ft)
The *Balboa* was a 115-m (375-ft) lumber steamer which was wrecked off George Town during the 1932 hurricane. Unable to be salvaged, she was a danger to shipping and was subsequently destroyed by blasting in

1957. The wreckage is strewn over a wide area making this a very popular site for exploration. It is surprising that even so close to the harbour, there is so much marine life to be found. This is one of the best night dives on the island due to its being in protected waters and still relatively undived with a profusion of marine life, particularly invertebrates.

43 CALLIE WRECK
★★★★★

Location: Shallow dive. Inshore from the Balboa in front of Surfside Watersports. See map page 38.
Access: Can be done by day boat, but more often from the shore, 30m (100ft).
Conditions: Easy and safe, apart from other localised boat traffic.
Minimum depth: 6m (20ft)
Maximum depth: 6m (20ft)
Sunk in 1944, the *Callie* was a 66-m (220-ft) four-masted schooner or barquentine, which had been converted to diesel engines. In 1957 she was registered as a shipping hazard and, like the *Balboa* (see Site 42), the British Corps of Army Engineers blew her up. She is now scattered all over the seabed. This is a very popular snorkelling site.

There is the remains of an even older wreck 100m (330ft) south of the *Callie* called the *Arbutus*. This ancient wooden vessel is now long gone and only the ballast stones remain. For those who want to dive this area, you can sometimes find artefacts, but you must obey the wreck laws of the Cayman Islands.

44 EDEN ROCK
★★★★★★

Location: Shallow dive. Slightly to the north and opposite Eden Rock Dive Centre, to the south of George Town. Marked by two single pin mooring buoys to the north and south of the reef. See map page 38.
Access: Can be done by local day boats, for those who are not able to swim out from the shore. Rinse tank and shower convenient for use after the dive.
Conditions: No current. Some coral damage and lower visibility due to the popularity of the site and proximity of George Town harbour. Visibility variable.
Minimum depth: 6m (20ft)
Maximum depth: 15m (50ft)
This labyrinth of inter-connecting tunnels and caves has deteriorated over the years, but is still popular with beginners and underwater photographers. The swim out over the ancient sand coral platform is studded by small coral boulders and the occasional sea fan. I was disappointed in the condition of the site after 18

months. Probably better to dive Eden Rock at night.

45 DEVIL'S GROTTO

★★★☆☆☆☆☆

Location: Shallow dive. Opposite Eden Rock and more to the south. Marked by both a double pin and single pin mooring buoy to the south and north of the reef. See map page 38.

Access: Boat or shore.

Conditions: No current, and low visibility, slightly better as you travel south.

Minimum depth: 6m (20ft)

Maximum depth: 13m (40ft)

Very similar to Eden Rock and a continuation of same: you can lose yourself exploring these gulleys and crevices with your 'buddy'. Tarpon are often seen 'resting' during daylight hours. Very popular location with everyone but showing obvious signs of deterioration, with some coral damage.

46 PARROT'S REEF

★★★☆☆☆☆

Location: Shallow dive. Opposite Parrot's Landing, south from Eden Roack along South Church Street. See

map page 38.

Access: Directly from the shore

Conditions: Can be moderate current over reef top. Visibility less than on northern wall.

Minimum depth: 8m (26ft)

Maximum depth: 15m (50ft)

Popular training dive, but also very good photographically. The sparse coral heads close to shore soon become more complex with depth, although the coral is not as good as at Devil's Grotto (Site 45) and is showing signs of damage. At 18m (60ft) you can find the remains of a small tug, the *Anna Marie* which used to be the *Atlantis* submarine's tender. It sank in stormy weather in October 1987 and is an interesting backdrop for your photographs.

47 SEAVIEW REEF (SUNSET REEF)

★★★☆☆☆☆

Location: Shallow dive. Directly out from the Sunset House Hotel. Single pin mooring buoy. See map page 38.

Access: Directly from the shore. Convenient showers allow you to rinse off your equipment after the dive.

Conditions: Visibility variable.

The wreck of the Oro Verde, Grand Cayman (Site 30, page 50).

Minimum depth: 10m (33ft)
Maximum depth: 14m (50ft)

This is a safe, easy dive, if a little crowded due to its popularity as a training site. Similar to Parrot's Reef (Site 46), Seaview Reef has some broken corals but not as severe as might be imagined. The coral growth is diverse, but there is not much of it. You can also dive the *Anna Marie* from this site, but it is a lengthy swim. Tame fish are well used to being fed by divers (but feeding is **not** recommended). The fish can be a nuisance because of this feeding. Popular for night diving. (See feature page 124.)

48 WALDOE'S REEF
★★★☆☆☆

Location: Opposite Coconut Harbout Resort. See map page 38.
Access: Long swim 80m (300 feet) from shore.
Conditions: Little current, visibility average.
Minimum depth: 10m (33ft)
Maximum depth: 15m (50ft)

This is a popular dive named after its most famous resident, a 2-m (6.5-feet) moray eel known as 'Waldoe'. This fish is quite tame and has been handled and fed over many years, but you should still approach him with caution. Many other tame fish including black grouper (*Mycteroperca bonaci*) and the great barracuda (*Sphyraena barracuda*).

49 ARMCHAIR REEF
★★★★

Location: Shallow dive. Single pin mooring buoy. See map page 38.
Access: Boat.
Conditions: Moderate current, but strong around the pinnacle. Visibility over 20m (66ft).
Minimum depth: 18m (60ft)
Maximum depth: Beyond 30m (100ft)
Similar to Site 51.

50 FRANK'S REEF (SMITH'S COVE)
★★★★

Location: Shallow dive. Single pin mooring buoy. See map page 38.
Access: Boat.
Conditions: Moderate current, but strong around the pinnacle. Visibility over 20m (66ft).
Minimum depth: 18m (60ft)

Maximum depth: Beyond 30m (100ft)
Similar to Site 51.

51 EAGLE RAY ROCK
★★★★

Location: Deep dive. On the end of Grand Cayman's West Side. Double pin mooring buoy. See map page 38.
Access: Boat.
Conditions: Moderate current, but strong around the pinnacle. Visibility over 20m (66ft).
Minimum depth: 18m (60ft)
Maximum depth: Beyond 30m (100ft)

This large 'L' shaped canyon festooned with orange sponges and black coral is named after the regular sightings of eaglerays which cruise the southern end of the wall.

This is quite an exposed site and dive operators rarely come to the wall, because many casual divers are unable to handle the current, which can be quite swift around the pinnacle.

Eagle Ray Rock is a lovely dive (similar to the wall off West Bay), and since it is under-dived it's well worth requesting if you feel comfortable with sudden strong currents.

52 BLACKIE'S HOLE (BLACK FOREST HOLE)
★★★★

Location: Deep dive. Further along same stretch of wall. Single pin mooring buoy. See map page 38.
Access: Boat. Last dive on West Side.
Conditions: Current along wall. Good visibility.
Minimum depth: 20m (66ft)
Maximum depth: Beyond 30m (100ft)

This is a beautiful wall with rope sponges (*Aplysinia sp.*), and the yellow tube sponge (*Aplysinia fistularis*), gorgonian sea fans and a myriad of fish including pairs of butterflyfish, angelfish, filefish, parrotfish and juvenile wrasse. Gobies and blennies can be found on most coral surfaces. Named for the profuse growth of black coral which grows on the more protected, deeper slopes of the wall.

A very fitting end to the diving along the west coast of Grand Cayman.

South Shore

Many of the sites listed are marked by buoys placed by the Department of the Environment. However, a large number of locations used regularly by the various dive centres along the South Shore and East End are not buoyed and there may be some confusion as to the exact location of the sites. The CIWOA also have their own name for some of these locations which may differ from those sites recognised by the DOE. This also adds to the confusion.

The DOE are committed to installing buoys at all the regularly used dive locations to minimise anchor damage. Where there is no permanent mooring, the dive boats will either hang off the reef and drift above the divers or they will place a sand anchor (non-grappling) into an empty sand patch to avoid coral damage.

The dive sites are numbered from Pull-and-be-Damned Point in the west all the way around East Side to Colliers Channel, located above the Morritts Tortuga Club.

The spur and groove reef along the South Shore is well defined, signifying the long-term severity of the prevailing weather which has shaped these islands. The wall tends to start much further out from the shore and at deeper depths than elsewhere on the island.

53 SOUTH TARPON ALLEY
★★★★

Location: Shallow dive. See map page 60.
Access: Boat.
Conditions: Strong currents and not always divable, because of the mooring. Visibility over 20m (66ft).
Minimum depth: 15m (50ft)
Maximum depth: 18m (60ft)
Similar to Site 54.

54 BIG TABLE ROCK
(KENT'S CAVES WEST)
★★★★

Location: Shallow dive. Southwest tip of Sand Key. Single pin mooring buoy. See map page 60.
Access: Boat.
Conditions: Strong currents and not always divable, because of the mooring. Visibility over 20m (66ft)
Minimum depth: 15m (50ft)
Maximum depth: 18m (60ft)
This is one of the least dived areas along South Shore, but perhaps some of the best diving due to the undersea topography. Dive operators are reluctant to moor on this buoy, because if the current is running, divers have extreme difficulty in coming back to the boat, especially in open water. Nurse sharks (*Ginglymostoma cirratum*) are fairly common, plus snapper, grunts, parrotfish and wrasse as well as queen angelfish.

55 LITTLE TABLE ROCK
(KENT'S CAVES EAST)
★★★★

Location: Shallow dive. Adjacent to Site 54. Single pin mooring buoy. See map page 60.
Access: Boat.
Conditions: Can be strong currents and surface chop which makes life difficult on the day boats. Visibility over 15m (50ft).
Minimum depth: 15m (50ft)
Maximum depth: 18m (60ft)
This is a very obvious spur and groove reef with good quality sea fans, plumes and soft corals on the reef crest. The reef is cut through with tunnels and crevices and there are big caverns with lots of fish. The caverns all tend to have resident grouper of some type or another and you can always find large numbers of shrimp and hermit crabs, particularly *Paguristes cadenati*.

56 SOUTHERN CROSS (RON'S WALL)
★★★★

Location: Deep dive, out from Kent's Caves opposite Sand Key. Single pin mooring buoy.
See map page 60.
Access: Boat.
Conditions: Can be strong current and windy.
Minimum depth: 20m (66ft)
Maximum depth: Beyond 30m (100ft)

The wall is vertical, but has a deep start to the dive. The reef crest rolls over into a series of overlapping coral plates which form overhangs sheltering a number of species of fish, and there are large soft corals, sponges and small schools of young barracuda. Rainbow parrotfish (*Scarus guacamaia*) are seen regularly moving over the reef, biting large chunks out of the living coral. Clumsy divers are not the only reason for coral damage!

PALACE (PALLAS) PINNACLE WEST
★★★★

Location: Deep dive. Single pin mooring buoy. See map below.
Access: Boat
Conditions: Can be surge and current; entry and exit may be difficult from boat. Visibility generally over 25m (80ft)
Minimum depth: 25m (80ft)
Maximum depth: Beyond 30m (100ft)
Similar to Site 59.

LITTLE PINNACLE (PALLAS PINNACLE CENTRAL)
★★★★

Location: Deep dive. Single pin mooring buoy. See map below.
Access: Boat
Conditions: Can be surge and current; entry and exit may be difficult from boat. Visibility generally over 25m (80ft)

Minimum depth: 25m (80ft)
Maximum depth: Beyond 30m (100ft)
Similar to Site 59.

59 BIG PINNACLE (PALLAS PINNACLE EAST)
★★★★

Location: Deep dive. This whole group is known as the Four Sisters. Single pin mooring buoy. See map below.
Access: Boat
Conditions: Can be surge and current; entry and exit may be difficult from boat. Visibility generally over 25m (80ft)
Minimum depth: 25m (80ft)
Maximum depth: Beyond 30m (100ft)
Each site is similar with huge, incredible coral pinnacles the shallowest of which tops at 21m (70ft). Each pinnacle is totally separated from the reef, with lots of black coral on the lower wall and large barrel sponges. One of the most obvious fish that you see on these dives is the small fairy basslet (*Gramma loreto*). This strikingly colourful fish, with its purple and violet head and brilliant golden rear body and tail, is a joy to watch. The arrow blenny (*Lucayablennius zingaro*) can also be found amongst the small coral and sponge growths.

60 PALACE WRECK REEF (PALLAS REEF)
★★★★☆☆☆☆

Location: Shallow dive near Caribbean Paradise Jetty.

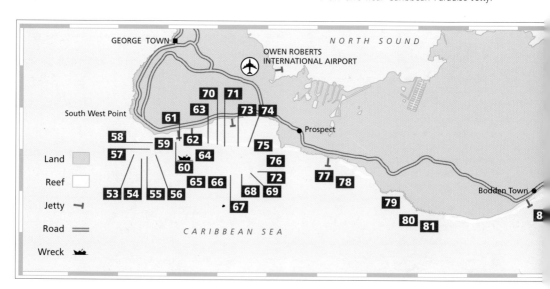

Single pin mooring buoy. See map below.
Access: Can be done by day boat or from the shore.
Conditions: Can be surge amongst coral channels.
Visibility 15m (50 ft).
Minimum depth: 6m (20ft)
Maximum depth: 15m (50ft)
The *Palace* was a Norwegian steel-hulled brigantine sunk when she hit a reef in 1903. Now very well broken up, it is home to a large and diverse assortment of fish and invertebrates. The surge of the ocean swell may be quite strong in this area and extra care should always be taken when diving around the remains of the wreck. The coral channels feature lots of overhangs and swimthroughs: very nice light for photography.

61 CHRISTINA'A REEF AND WALL
★★★★

Location: Both shallow and deep dive midway along South Sound. Two single pin mooring buoys. See map below.
Access: Boat.
Conditions: Can be exposed and current experienced on deeper site. Sheltered within the confines of the spur and groove reef. Visibility 25m (80ft).
Minimum depth: 20m (66ft)
Maximum depth: Beyond 30m (100ft)
The dive boats always put a line out into the water to aid any divers on the surface getting back to the boat because of the current. Down below amidst the spur and groove reef formations are large sea fans and black corals. Rope sponges and other varieties of tube sponges can also be found and all dotted with small blennies and gobies. The large hermit crab (*Paguristes punticeps*) can

NOMENCLATURE

The scientific name or nomenclature of a particular animal is very important. When diving in various parts of the world, or even in the same region, you may come across several different common names for the same creature. This can be confusing. Scientists prefer that, when identifying or describing a particular animal, you use its scientific or specific name. There are a number of superb identification books available for today's amateur marine biologist; see Bibliography.

be found as well as the channel crab (*Mithrax spinosissimus*). Lots of tunnels and swimthroughs.

62 DEDE'S GARDENS
★★★★

Location: Shallow dive. Single pin mooring buoy. See map below.
Access: Boat from main channel.
Conditions: Fairly sheltered, but more of a winter dive due to seasonal weather conditions. Visibility over 15m (50ft).
Minimum depth: 8m (25ft)
Maximum depth: 17m (55ft)
Similar to Site 64.

63 GARY'S REEF
★★★★

Location: Shallow dive. Single pin mooring buoy. See map below.

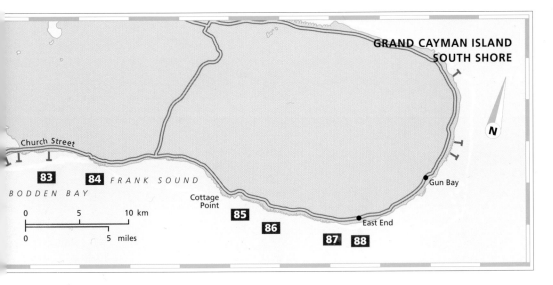

GRAND CAYMAN ISLAND
SOUTH SHORE

N

Church Street

83 **84** *FRANK SOUND*
BODDEN BAY

Cottage
Point

85

86

Gun Bay

East End

87 **88**

0   5   10 km

0   5 miles

Access: Boat from main channel.
Conditions: Fairly sheltered, but more of a winter dive due to seasonal weather conditions. Visibility over 15m (50ft).
Minimum depth: 8m (25ft)
Maximum depth: 17m (55ft)
Similar to Site 64.

64 PIRATES COVE
★★★★

Location: Shallow dive. West of Christina's Reef and Wall (Site 61) along South Sound fringing reef. Single pin mooring buoy. See map page 60.
Access: Boat from main channel.
Conditions: Fairly sheltered, but more of a winter dive due to seasonal weather conditions. Visibility over 15m (50ft).
Minimum depth: 8m (25ft)
Maximum depth: 17m (55ft)
There is virtually no shore access due to the exposed ironstone and very rocky entry through the surf. (The rock which makes up the old limestone shore line is known as 'ironstone'; when a large section of the shore is made up of this rock, it is known as 'ironshore'.) It is a standard spur and groove reef with a mini wall on the inside of the barrier reef which drops lower.

It is important to remember when diving the outer wall, that once you start to ascend to the reef crest, do not be tempted to drop back down to the sand flat towards the shore, as this is still fairly deep and you may go beyond your safe dive time limit. Good quality corals on the outer reef wall as well as large and different species of sponges.

65 NED'S TUNNELS (CROSSROADS)
★★★★

Location: Deep dive. Single pin mooring buoy. See map page 60.
Access: Boat.
Conditions: Surge on top makes it difficult to get back into a smaller day boat. Visibility over 20m (66ft).
Minimum depth: 20m (66ft)
Maximum depth: Beyond 30m (100ft)
Similar to Site 66.

66 OLLEN'S OFFICE
★★★★

Location: Deep dive, east along same reef, but before

Hole-in-the-Wall (Site 67). Single pin mooring buoy. See map p. 60.
Access: Boat.
Conditions: Surge on top makes it difficult to get back into a smaller day boat. Visibility over 20m (66ft).
Minimum depth: 20m (66ft)
Maximum depth: Beyond 30m (100ft)
Lots of yellow tube sponges and star coral (*Monastrea annularis*) on the reef crest and Graham's sheet coral (*Agaricia grahamae*) cascading into the depths. Red boring sponges cover large areas and lots of crevices, with bigeye (*Priacanthus arenatus*) lurking in the shadows. Squirrelfish tend to keep bigeyes company and this type of colour association is common with many of the reef inhabitants of the Cayman Islands.

67 HOLE-IN-THE-WALL (EYE OF THE NEEDLE)
★★★★

Location: Deep dive. Out of Red Bay Cut to the first single pin mooring buoy to the west. See map page 60.
Access: Boat.
Conditions: Exposed site and current experienced due to the proximity of the channel, best on an incoming tide. Visibility variable, depending on direction of tide.
Minimum depth: 22m (74ft)
Maximum depth: Beyond 30m (100ft)
This is a massive valley structure which becomes a huge hole that falls off the wall, which is vertical and deeply incised. Sheet corals form natural overhangs all along this section, and there are large yellow tube sponges and tall soft corals. There is always a constant movement of rainbow parrotfish. Very good scenic and wide angle photographic dive.

68 PHANTOM'S LEDGE
★★★★

Location: Deep dive. Single pin mooring buoy. See map page 60.
Access: Boat.
Conditions: Exposed on surface, generally windy and ocean swell on surface. Visibility 25m (80ft).
Minimum depth: 20m (66ft)
Maximum depth: Beyond 30m (100ft)
Similar to Site 69.

Opposite: *A school of Blackbar Soldierfish (Myripristis jacobus).*

69 GARY'S WALL
★★★★

Location: Deep dive. East out of Red Bay Cut. Single pin mooring buoy. See map page 60.
Access: Boat.
Conditions: Exposed on surface, generally windy and ocean swell on surface. Visibility 25m (80ft).
Minimum depth: 20m (66ft)
Maximum depth: Beyond 30m (100ft)
Typical South Sound deep spur and groove reef system, very similar to the southern shore sites along Cayman Brac and Little Cayman. Dramatic vertical wall deeply incised with gulleys and canyons. The crest folds over the top revealing interesting small sea fans and large magnificent featherduster worm (*Sabellastarte magnifica*). Shafts of light come through the top, making for some interesting upwards angled photographs.

70 RED BAY CAVES
★★★★

Location: Shallow dive. Single pin mooring buoy. See map page 60.
Access: Boat. Too far out from the shore to swim, although some foolhardy types have been seen to try!
Conditions: Exposed on surface with swell and surge. Visibility reduced due to water movement.
Minimum depth: 8m (25 ft)
Maximum depth: 15m (50 ft)
Similar to Site 71.

71 BULL WINKLE'S REEF
★★★★

Location: Shallow dive. Two single pin mooring buoys to the east and west of the reef off Red Bay. See map page 60.
Access: Boat. Too far out from the shore, although some foolhardy types have been seen to try!
Conditions: Exposed on surface with swell and surge. Visibility reduced due to water movement.
Minimum depth: 8m (25 ft)
Maximum depth: 15m (50 ft)
More like cave-type formations, rather than swimthroughs. Not as spectacular as Kent's Caves, but still very nice indeed. Relatively underdived, making the coral structures that much more attractive. Large aggregations of bluestriped grunt (*Haemulon sciurus*) interspaced with schoolmaster snapper (*Lutjanus apodus*). Barred hamlet (*Hypoplectrus puella*) can be

---

found and the beaugregory (*Stegastes leucostictus*).

72 3D (DANGEROUS DAN DROP-OFF)
★★★★

Location: Deep dive. East of Red Bay opposite Prospect Point. Single pin mooring buoy. See map page 60.
Access: Boat.
Conditions: Exposed site with current and choppy conditions on surface. Easier during winter months.
Minimum depth: 20m (66ft)
Maximum depth: Beyond 30m (100ft)
A very dramatic start to the wall, 3D features large coral buttresses cut with ravines and underhanging coral gardens. The top of the reef crest is a constant moving shoal of blue chromis (*Chromis cyanea*). Juvenile wrasse, particularly the younger yellow form of the spotfin hogfish (*Bodianus pulchellus*) and the bluehead wrasse (*Thalassoma bifasciatum*) are common. Superb photographic location, underdived.

73 JAPANESE GARDENS (WEST)
★★★★

Location: Shallow dive. Single pin mooring buoy. See map page 60.
Access: Boat.
Conditions: Sheltered but can be windy. Rarely affected by current, but surge can be quite strong. Visibility over 15m (50 ft).
Minimum depth: 8m (30ft)
Maximum depth 17m (55ft)
Similar to Site 75.

74 ORIENTAL GARDENS (BARRACUDA RON'S PASS)
★★★★★

Location: Shallow dive. Single pin mooring buoy. See map page 60.
Access: Boat.
Conditions: Sheltered but can be windy. Rarely affected

by current, but surge can be quite strong. Visibility over 15m (50 ft).
Minimum depth: 8m (30ft)
Maximum depth: 17m (55ft)
Similar to Site 75.

75 CHINESE GARDENS (JAPANESE GARDENS EAST)

★★★★★

Location: Shallow dive on other side of Red Bay East, through a break in the reef. Single pin mooring buoy. See map page 60.
Access: Boat.
Conditions: Sheltered but can be windy. Rarely affected by current, but surge can be quite strong. Visibility over 15m (50 ft).
Minimum depth: 8m (30ft)
Maximum depth: 17m (55ft)
This is a very lovely dive indeed, with acres of untouched staghorn coral (*Acropora cervicornis*) and the fused staghorn coral (*Acropora prolifera*), as well as magnificent soft corals including the bipinnate sea plume (*Pseudopterogorgia bipinnata*). The rose blenny (*Malacoctenus macropus*) is very evident as is the peppermint goby (*Coryphopterus lipernes*). Schooling fish are everywhere including several species of snapper, grunts and jacks.

76 TIN CITY

★★★★★★☆☆☆☆

Location: Shallow dive. See map page 60.
Access: Boat or by public access from the beach.
Conditions: Sheltered location, can suffer from surge. Visibility reduced.
Minimum depth: 10m (33ft)
Maximum depth: 15m (50ft)
Similar to Site 78.

77 SPOTTS CAVES (SPOTTS REEF)

★★★★★★☆☆☆☆

Location: Shallow dive. Single pin mooring buoy. See map page 60.
Access: Boat or by public access from the beach.
Conditions: Sheltered location, can suffer from surge. Visibility reduced.

Venus sea fan, Gorgonia flabellum.

Minimum depth: 10m (33ft)
Maximum depth: 15m (50ft)
Similar to Site 78.

BATS CAVE REEF
★★★★★★☆☆☆☆

Location: Shallow dive. East of Bat Cave Channel, opposite Coral Cay Condominiums. Single pin mooring buoy. See map page 60.
Access: Boat or by public access from the beach.
Conditions: Sheltered location, can suffer from surge. Visibility reduced.
Minimum depth: 10m (33ft)
Maximum depth: 15m (50ft)
This is a very extensive cave and tunnel system, reputed by some to be the best on the island. Both staghorn and elkhorn coral (*Acropora palmata*) in profusion: this species in particular always appears to have snapper resting underneath. Horseyed jacks (*Caranx latus*) and Bermuda chubb (*Kyphosus sectatrix*) are also common. Tarpon can be found cruising the entrances of the tunnels and there are numerous lobster and shrimps.

PEDRO'S REEF
★★★★

Location: Shallow dive. Opposite Pedro's Castle on inner reef. Single pin mooring buoy. See map page 60.
Access: Boat, but can be done as a shore dive, if a little difficult.
Conditions: Sheltered, no current, inside a cove. Visibility over 15m (50ft).
Minimum depth: 14m (45ft)
Maximum depth: 20m (66ft)
Pedro's reef has some very nice small caverns with elkhorn coral on the crests of the spur and groove reef. Spotted spiny lobster (*Panulirus guttatus*) can be found here as well as the split-crown featherduster worm (*Anamobaea orstedii*) as well as Christmas tree worms. Large numbers of fish. A beautiful dive. The further east you travel, the more virgin the location. These sites involve long boat rides which both the average paying guest and the dive shop are unwilling to do.

Divers at the Sandbar, Grand Cayman.

PEDRO'S PINNACLES
★★★★

Location: Deep dive. Single pin mooring buoy. See map page 60.
Access: Boat.
Conditions: Can be exposed to weather, best done during the winter months. Visibility generally over 25m (80ft)
Minimum depth: 20m (66ft)
Maximum depth: Beyond 30m (100ft)
Similar to Site 81.

TEACHER'S CAVERNS
(RUTTY'S CAVES)
(CARDIAC TUNNELS)
(TEACH'S CAVERNS)
★★★★

Location: Deep dive. East of Pedro's Castle. See map page 60.
Access: Boat.
Conditions: Can be exposed to weather, best done during the winter months. Visibility generally over 25m (80ft)
Minimum depth: 20m (66ft)
Maximum depth: Beyond 30m (100ft)
This is a steeply sloping drop-off comprising several large coral mounds, cut with sand chutes with numerous caves, gulleys and swimthroughs. Very good coral and sponge formations. Not as many fish as on some of the other locations and the coral formations of the spur and groove reef are rather like the south shore of Little Cayman. Occasional green turtle (*Chelonia mydas*) cruise the reefs and a good chance of seeing some of the larger pelagic fish.

The name Teach relates to the infamous pirate Blackbeard – Edward Teach.

PAUL'S WALL
★★★★

Location: Deep dive. Named after Paul Humann. See map page 60.
Access: Boat.
Conditions: Can be exposed on the corner with a strong current running into Betty Bay. Visibility over 20m (66ft)
Minimum depth: 20m (66ft)
Maximum depth: Beyond 30m (100ft)
Similar to Site 84.

LIGHTHOUSE WALL
★★★★

Location: Deep dive. See map page 60.
Access: Boat.
Conditions: Can be exposed on the corner with a strong current running into Betty Bay. Visibility Over 20m (66ft)
Minimum depth: 20m (66ft)
Maximum depth: Beyond 30m (100ft)
Similar to Site 84.

WAHOO WALL
★★★★

Location: Deep dive. Opposite Lighthouse Restaurant at Betty Bay Point. See map page 60.
Access: Boat.
Conditions: Can be exposed on the corner with a strong current running into Betty Bay. Visibility Over 20m (66ft)
Minimum depth: 20m (66ft)
Maximum depth: Beyond 30m (100ft)
There is a large flat sandy area leading to the reef crest. Deeply incised spur and groove reef with large star coral and pillar coral (*Dendrogyra cylindrus*). Several species of Brain coral are to be found in the same vicinity (*Diploria spage*). Steep wall with not too many fish, but the usual chromis, blennies and gobies – the top of the reef crest is always a 'cloud' of small fish. The 'Wahoo' name comes from the occasional sighting of these pelagic fish.

IRON SHORE GARDENS
★★★★★

Location: Shallow dive. East past Cottage Point along Half Moon Bay. See map page 60.
Access: Boat.
Conditions: Sheltered location, no current and little surge. Visibility 15m (50ft)
Minimum depth: 8m (30ft)
Maximum depth: 14m (45ft)
These old coral formations have many caves and swimthroughs, with large groups of schooling fish and numerous species of soft corals in the shallows. The many small caverns are always interesting to explore, with a good chance to see lobster and moray eels. The yellow stingray can be found here (*Urolophus jamaicensis*). The coral formations are all twisted and convoluted, with some excellent quality coral growths of staghorn, brain, star and acropora species dominating.

86 TUNNELS OF LOVE (RIVERS OF SAND) (EEL GARDENS)
★★★★

Location: Deep dive. Between Cottage Point and Blow Holes. See map page 60.
Access: Boat.
Conditions: Fairly sheltered, but can experience current and choppy surface water.
Minimum depth: 16m (55ft)
Maximum depth: Beyond 30m (100ft)

The *Aggressor* also has an anchor drop site in this area which they call Rock Piles, being opposite where the blasting has been carried out on the shore; it is 16m (55ft) to the seabed. There are large numbers of garden eels as well as conch shell (*Strombus gigas*) and the milk conch (*Strombus costatus*). Steeply sloping to the deeper wall where the various sand chutes plummet over the edge. Barracuda are seen regularly.

Colourful sponges and coral hydroids are a spectacular sight.

87 THREE SISTERS
★★★★

Location: Deep dive. See map page 60.
Access: Boat.
Conditions: Exposed on corner to wind, current and surface swell, care must be taken. Visibility over 25m (80ft).
Minimum depth: 25m (80ft)
Maximum depth: Beyond 30m (100ft)
Similar to Site 88.

88 DISAPPEARING CANYON
★★★★

Location: Deep dive. Opposite Panorama Vista Estates. See map page 60.
Access: Boat.
Conditions: Exposed on corner to wind, current and surface swell, care must be taken. Visibility over 25m (80ft).
Minimum depth: 25m (80ft)
Maximum depth: Beyond 30m (100ft)
This site features dramatic canyons cut through the deep spur and groove reef forming large coral buttresses. A spectacular. The reef crest comprises a number of hard stony corals; these soon tumble over the wall forming interesting overhangs where bigeyes and squirrelfish can be found.

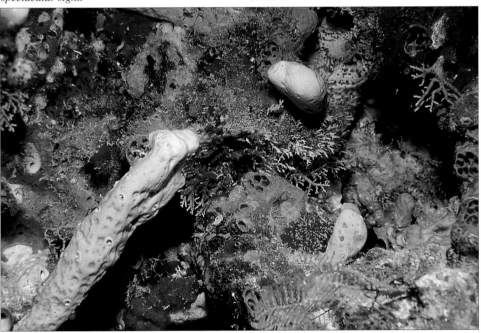

East End

The East End Wall appears more broken than other areas around the island due to the long-term effects on the reefs of the prevailing wind from the southeast. The diving is around the inner fringing reef due to the wall being so far offshore and so deep.

The deeper wall dives listed appear on both the north and south shore corners; there is no deep wall diving directly off East End.

The deepest dives will be on the mini wall which is in fact the inner fringing barrier reef which has built up to protect the east end of the island from the worst of the Caribbean swells. The spur and groove formations here are very typical, but more gently sloping than in other areas.

> **GOLDEN DIVING RULES**
>
> - Avoid touching coral with hands, fins, tanks, etc.
> - Do not wear gloves
> - Never stand on coral
> - Do not collect any marine life
> - Avoid overweighting and practice buoyancy control
> - Do not feed the fish alien, harmful foods
> - Watch your equipment consoles do not drag on the coral
> - Do not use spear guns
> - Do not molest marine life, in particular turtles, puffer fish and sea urchins
> - Do not climb inside barrel sponges

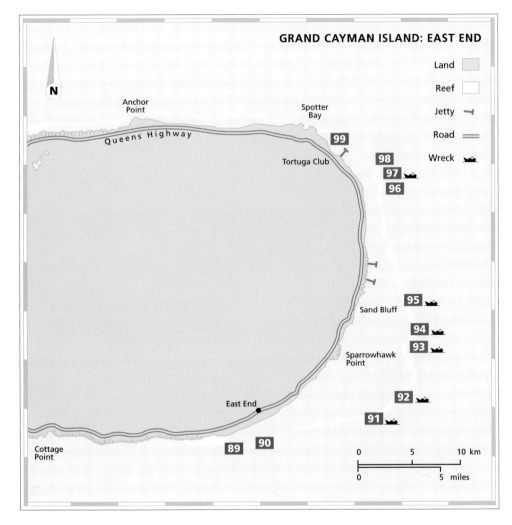

89 THE MAZE (MAZES)
★★★★

Location: Deep dive. Opposite South Channel. See map page 69.
Access: Boat, too far from shore.
Conditions: Very exposed on the corner which suffers greatly from current and inclement weather. Visibility over 25m (80 ft).
Minimum depth: 20m (66ft)
Maximum depth: Beyond 30m (100ft)
The Maze features a large number of swimthroughs which weave through fissures and caves into semi-darkness and out again onto the 'blue' of the wall. There are two resident bull sharks (*Carcharinus leucas*) in the area. Large pinnacles of brain coral, black coral fans and deep water gorgonian fan corals (*Iciligorgia schrammi*) are to be found. This is one of the deepest dives off East End due to the more gradual sloping seabed as you travel towards the north.

90 GROUPER GROTTO
★★★★

Location: Shallow dive. Opposite and left of South Channel. See map page 69.
Access: Boat.
Conditions: Exposed and there can be quite strong currents due to the proximity of the channel.
Minimum depth: 15m (50ft)
Maximum depth: 20m (66ft)
As you enter the top of the reef crest there are numerous caves and tunnels, with Nassau grouper and several species of jacks in evidence. The high buttressed coral blocks are full of interesting fissures and large caves. Large stands of elkhorn coral can be found on the reef crest as well as several species of sea fans and plumes. Some fans are being overgrown with fire coral.

91 RIDGEFIELD REEF
★★★★★★★

Location: Shallow dive in Eastern Channel. See map page 69.
Access: Boat.
Conditions: Very exposed in Eastern Channel and subsequent strong current encountered. Care should be taken prior to snorkelling and local advice sought over the best and most protected areas.
Minimum depth: 15m (50ft)
Maximum depth: 18m (60ft)

The *Ridgefield* was a Liberian freighter weighing 7332 tonnes (7217 tons), some 133m long by 17m wide (441ft x 57ft). Built originally as a Liberty Ship, at the New England Ship Building Corporation in Portland, Maine in 1943, she went through four name changes before eventually running aground on 18 December 1962. This is an excellent snorkelling site with lots of fish. The wreck is now slowly becoming encrusted in corals and sea fans.

92 RUMARCI REEF (RUMANDI REEF — WRECK)
★★★★

Location: Shallow dive. To the left of Eastern Channel. See map page 69.
Access: Boat.
Conditions: Can be surge and current, so care must be taken around the wreckage.
Minimum depth: 5m (16ft)
Maximum depth: 10m (33ft)
You can distinguish the boiler, ribs and engines scattered all over this reef.

There are large aggregations of sergeant majors, snapper, bar jacks (*Caranx ruber*) and the occasional small nurse shark. The more exposed metal surfaces are well encrusted with coral growths and their attendant blennies, gobies and tube worms.

93 SHARK ALLEY
★★★★

Location: Deep dive. In the middle of the Eastern Channel. See map page 69.
Access: Boat.
Conditions: Very strong rip tide in the channel, so timing is critical. Visibility variable.
Minimum depth: 15m (50ft)
Maximum depth: 18m (60ft)
Exciting dive due to the difficulties encountered. The sides of the channel are quite steep and deeply indented with sheltered areas from the current, with coral boulders amid-stream. Large coral buttresses provide shelter for fish and divers and the whole areas is very much 'alive' with beautiful pristine corals and sponges.

There are small caves with tarpon and grouper. You can often see a variety of sharks and rays here.

It is often safer to dive this channel when there is an incoming tide which flows into the relative safety of the inner lagoon.

Opposite: *The Caymans are renowned for schools of silversides.*

94 OLD WRECK HEAD
★★★★★

Location: Shallow dive. Opposite Gun Bay. See map page 69.
Access: Boat.
Conditions: Exposed location on the point, with current, but sheltered in the caves. Visibility usually in excess of 25m (80ft)
Minimum depth: 10m (33ft)
Maximum depth: 18m (60ft)
Similar to Site 96.

95 LOST VALLEY
★★★★★

Location: Shallow dive. Opposite Sand Bluff. See map page 69.
Access: Boat.
Conditions: Exposed location on the point, with current, but sheltered in the caves. Visibility usually in excess of 25m (80ft)
Minimum depth: 10m (33ft)
Maximum depth: 18m (60ft)
Similar to Site 96.

96 SNAPPER HOLE
★★★★★

Location: Shallow dive. South east of Morritts Tortuga Club. Protected Location. See map page 69.
Access: Boat.
Conditions: Exposed location on the point, with current, but sheltered in the caves. Visibility usually in excess of 25m (80ft)
Minimum depth: 10m (33ft)
Maximum depth: 18m (60ft)
One of the top dive sites in Grand Cayman, Snapper Hold has an absolute mass of large caves and fissures in the reef structure.

Tarpon are always around and the reef has excellent coral growth with large stands of elkhorn coral. There is an old anchor – of unknown origin and age – and ring, well embedded and encrusted in all manner of growth in the top of the reef.

Absolutely fascinating dive, but difficult to find: you must use an experienced boat handler who is familiar with the exact location.

This is a protected site for the large numbers of breeding snapper and grouper that can be found, subsequently this area is very rarely dived.

97 TWO WRECKS
★★★★★★★★★

Location: Shallow dive. Opposite Tortuga Club (Site 99). See map page 69.
Access: Boat.
Conditions: This site has to be flat calm with no wave action to be dived safely. Visibility around 15m (50ft)
Minimum depth: 4m (12ft)
Maximum depth: 12m (40ft)
The two wrecks of the name are the *Mary Belle* , and the *Methuslan* which is on top of the other. The *Mary Belle* was a steel steamship (her origin, size and cargo are unknown) and the *Methuslan* was a steel sailing boat with three masts. There are piles of anchor chain and an anchor on this shallow reef dive.

When conditions are right, this is a superb snorkelling site with lots of different species of schooling fish. Care should be taken around the wreckage in case you snag your equipment.

98 THE CASTLE (CINDERELLA'S CASTLE)
★★★★★

Location: Shallow dive. Out from the Morritts Tortuga Club. See map page 69.
Access: Boat.
Conditions: Can be choppy surface conditions and very windy. Visibility good.
Minimum depth: 10m (33ft)
Maximum depth: 18m (60ft)
There are a large number of caves and ravines with excellent growths of elkhorn coral on the crest. Very friendly population of grouper including large Nassau grouper. Very scenic dive for photography with a huge coral buttress festooned in all manner of marine life.

99 TORTUGA CLUB

★★★★★

Location: Under the jetty and platform next to Tortuga Dive Centre. See map page 69.

Access: Directly from the sandy beach or off wooden platform.

Conditions: Perfect, flat calm, shallow but visibility variable.

Maximum depth: 1m (3ft)

This is one of those snorkel dives which must be seen to be believed. During early summer, hundreds of thousands of silverside minnows congregate under the shade and seeming protection of the wooden platform built out into the shallow lagoon, next to the Tortuga Dive Centre. These tiny fish move away, just out of armlength. Large Tarpon cruise these shallows and look

CORAL CUTS AND ABRASIONS

Care should always be taken underwater to avoid blundering into the coral accidentally. Cuts or abrasions from old pieces of wreckage can be particularly nasty, especially if you are stung by fire coral at the same time. Wounds should be treated and sterilised immediately on exiting the water. The dive boats all have medical supplies on board, but in some instances a visit to the local hospital may be required due to the high amounts of planktonic bacteria to be found in warm water.

intimidating as they circle the shoal and try to dissect the larger groupage into a more manageable size to attack.

The elegant Pudding wife, Halichoeres radiatus, is generally quite shy and difficult to approach.

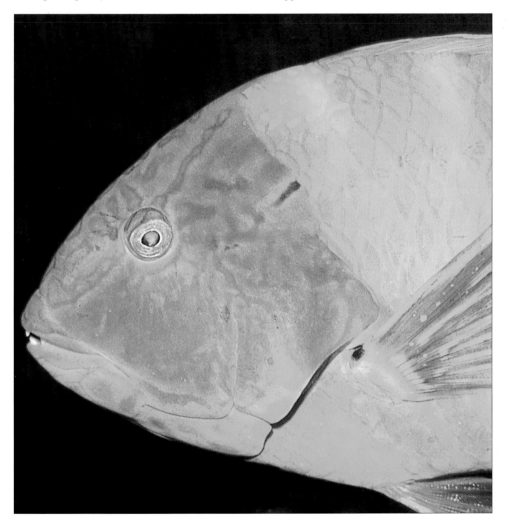

Virtually every small section of coral reef in the Cayman Islands (and indeed everywhere else where there are reefs) will have cleaning stations, whether you are aware of them or not. These are areas where larger fish come to be 'cleaned' of parasites and any diseased scales or skin by a number of different reef inhabitants. It is common to see predators and prey lining up at cleaning stations, all enmity temporarily forgotten. This social truce is integral to the survival of the fish populations on the reef.

Cleaner shrimps are very common and in fact virtually all of the species of shrimp in the Cayman Islands act as cleaning shrimps. The largest are the peppermint shrimp (*Lysmata wurdmanni*) and the coralbanded shrimp (*Stenopus hispidus*). They tend to live in and around a variety of sponges on the reef wall and will signal to the waiting fish with a wave of their antennae that they are open for business. Doing a similar job on some of the larger grouper and moray eels is the striped cleaner shrimp (*Lysmata grabhami*) – they climb into the mouths of these fish and clean any debris from the teeth.

Pederson's cleaner shrimp (*Periclimenes pedersoni*) lives in association with a number of anemones and is fairly common – and also totally unafraid. If you extend your hand slowly, it will approach you and attempt to clean you too! This species has been known to clean human wounds and infections successfully. To attract fish into their cleaning territory, they sway their bodies and flick their antennae similar to the spotted cleaner shrimp (*Periclimenes yucatanicus*).

Members of the wrasse family are more commonly associated with cleaning stations. Some act as roving cleaners of no fixed territory and will try their luck for a free meal of parasites from any fish that they happen to

meet. The juveniles of the bluehead wrasse (*Thalassoma bifasciatum*) are yellow with a black spot at the front of the dorsal fin. Similarly the juveniles of the spotfin hogfish (*Bodianus pulchellus*) are seen to school with the Bluehead wrasse and will perform a similar function as they rove the tops of the reef crests.

The Spanish hogfish (*Bodianus rufus*) is much more territorial and invites larger fish to come into the cleaning station by a vertical posturing in the water column away from the reef. Jacks, normally a predator, will approach the hogfish and signal intent to be cleaned by standing on its tail, extending the jaw and opening the mouth. The Hogfish performs similarly before the cleaning process can take place.

The most common of all the cleaners in the Cayman Islands is the cleaning goby (*Gobiosoma genie*). These tiny fish with their blue and white striped body and the yellow 'V' on their heads swarm all over the hard stony corals waiting for fish to approach their protected area of the reef. Tiger grouper (*Mycteroperca tigris*) will signal its intent to be cleaned by swimming into this enclave and opening its mouth and gill covers wide. The gobies soon enter every available space and clean off any debris, decaying skin or infection. When danger approaches the grouper will close its mouth and gills, but still leave enough room for the gobies to exit and retreat to safety before the grouper swims off.

Opposite: *A Tiger grouper opens its mouth and gills wide to a cleaning goby.*
Below left: *Pederson's cleaner shrimp, Periclimenes pedersoni.*
Below right: *Cleaning goby, Gobiosoma genie.*

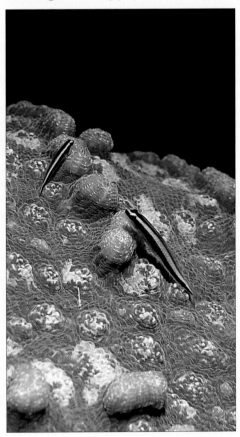

North Wall

The North Wall (sometimes known as North Side) is justifiably world famous for the sheer drama of the drop-off. The area could possibly be split into a further three sections, but for ease and convenience I have included the whole area from Colliers Channel in the east to the Turtle Farm in the west.

There are a huge variety of options along North Side – the fringing reef dives, the wall of course, and the more sheltered shallow lagoon behind the exposed inner fringing reef. The area along North Shore is more susceptible to adverse conditions and therefore is only frequented by a few of the more specialised dive centres and subsequently less dived and in more pristine condition.

The fascination for the area is obvious after your first visit. The wall or drop-off is indeed dramatic and awesome to the extreme, with a higher than average chance to see eaglerays, turtles, sharks and barracuda. The shallower area around Stingray City and the Sandbar are perhaps even more amazing – the attraction being the encounters you will have with the hundreds of wild stingrays which are in residence. The weather may not always be in your favour and the journey to the outer wall a bit choppy, but if the opportunity arises for you to dive this area, then do not hesitate – this is world–class diving at its best.

The drop-off starts at the reef crest around 15m (50ft) and 'folds' over into the blue. The wall is more vertical as you travel east. The dive centres who concentrate on this wall (such as Indies Divers) are constantly exploring for new sites and the Department of Environment is committed to installing at least a further 100 mooring buoys around the Cayman Islands within the next five years.

FIRE CORAL

For many first time divers and snorkellers, their introduction to fire coral (Millepora alcicornis) can be a painful and somewhat unforgettable experience.

Fire coral is not actually a true coral but a member of the Hydroid or sea fern family. They have a hard calcerous skeleton either branching or in bony plates from *Millepora complanata*. The 'coral' is covered in thousands of tiny barbed hooks which can penetrate the skin with ease and leave large irritations on the skin which can last for several days. They can be found in most areas of the reef and will often completely overgrow a gorgonian fan coral. As always, if in doubt, do not touch.

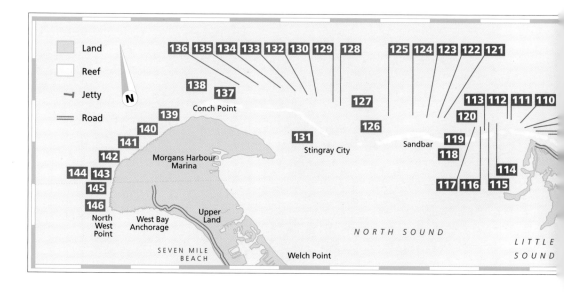

CABANA WALL
★★★★

Location: Deep dive. Out of Colliers Channel and just to the north on the start of the wall. See map below.
Access: Boat.
Conditions: Very exposed site and very deep. Visibility over 30m (100ft)
Minimum depth: 25m (80ft)
Maximum depth: Beyond 30m (100ft)
This is probably the last wall dive location at this end of the island that you are able to dive due to the restrictions of the depth and the seriousness of the dive. Beyond this is Coxon Bank, a steeply sloping plain, used by generations of fishermen. There is not much time to explore at these depths, but the corals are in good condition.

TURTLE PASS
★★★★

Location: Shallow dive. To the north of Colliers Channel. See map below.
Access: Boat
Conditions: Can be quite strong current sweeping around northern reef and into the lagoon. Very exposed to wind and wave action. Visibility over 25m (80ft)
Minimum depth: 20m (66ft)
Maximum depth: Beyond 30m (100ft)
There is a distinctive small tunnel which starts on the sand plain and gradually becomes a huge fissure with a number of caves on the wall. Very good chance to see turtles along this stretch. Good quality corals bordering this canyon, but be careful not to knock against the coral sea fans as you swim through to the outer wall. Many varieties of fish.

VALLEY OF THE DOLLS
★★★★

Location: East of Anchor Point opposite Great Bluff. See map below.
Access: Boat.
Conditions: Exposed northern reef and a long boat ride, but well worth it. Choppy surface conditions, very clear underwater. Moderate current.
Minimum depth: 20m (66ft)
Maximum depth: Beyond 30m (100ft)
Very nice vertical reef, plunging into the depths. Corals are pristine due to the travelling time in small boats; certainly no diver pollution here. Excellent drift dive along the wall. Some very large snapper and jewfish along this area. Good for invertebrates.

BLACK ROCK WALL
★★★★★

Location: Deep dive. Close to Anchor Point, beyond shallower fringing reef. See map below.
Access: Boat.
Conditions: Current on dive, very clear visibility, choppy on surface.
Minimum depth: 20m (66ft)
Maximum depth: Beyond 30m (100ft)
This is an excellent wall deeply undercut by steep fissures, with brightly coloured rope corals and

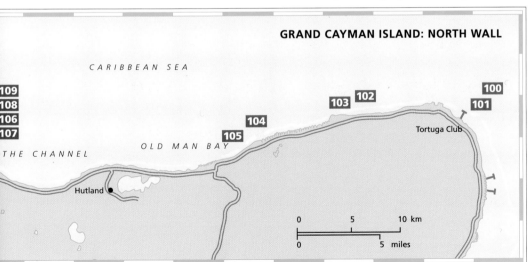

GRAND CAYMAN ISLAND: NORTH WALL

CARIBBEAN SEA

109 108 106 107

THE CHANNEL

OLD MAN BAY

Hutland

104
105

103 102 100 101

Tortuga Club

0   5   10 km

0   5 miles

encrusting sponges. A relatively undived reef in pristine condition. This is a superb night dive and you can always see two very large basket starfish (*Astrophyton muricatum*). This particular species of the starfish family is particularly sensitive to light. If you play your torch light over the starfish's multi-branching arms, they will quickly roll up into a tight ball and the animal will try and move away from the light. Be sensitive and sympathetic in your approach of these interesting echinoderms.

104 BABYLON
★★★★★

Location: Deep dive. Lying west of Old Man Bay opposite Little Spot Point. See map page 76.
Access: Boat.
Conditions: Moderate current, good visibility, over 30m (100ft). Choppy on surface.
Minimum depth: 15m (50ft)
Maximum depth: Beyond 30m (100ft)
Babylon features lots of black coral everywhere, especially in the ravines between the pinnacle and the wall, as well as long, brilliantly coloured rope sponges. There is a huge 3m (10ft) black tube sponge (*Aplysinia archeri*) which grows vertically and the corals are in pristine condition. Very good photographically: looking up you can see large schools of Creole wrasse (*Clepticus parrai*) and blue chromis (*Chromis cyanea*). This is a spectacular wall dive favoured by a number of the faster day boats which operate out of South Sound, but it is a long way to travel and conditions must be near perfect.

105 DARBY'S FANTASY
★★★★★

Location: Deep dive. Opposite Old Man Bay town. See map page 76.
Access: Boat.
Conditions: Quite an exposed site and rather windy. Excellent underwater visibility.
Minimum depth: 20m (66ft)
Maximum depth: Beyond 30m (100ft)
The vertical wall, steeply undercut in places, starts at only 14m (45ft). There is a small ledge at 30m (100ft) before it drops into the blue. Excellent and very diverse marine life all along this stretch of reef. Sadly, one of the first Caymanian dive masters died off this point.

Opposite: *Spectacular corals are a common sight in Cayman waters.*

106 DELLA'S DELIGHT
★★★★

Location: Shallow dive. Northeast of Cayman Kai resort on inner fringing reef. Single pin mooring buoy. See map page 76.
Access: Boat.
Conditions: Exposed site, moderate current. Visibility over 15m (50ft)
Minimum depth: 16m (55ft)
Maximum depth: 20m (66ft)
This is a good reef with lots of large coral pinnacles and swimthroughs and is relatively undived due to its physical location. Excellent, not just as a second dive, with lots of marine life including rays. The corals are in fine condition and you will find goldentail morays and several species of chromis in the convoluted nooks and crannies of the reef.

107 ANDES REEF
★★★★

Location: Shallow dive. Northwest of Della's Delight (Site 106) continuing westwards on fringing reef. Single pin mooring buoy. See map page 76.
Access: Boat.
Conditions: Can be windy with surface chop on sea. Moderate current, poorer underwater visibility.
Minimum depth: 6m (20ft)
Maximum depth: 10m (33ft)
Named after Mr and Mrs Andes who have a house opposite the site, this is a good shallow dive with lots to see. Coral growths are excellent with a wide variety as you would expect from this fairly exposed location including brain, acropora and star corals. This is a more protected area, but the proximity of the large sandy plain often reduces the visibility. Several of the coral heads host cleaning stations.

108 ANDES WALL
★★★★

Location: Deep dive. North of Andes Reef (Site 107). Single pin mooring buoy. See map page 76.
Access: Boat. Down to mooring pin at 15m (50ft). Through steep ravine and archway to the pinnacle out on the wall.
Conditions: Exposed on the surface and there may be a large oceanic swell. Do not delay entering and leaving water. Visibility over 25m (80ft)
Minimum depth: 18m (60ft)
Maximum depth: 30m (100ft)

Andes Wall is in good condition, but shows some signs of coral damage from winter storms. Sponges are everywhere; the fish are more timid here, but there are plenty of them. This is a very good site indeed with a dramatic deep ravine and several swimthroughs. This area is still relatively undived and in much better condition than some of the other sections of the reef.

109 PENNY'S ARCH
★★★★

Location: Shallow dive. Due west of Andes Wall (Site 108). Single pin mooring buoy. See map page 76.
Access: Boat. Down mooring line onto reef plateau at 8m (25ft).
Conditions: Can be windy on corner with rough seas. Fair underwater visibility.
Minimum depth: 9m (30ft)
Maximum depth: 18m (60ft)
Archway is situated east to the edge of the coral plateau and over the crest. Be careful of your fin strokes in this

area as the corals are extremely fragile. You can always find large fish awaiting the cleaning stations. Juvenile Spanish hogfish (*Bodianus rufus*), a species of wrasse, also act as cleaner. When the black jacks approach them (*Caranx lugubris*), they stand on their tails and open their mouths and 'kiss' the wrasse first (See feature page 74.).

110 WHITE STROKE CANYON
(GRAND CANYON)
★★★★

Location: Deep dive. Near Rum Point Channel. Double pin mooring buoy. See map page 76.
Access: Boat.
Conditions: Visibility may be impaired due to sandy location and other divers!
Minimum depth: 15m (50ft)
Maximum depth: 20m (66ft)

The Cayman Islands are surrounded by magnificently clear, aquamarine waters.

The name is derived from the number of spur and groove reef formations which appear like exclamation marks when viewed from above. These reef formations continue out to the wall and over into the blue. This is a good area to see slipper lobsters and many other invertebrates. The fingers are filled with old coral rubble where you will find yellowhead jawfish, harlequin pipefish (*Micrognathus crinitus*) and yellow goatfish (*Mulloidichthys martinicus*).

Most divers tend to avoid these coral rubble areas and concentrate either over the edge of the more vertical wall or on the top of the reef crest to avoid decompression penalties, but the coral rubble fingers are well worth exploring and yield higher than average photographic opportunities.

111 QUEEN'S THRONE
★★★★★★★★

Location: Shallow dive. 80m (300 ft) south of White Stroke Canyon (Site 110). Single pin mooring buoy. See map page 76.
Access: Boat.
Conditions: Moderate to slight current, sheltered around pinnacles, good visibility.
Minimum depth: 5m (17 ft)
Maximum depth: 15m (50 ft)
Queen's Throne is a very nice mini wall or terrace where the coral pinnacles rise to within 5m (17ft) of the surface. A large green moray eel (*Gymnothorax funebris*) is said to inhabit this reef; I didn't see it, but there is plenty of everything else and the fish appear eager to be photographed. Cleaning stations in evidence and the greater soapfish (*Rypticus saponaceus*) appears to be asleep on the bottom amongst the coral heads — curious behaviour for a fish during the day, as it lies on its side and sometimes upside down.

112 NO NAME WALL
★★★★

Location: Deep dive. North of Rum Point Channel and west to the second single pin mooring buoy. See map page 76.
Access: Boat.
Conditions: Moderate current in open water, sheltered in ravines. Can be choppy on surface. Visibility over 25m (80ft)
Minimum depth: 15m (50ft)
Maximum depth: 27m (90ft)
This is actually a series of four perpendicular ravines that start in 15m (50ft) of water and plunge over the wall at 27m (90ft). Limit your dive to this depth only, due to the

seriousness of the dive. The wall has large stands of black coral, rope sponges and many species of fish. Look out for arrow blennies (*Lucayablennius zingaro*) and the cleaning goby (*Gobiosoma genie*).

The tops of these buttresses are steeply sloping and always appear to be in rather poor condition at first glance, but when you stop swimming around and look closely at the corals and sea fans, you will see all manner of interesting vignettes into the lives of many species of fish.

Remember when swimming over the corals, to be careful of your buoyancy, and be certain that none of your equipment is dragging below you.

113 PINNACLE REEF
★★★★

Location: Shallow dive. Very close to Queen's Throne (Site 111). Single pin mooring buoy. See map page 76.
Access: Boat.
Conditions: Sheltered in gulleys around pinnacles, moderate current in the open water areas. Visibility 15m (50ft)
Minimum depth: 8m (30ft)
Maximum depth: 13m (40ft)
The coral pinnacles here rise from 13m (40ft) to near the surface. This is a spur and groove reef, with sand ravines which run off over the wall and now has a spectacular amount of fish and invertebrates. There is a very nice swimthrough northwest of the mooring pin with a number of natural shelves in the reef. This location is well known for its lobster and various species of blenny including the tiny blackedge triplefin (*Enneanectes atrorus*) which seem to prefer their cocky stance on the strawberry vase sponge (*Mycale laxissima*).

114 HAUNTED HOUSE
★★★★

Location: Deep dive. To the east of Rum Point Channel. Single pin mooring buoy. See map page 76.
Access: Boat.
Conditions: Moderate current on the outer wall, sheltered in the reef system. Perhaps not as clear as outer wall.
Minimum depth: 21m (70ft)
Maximum depth: Beyond 30m (100ft)
At Haunted House, two coral buttresses 50m (165ft) apart form the 'mouth' of a huge amphitheatre-type formation indented into the reef. These interesting coral structures feature some huge black coral trees and very large black barrel sponges. Good chance to spot eaglerays, turtles and interesting coral structures.

115 GAIL'S MOUNTAIN
★★★★★

Location: Deep dive. Out of Sand Bar Cut and east to the third single pin mooring buoy. See map page 76.
Access: Boat. Down mooring line to sand plain directly behind 'mountain'.
Conditions: Moderate current, open water.
Minimum depth: 15m (50ft)
Maximum depth: 20m (66ft)
Although this site plummets off the wall in a series of spectacular coral formations, it is best to stay around the top of the 'mountain' at around 17m (56ft). The area has the appearance of a pyramid and is deeply indented by surrounding ravines. Superb dive amongst lush coral and sponges; good light for photographs.

When approaching this single pinnacle from the edge of the reef it appears to tower out into the blue. There are some large caves lower down on its slopes, but on this dive is all too easy to go beyond the recommended safe limits and extra care should always be taken.

116 CHINESE WALL
★★★★

Location: Deep dive. Out of Sandbar Cut and east to second single pin mooring buoy. See map page 76.
Access: Boat, down mooring line onto sand plain at apex of the descending reef.
Conditions: Moderate to strong current, exposed on surface. Visibility over 25m (80ft)
Minimum depth: 20m (66ft)
Maximum depth: Beyond 30m (100ft)
You enter the canyon through a cave-like opening which leads to the outer reef: follow reef around to your right to find another three coral buttress formations deeply incised. Profuse marine life with black coral, sponges, trumpet fish and cow fish. Look for the cleaning stations where you will find grouper and jacks queuing up to be cleaned by the tiny wrasse or shrimps. There is a resident nurse shark which can be seen occasionally at the top of the wall under the overhang.

117 ROBERT'S WALL
★★★★

Location: Deep dive. Directly opposite Sandbar Cut. Single pin mooring buoy. See map page 76.
Access: Boat.
Conditions: Moderate current, excellent visibility,

UNACCEPTABLE PRACTICE

Unfortunately some of the day boat staff at the Sandbar appear to take liberties with the stingrays (Stingray City is used more by the *Aggressor* and not by the day snorkel boats) and snorkel guides have been seen lifting the stingrays out of the water onto a boat to show the tourists. The heads of the fish are also lifted up out of the water to allow people to photograph their faces and underside. This practice must stop – the fish are definitely distressed by it and it is incredible that there have not been any serious accidents.

---

generally well over 30m (100ft).
Minimum depth: 18m (60ft)
Maximum depth: Beyond 30m (100ft)
This is an excellent wall with wide spur and groove formations. A swimthrough can be found at 30m (100ft) and a wider hole above at 23m (85ft). Be careful of your exhalations as you pass through these arches. There are some wide lettuce corals (*Leptoseris cucullata*) and scroll Coral (*Agaricia undata*), which create overhangs. Lots of yellow sponges and prolific marine life.

118 SANDBAR
★★★★★★★★★★★

Location: West of Sandbar Cut on inside of protective fringing reef. See map on page 76.
Access: Boat.
Conditions: Easy, safe, shallow dive, no current to speak of but poor visibility due to divers, very shallow in places.
Minimum depth: 1m (3ft)
Maximum depth: 4m (13ft)
This is the alternative site to Stingray City (Site 131, page 86) – and some say it is a better site. These are either the same stingrays (*Dasyatis americana*) or in fact an entirely different pack who have managed to train humans into bringing them a delightful mixture of frozen squid to supplement their normal diet of crustaceans, molluscs and marine worms. This is the preferred location for all of the day dive boats and snorkelling boats. The depth actually rises to no more than 1m (3ft) on the Sandbar, so tourists can stand in this shallow area and be mobbed by the stingrays. You will have heard about this area, seen film on it and read the description in *National Geographic* – but nothing can compare to your own personal experience.

Opposite: *Favites coral and a sea fan contribute to this colourful display.*

119 STINGRAY ALLEY

★★★★☆☆☆☆☆☆

Location: Northeast of the Sandbar (Site 118) inside the protective reef crest. See map page 76.
Access: Boat.
Conditions: Sheltered, calm, shallow dive, no current. Visibility variable due to water movement.
Minimum depth: 4m (13ft)
Maximum depth: 5m (16ft)
This site is used by a couple of the day boats when waiting for the necessary surface interval between the first and second dives to the outer wall. This location is also an excellent shallow dive on to a row of eight large mushroom-shaped coral heads. When the stingrays get fed up with the snorkellers they pass up and down these coral heads and are not nearly as aggressive as they are around the Sandbar. There is a resident green moray as well as a number of much smaller goldentail moray eels (*Gymnothorax miliaris*).

120 DREAM WEAVER REEF

★★★★★

Location: Deep dive. Out of Sandbar Channel west to first single pin mooring buoy. See map page 76.

Access: Boat.
Conditions: Slight to moderate current, reduced visibility due to sandy location.
Minimum depth: 16m (55 ft)
Maximum depth: 23m (75 ft)
Although very similar along much of its length, the North Wall in this section has many different points of interest – there is just no way that you can take it all in. Dream Weaver Reef has a series of shallower coral pinnacles which lead into the spur and groove reef typical of this area and plunge over the wall into the abyss. There is a nice tunnel at the top of the reef crest and several swimthroughs. Very good coral growth and quite dramatic along the wall.

121 3B'S WALL (BUSH'S BLUNDERING BUBBLE!)

★★★★

Location: Deep dive. West and further out from Dream Weaver Reef. (Site 120). Single pin mooring buoy. See map page 76.
Access: Boat. Down to mooring pin then east to a large star coral.
Conditions: Moderate current. Potentially very deep dive. Visibility over 25m (80ft).
Minimum depth: 20m (66ft)

Maximum depth: Beyond 30m (100ft)

Huge coral buttresses dominate this wall plunging into the depths. Large tube and vase sponges abound and every overhang appears to have black coral and gorgonian sea fans. Lots of very colourful fish inhabit the deeper recesses such as big eye and squirrelfish (*Holocentrus adscensionis*).

122 HAMMERHEAD WALL (HAMMERHEAD HILL EAST)
★★★★★

Location: Deep dive. East along the North Wall, midway between Sandbar Channel and Main Channel. Double pin mooring buoy. See map page 76.
Access: Boat. Mooring pin is on the coral plateau.
Conditions: Moderate current, good visibility.
Minimum depth: 18m (60ft)
Maximum depth: 30m (100ft)

Favoured by the larger live-aboard boats, Hammerhead Wall features a large coral pinnacle jutting out from the wall which is covered in excellent coral growth. There is a very good chance to spot eaglerays and yes, the elusive hammerhead shark (*Sphyrna lewini*). Blue chromis form a perpetual motion above your head and there are always large numbers of parrotfish and wrasse. The light is excellent for photographs.

123 LESLIE'S CURL
★★★★★

Location: Deep dive. East out of Main Channel to third single pin mooring buoy. See map page 76.
Access: Boat. Down to mooring pin on the crest of the spur and groove reef.
Minimum depth: 17m (55ft)
Maximum depth: Beyond 30m (100ft)

Here is a large tunnel or swimthrough and the reef crest appears to 'curl' over into the abyss, creating a large number of overhangs where many varieties of black coral can be found. These locations are also good for finding the painted tunicate (*Clavelina picta*) and a few green tunicates or sea squirts (*Ascidia sydneiensis*).

124 LEMON DROP-OFF (LEMON WALL)
★★★★

Location: Deep dive. Eastern edge of Main Channel. Single pin mooring buoy. See map page 76
Access: Boat.

Conditions: Slight to moderate current, surface choppy, calm beneath. Visibility good.
Minimum depth: 17m (55ft)
Maximum depth: Beyond 30m (100ft)

This site consists of three large pinnacles and sand chutes with gorgonian sea fans, rope sponges and many colourful fish on the reef. The top of the reef crest seems a bit sparse in good coral growth due to the movement of sand over the edge. This dive is much better once you drop over the wall. The coral rubble in the grooves is home to sand tilefish (*Malancanthus plumieri*) and lizardfish (*Synodus intermedius*). An excellent dive.

125 CHANNEL'S END REEF (MAIN CHANNEL REEF) (LEMON REEF)
★★★★

Location: Shallow dive. Close to Eagle Ray Pass. See map page 76.
Access: Boat.
Conditions: Visibility around 15m (50ft)
Minimum depth: 13m (40ft)
Maximum depth: 20m (66ft)

A dramatic drop through open water onto a patch reef and spur and groove reefs makes this an excellent second dive without travelling too far in the boat. With lots of very good coral growth, it is relatively underdived. Very good for close up photography amongst the wide coral rubble valleys. You will find yellowhead jawfish (*Opistognathus aurifrons*) and sand gobies (*Coryphopterus dicris*). Large sea fans and plumes, although some of the gorgonian sea fans appear to have holes in them and are straggly in appearance.

126 EAGLE RAY PASS
★★★★★

Location: Deep dive. Directly out from Main Channel which cuts into North Sound. Single pin mooring buoy. See map page 76.
Access: Boat. Down to sand patch and into the lip of the canyon.
Conditions: Little or no current in the ravine. Choppy surface conditions. Visibility good.
Minimum depth: 23m (75ft)
Maximum depth: Beyond 30m (100ft)

The entrance to the pass is at 23m (75ft) on a steeply sloping sand plain which cuts through the reef and

Opposite: *Divers relaxing at the jetty, East end, Grand Cayman.*

plummets into the depths. The coral buttresses are indeed dramatic as they rise vertically on both sides. Very good chance to see the spotted eagleray foraging in the sand with its pointed nose, like a pig searching for truffles.

127 BLACK FOREST (NORTH)
★★★★

Location: Deep dive. Continuing west along North Wall towards North Point. Single pin mooring buoy. See map page 76.
Access: Boat.
Conditions: Excellent visibility, over 30m (100ft), slight current.
Minimum depth: 20m (66ft)
Maximum depth: Beyond 30m (100ft)
Here there is a large number of coral pinnacles, buttresses and a sand chute all tightly packed together. As the name suggests there is a profuse growth of black coral in the canyons. On the top of the wall can be seen 'clouds' of blue chromis and creole wrasse. The edge of the reef crest is also a favourable area to spot Scorpionfish, as well as in the coral rubble valleys.

128 PRINCESS PENNY'S WALL (PRINCESS PENNY'S PINNACLE)
★★★★

Location: Deep dive. Further west towards North Point. Single pin mooring buoy. See map page 76.
Access: Boat.
Conditions: Moderate current. Exposed on surface.
Minimum depth: 14m (46ft)
Maximum depth: Beyond 30m (100ft)
Very similar to Site 127 but with a large coral pinnacle set off the wall. This whole wall is awesome and second only to the very similar walls in the Red Sea, where even some of the species are the same, such as the coralbanded shrimp (*Stenopus hispidus*). This dive site is dedicated to the memory of Penny Ventura, a dive master, who sadly lost her fight against cancer. A plaque can be found at the bottom of the mooring, placed in her memory.

129 TARPON ALLEY WEST AND EAST
★★★★★

Location: Deep dive. Opposite and to the east of Stingray City Channel. Double and single pin mooring buoys. See map page 76.

Access: Boat.
Conditions: Moderate current in open, sheltered in canyons. Exposed on surface.
Minimum depth: 18m (60ft)
Maximum depth: 30m (100ft)
Three large coral buttresses drop and wind down the steeply inclined wall, where there are a couple of caves and various winding channels, all covered in marine life. The name is derived from the territorial school of tarpon which live in the grottos on the reef crest. There are a couple of caves and various winding channels, all covered in marine life. A hammerhead shark has also been seen here as well as the Caribbean reef shark (*Carcharinus perezi*). This site is also favoured by the *Aggressor* live-aboard.

130 VALLEY OF THE RAYS
★★★★

Location: Deep dive. Directly out from Stingray City Channel. See map page 76.
Access: Boat.
Conditions: Moderate current and preferably dived on an incoming tide. Visibility variable.
Minimum depth: 18m (60ft)
Maximum depth: Beyond 30m (100ft)
This is a deep cleft sand chute cutting through the wall. There is a good possibility of seeing rays here and not just common stingrays and eaglerays – you may also find the torpedo or electric ray (*Torpedo nobiliana*). Yellow goatfish and the spotted goatfish (*Pseudupeneus maculatus*) can be seen 'digging' in the sand with their adapted pelvic fins or barbels. When they are not searching for food, they can be found resting on the sandy bottom.

131 STINGRAY CITY
★★★★★★★★★★★

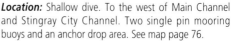

Location: Shallow dive. To the west of Main Channel and Stingray City Channel. Two single pin mooring buoys and an anchor drop area. See map page 76.
Access: Boat.
Conditions: Calm, low visibility dive.
Minimum depth: 3m (10ft)
Maximum depth: 4m (13ft)
Superb world-renowned dive – with over 200 of the southern stingray (*Dasyatis americana*)! This is one of those unforgettable dives: interaction with wild creatures is always special, but the stingrays on this site are superb and far better than advertised! See feature on p 100.

Above: *The distinctive Trumpetfish, Aulostomus maculatus is fairly common around Cayman reefs.*
Below: *Spotted Lobster, Panulirus guttatus.*

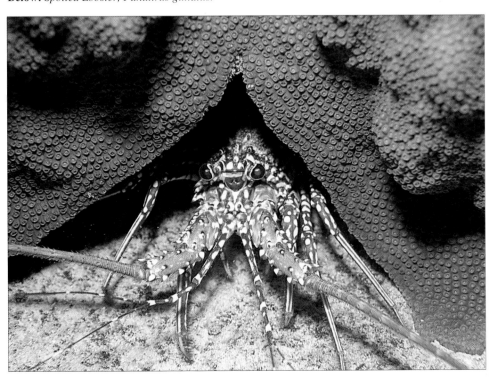

132 JOSH'S CANYON
★★★★

Location: Deep dive. First single pin mooring buoy west from Stingray City Channel. See map page 76.
Access: Boat.
Conditions: Choppy surface conditions, moderate current. Visibility over 25m (80ft)
Minimum depth: 18m (60ft)
Maximum depth: Beyond 30m (100ft)
Similar to Site 133.

133 MAIN STREET (PETE'S RAVINE)
★★★★

Location: Deep dive. First single pin mooring buoy west from Stingray City Channel. See map page 76.
Access: Boat.
Conditions: Choppy surface conditions, moderate current. Visibility over 25m (80ft)
Minimum depth: 18m (60ft)
Maximum depth: Beyond 30m (100ft)
Again, the depth here is unlimited: the ravine is much steeper and deeper than others along the wall. The coral formations are massive and all of the promontories are evident on the reef crest. As you approach the western corner of the wall, the chance to see rays and turtles increases, so do not spend all your time looking for them on the reef – just remember to look over your shoulder occasionally.

134 HOLE IN THE WALL
★★★★

Location: Deep dive. Further west along same wall. See map page 76.
Access: Boat. Drop to 18m (60ft) to mooring pin.
Conditions: Moderate current. Good visibility.
Minimum depth: 20m (66ft)
Maximum depth: Beyond 30m (100ft)
This is a very serious dive, and not suitable for a recreational diver.

Large coral pinnacles or buttresses loom up into the blue creating dramatic overhangs deeply incised with crevices. Large coral formations feature, as do many varieties of sponge.

The reef here is of very good quality overall. Creole wrasse and blue chromis form a moving bank of fish on top of the reef crest which is an incredible sight.

135 BLUE PINNACLES (TWO FINGERS)
★★★★★

Location: Deep dive. Due north of Palmetto Point. Single pin mooring buoy. See page 76.
Access: Boat.
Conditions: Moderate current. Good visibility.
Minimum depth: 18m (60ft)
Maximum depth: Beyond 30m (100ft)
This location has a pair of huge exaggerated coral buttresses which spread out into the open sea. There are large gulleys and canyons, very good quality coral and some very large sea fans (*Nicella goreaui*) on the top of the crest and long sea whips (*Ellisella elongata*).

136 BEAR'S CLAW (BEAR'S PAW)
★★★★

Location: Deep dive. West of Big Channel on the outside of inner fringing reef. Single pin mooring buoy. See map page 76.
Access: Boat.
Conditions: Calm, sheltered area. Visibility less than outer wall.
Minimum depth: 8m (30ft)
Maximum depth: Beyond 30m (100ft)
Although the maximum depth is listed at 12m (40ft), the spur and groove reef will continue out to the wall. There are long coral fingers and it is very easy to find yourself travelling too deep along the steeply sloping reef. There is a large overhang to the west of the mooring line. This is an excellent second dive, without having to move too far. There is profuse marine life, particularly juveniles.

137 GHOST MOUNTAIN
★★★★

Location: Deep dive. Due north of Conch Point. Single pin mooring buoy. See map page 76.
Access: Boat.
Conditions: Moderate current. Clear water.
Minimum depth: 25m (83ft)
Maximum depth: Beyond 42m (140ft)
Due to the potential dangers encountered on this dramatic deep dive, it is always recommended that you are accompanied by a qualified guide. This single coral pinnacle thrusts up from the sloping spur and groove reef system. The coral head is covered in superb coral

formations and sponges. Schools of jacks frequent a cave lower down the pinnacle as well as squirrelfish and angelfish. Best done with a small group of very competent divers. Quite breathtaking.

SPONGE POINT (GROUPER POINT)

★★★★

Location: Deep dive. North west of Spanish Cove. See map page 76.
Access: Boat.
Conditions: Strong current on outer edges and surface generally choppy due to exposed nature of site. Visibility over 25m (80ft)
Minimum depth: 10m (33ft)
Maximum depth: Beyond 30m (100ft)
On the eastern extremities of Spanish Bay Reef this 'Y' shaped ravine cuts through the coral crest creating a coral pinnacle at the bottom rising some 10m (33ft) above the sloping sandy floor at 30m (100ft). Highlights include some very large gorgonian fan corals, large numbers of Nassau grouper and a large variety of colourful sponges. This is a very colourful dive, particularly as a second, late morning, dive.

139 SPANISH BAY REEF

★★★★★★★★★

Location: Shallow dive. Directly out from the marina at Spanish Bay Reef Resort. See map page 76.
Access: From shore about a 100m (330ft) swim.
Conditions: Be careful of boat traffic if swimming on the surface.

Minimum depth: 8m (30ft)
Maximum depth: 18m (60ft)
A few of the coral buttresses are so closely packed together here, they are like smaller versions of Hepp's Pipeline (Site 144). This is a mini wall which extends southeast towards the Turtle Farm. An easy dive well suited for novice divers and popular with underwater photographers, with a wide range of invertibrates and fish to be found. Pairs of spotfin butterflyfish (*Chaetodon ocellatus*) and foureye butterflyfish (*Chaetodon capistratus*) can be seen in several locations. Some broken coral due more to the exposed nature of the site than to diver damage.

140 LITTLE TUNNELS

★★★★★★★

Location: Shallow dive. Further south west along same mini wall from Spanish Bay Reef (Site 139). See map page 76.
Access: Boat, but can be reached from the shore.
Conditions: Slight current on the surface but sheltered amongst the coral heads. Visibility 15m (50ft)
Minimum depth: 8m (30ft)
Maximum depth: 20m (66ft)
The reef is cut in many areas offering a prolific number of routes in, out, under and through a variety of large coral formations. The tunnels are actually short narrow ravines which are at right angles to the mini wall. Lots of wrasse and parrotfish around as well as some of the more colourful reef inhabitants.

The fine hairs along the body of the Bearded fire worm, Hermodice carunculata, can inflict a painful skin irritation.

141 SCHOOLHOUSE REEF
★★★☆☆☆☆

Location: Shallow dive. East of the Turtle Farm. The associated Cemetery Reef is found in the same area and both are named after their land counterparts as location markers. They are at the southern end of Boatswain's Bay. See map page 76.

Access: Spanish Bay has quite a nice stretch of beach and access can be had across the beach and over the various clumps of patch coral.

Conditions: Can be choppy on surface, slight to moderate current. Visibility 15m (50ft)

Minimum depth: 10m (33ft)

Maximum depth: 5m (50ft)

This whole area is enjoyed by swimmers and snorkellers. These spur and groove reefs are home to quite a large number of juvenile fish, and sea urchins can be found under a few of the dead coral slabs. Remember that if you do have to turn up a coral slab, be very careful in replacing it back down exactly the same way, because some marine creatures could be killed during this process. Better still, leave everything alone.

When diving this reef at night, be sure to look out for the balloonfish (*Diodon holocanthus*) and juvenile queen triggerfish (*Balistes vetula*). There are large numbers of the red night shrimp in the coral crevices, and their green reflective eyes seem to wink in the lights of your dive torches.

142 CEMETERY REEF
★★★☆☆☆☆

Location: Shallow dive. Mini wall before you reach Trinity Caves (Site 12) out from the public beach along Boggy Sand Road and opposite Cemetery Road. See map page 76.

Access: From the beach or boat.

Conditions: Little or no current. Visibility reduced.

Minimum depth: 12m (40ft)

Maximum depth: 15m (50ft)

This is a quiet, easy dive along a mini wall, a well dived location with lots of marine life including sergeant majors in the shallows as well as filefish and angelfish. The area appears a bit battered (being on the rather exposed northwestern corner of Grand Cayman) and is a popular site for trainees and night diving – the coral damage in this location may be a direct result of this.

Be especially careful of your buoyancy during night dives and be sure your equipment consoles are all securely tucked away to avoid damaging the coral.

---

143 HEPPS WALL
★★★★

Location: Deep dive. Further out towards edge of drop-off. Single pin mooring buoy. See map page 76.

Access: Boat.

Conditions: Slight to moderate current. Visibility over 25m (80ft)

Minimum depth: 18m (60ft)

Maximum depth: Beyond 30m (100ft)

The topography here is similar to Cemetery Reef (Site 142) and it also has lots of invertebrates and fish. This is rather exposed on the corner and you may not get the chance to dive here. However, if you do there is a very high chance of seeing large pelagics moving past. This high profile wall, with its large stands of soft corals. The sand chute between the mounds is akin to a ski slope and was actually used as just that for an advertising photograph for the Cayman Islands.

144 HEPP'S PIPELINE
★★★☆☆☆☆

Location: Shallow dive. Fairly close to the shore and about 300m (1000ft) north of the Turtle Farm. There are two mini walls running parallel to the shore separated by a sand plain. Single pin mooring buoy. See map page 76.

Access: Can be made at the north end of the beach and swimming out to the buoy which is at the start of a sand chute which leads down to the dive. Alternatively by small day boat to the mooring buoy and again follow the same pattern. It is recommended to start at the north and swim towards the south on the lower wall then back north again to the mooring buoy.

Conditions: There may be a current on this corner, but

Opposite: *The incredible Atlantic Manta, Manta birostris (see feature page 100).*

it is no problem once in the 'pipeline'. This sand plain is approximately 0.5km (0.25 mile) long. Visibility is generally around 18m (60ft). Although this lower end of Spanish Bay is exposed, there may be a little surface chop, so care must be taken when entering from the shore. It may also prove difficult for some snorkellers. Visibility 15m (50ft)

Minimum depth: 10m (33 ft)
Maximum depth: 20m (66 ft)

There is luxuriant coral and sea fan growth on the upper reaches of the reef, testimony to the current. The reef structure of tunnel-like formations and the separating sand patch between the two reef make for a good variety of marine life. This is superb for macro photography, but there are also large barrel sponges and rope sponges on the overhangs. There is also a large colony of garden eels on the sand plain. This is a superb dive site for all levels and the proximity to the shore make it ideal for snorkellers.

145 TURTLE FARM REEF

★★★★★★☆☆☆☆

Location: Shallow dive. Just a short swim out from the beach in front of and just a little east of the Turtle Farm. This is a small but steep mini wall and is easily found.

See map page. 76

Access: Few dive boats actually stop here due to its location – so close to the shore and the Turtle Farm. It can be a bit of a scramble from the shore, but it is well worth the bother and the walk involved.

Conditions: This site is fairly unprotected and there can be quite a lot of surface chop on the water making it a little uncomfortable during certain conditions. Current can also be encountered here, but it is quite manageable. Visibility may be reduced due to the effluent discharge from the Turtle Farm.

Minimum depth: 12m (40ft)
Maximum depth: 18m (60ft)

There would appear to be a higher than average concentration of fish in this area and quite luxuriant coral growth due to the Turtle Farm outflow. This is primarily organic in nature and subsequently a lot of algae is also present. There are some quite large specimens of anemones and their associated shrimps and other small fish.

Schools of juvenile wrasse flit amongst the coral plumes and fans. Several small specimens of goby and blenny can be found including the sailfin blenny (*Emblemaria pandionis*). Lobster can be spotted in the fissures and cracks which run the length of this reef.

Divers swim alongside the Atlantis submarine (see page 23).

HOW TO GET THERE

Eleven scheduled air carriers fly into Grand Cayman. The national airline of the Cayman Islands is Cayman Airways; depending on the time of year, it flies three or four times each day from Miami. Other services from the USA include: Orlando, twice a week; Houston, three times each week; Tampa three to four times each week; Kingston, Jamaica, four times each week. Cayman Airways operate daily internal flights between Grand Cayman and Cayman Brac.

Cayman Airways Ltd
PO Box 1101G, Airport Road, George Town; tel toll free 800–G–CAYMAN. Reservations tel 949–2311; Administration tel 949–8200/fax 949–0082. Cayman Brac reservations; tel 948–2535.

Air Jamaica fly from Grand Cayman to Kingston and Montego Bay daily; tel 949–0888.

American Airlines fly into Grand Cayman three times a day from Miami. American Airlines, PO Box 31113SMB, Owen Roberts International Airport; Reservations tel 949–8799/fax 949–8247.

Northwest Airlines have one flight daily from Miami. Northwest Airlines Inc, PO Box 1059G, Owen Roberts International Airport; Reservations tel 949–2955/fax 949–2957.

US Air fly directly from Charlotte, North Carolina and from Tampa, Florida to Cayman. U.S. Air Inc, Owen Roberts International Airport; Toll free 800–622–1015; Reservations tel 949–7488/fax 1–703–418–7168.

Islena fly direct between La Ceiba, Honduras and Cayman, c/o Jefferson Travel Services; tel 949–6062/fax 949–8942.

British Airways have three regular non–stop weekly services from London direct to Grand Cayman. For the first time the major cities of Europe and the east have the option of one change at London instead of having to change carrier also at Miami. Cayman Airways are the handling agents. British Airways, Owen Roberts International Airport; Reservations tel 949–2311.

American Trans Air operate a weekly Sunday service from Indianapolis via Cincinnati; tel toll free 800–225–2995. Reservations tel 317–248–8308.

Charter Flights
Grand Cayman is also served by a number of charter flights, especially in the winter season. These link to other major conurbations such as Boston, Chicago, Minneapolis, Indianapolis, Boston and Toronto. Charters also operate to Cayo Largo and Cuba on a more infrequent basis.

Island Air operate the daily service to Cayman Brac and Little Cayman. PO Box 1991 G, Island Air Hangar, Owen Roberts International Airport; tel 949–0241. Reservations tel 949–5252/fax 949–7044.

Baggage allowance
You may check in up to 20 kg (55 lb) of baggage per passenger free of charge. It may be possible to gain extra baggage allowance by contacting the airline directly before your intended travel date. Excess baggage will be charged and is guaranteed to arrive at the destination within 24 hours of checking in. Most International scheduled flights – but not charter flights – now allow you two items of luggage in the hold (irrespective of weight) and one item of hand luggage (up to the maximum size that can be stowed in the overhead lockers) .

Think twice about bringing absolutely every bit of diving and photographic equipment with you. All dive centres offer first-class equipment for rent, including wetsuits, regulators, buoyancy compensators (BCs), masks, fins and snorkels, and have ample supplies of air tanks and weight belts with weights. All the equipment is fully serviced, sanitized and operational.

WHERE TO STAY

There is a wide range of hotels, condominiums, cottages and guest houses in the Cayman Islands, which offer visitors more than 2,000 hotel rooms alone.

Most hotels offer diving, which may be owned by the company or leased out through a concession agreement with a major watersports operator. There are also specialist hotels catering solely for divers.

All the major hotels offer restaurants, bars and swimming pools. Others also offer nightclubs, tennis courts and a beach, along with the usual ancillary services, such as cable TV. With more than 300,000 tourists arriving by air each year, the range of accommodation is more than adequate, at prices to suit all tastes.

Possibly the most popular type of accommodation for repeat visitors is a condominium. The condos are self-catering to allow you more flexibility, and your culinary needs will be amply catered for by the local supermarkets or by any one of the vast range of restaurants.

Cottages and guest houses tend to be more intimate and all are furnished to the very highest standard. For details of the full range of these, or for additional information on any of the accommodation offered, you should get in touch with the **Department of Tourism**, The Pavilion, Cricket Square, PO Box 67; tel 949–0623/fax 949–4053 or contact the hotels directly at the addresses given below:

Upper price range
Grand Pavilion Hotel
PO Box 30117, Seven Mile Beach; U.S. res: toll free 800–HERITAGE; tel 945–5656/fax 945–5353. Grand style accommodation, though not much Caribbean flavour. All facilities with various bars and restaurants.

Holiday Inn Grand Cayman
PO Box 904, Seven Mile Beach, tel toll free 800–421–9999, US res: 1–901–767–5046, tel 945–4444/fax 945–4213. Beach front, two restaurants, three bars, a freshwater pool, car hire and all water sports.

Hyatt Regency Grand Cayman
PO Box 1588, Seven Mile Beach; tel toll free 800–233–1234, tel 949–1234/fax 949–8528. Across the road from Seven Mile Beach, three restaurants, four bars, a large freshwater pool, a pool-side barbecue, tennis, water sports, gift shops, car rental.

Caribbean Club
PO Box 30499, Seven Mile Beach; tel toll free 800–327–8777, tel 945–4099/fax 945–4443. Villas with all services, on Seven Mile Beach, restaurant and bar.

Westin Casuarina Resort
Seven Mile Beach; tel toll free 800–228–3000, tel 945–3800/fax 949–5825. Latest hotel to be built along Seven Mile Beach. Excellent quality, freshwater pool, bars and restaurants.

Grand Cayman Marriott Beach Resort
PO Box 30371, West Bay Road, Seven Mile Beach; tel toll free 800–333–3333, tel 949–0088/fax 949–0288. Luxurious beachside hotel on five floors, recently undergone extensive renovation.

Spanish Bay Reef Resort
PO Box 903, George Town; res: 949–8100, tel 949–3765/fax 949– 1842. Caribbean feel, suitable for couples, complimentary jeeps and bicycles included in package, poolside afternoon tea, rooms in small villas.

Treasure Island Resort
PO Box 1817, Seven Mile Beach; tel toll free 800–203–0775, tel 949–7777/fax 949–8489/8672. Two freshwater pools, poolside bars and restaurants.

Morritts Tortuga Club and Resort
PO Box 496 G, East End; res: 1–813–559–8813, tel toll free 800–447–0309, tel 947–7449/fax 947–7669. Well kept and quiet – get away from it all style – but out of the way. Three-storey wooden-built apartment/hotel, poolside bar and full water sports.

Indies Suites
PO Box 2070, Seven Mile Beach: tel toll free 800–654–3130, tel 945–5025/fax 945–5024. Excellent suites (only all-suite hotel in the Caymans) and very good diving services. Couples mainly, and honeymoon specials. Fairly attractive, central pool, Jacuzzi and bar. Wrong side of Seven Mile Beach.

Medium price range
Beach Club Resort
PO Box 903, George Town; tel 949–8100/fax 949–5167. Two-storey beachfront, with freshwater pool, restaurant and bar on beach terrace, plus excellent stretch of beach and full water sports.

Sunset House
PO Box 479, George Town; tel toll free 800–854–4767, tel 949–7111/fax 949–7101. Two-storey with peach exterior, some rooms are fairly basic. Pool and terrace overlook sea, popular bar. Diving and photo shop on premises.

Sleep Inn Hotel
PO Box 30111, West Bay Road, Seven Mile Beach; tel toll free 800–SLEEP–INN, tel 949–9111/fax 949–6699. Lacks Caribbean atmosphere, has pool and is not actually on beach, though near.

Coconut Harbour
PO Box 2086, South Church Street; tel toll free 800–552–6281, tel 949– 7468/fax 949–7117. A favourite for divers, pool-view and ocean-front apartments, restaurant, bar and freshwater pool and Jacuzzi.

Lower price range
Best Western Sammy's Airport Inn
PO Box 236, Owen Roberts Drive; tel 945–2100/fax 945–2330. Typical airport hotel – could be anywhere – lacking in atmosphere, fairly quiet except for noise of air traffic.

Seaview Hotel
PO Box 260; tel 945–0558/fax 945–0559. Grand Cayman's oldest hotel, recently totally restored; with pool, restaurant and bar. Dive school on site.

Ambassadors Inn
PO Box 1789, Jackson Point; tel toll free 800–648–7748, tel 949–7577/fax 949–7050. Friendly atmosphere, simple rooms, freshwater pool and snack bar. Dive centre on site, popular with divers.

Cayman Diving Lodge
PO Box 11, East End; US res: 800–TLC–DIVE, tel 947–7555/fax 947–7560. Comfortable and informal, out-of-the-way location, restaurant and bar, popular with divers.

Coral Caymanian Hotel
PO Box 30611; tel 945–5622/fax 945–5931. Located on Seven Mile Beach, offering spacious budget accommodation.

John Silver's Inn
West Bay Road, PO Box 1083G; tel 949–4242/fax 949–3347. Close to Turtle Farm, out of the way but good quality for the money, excursions available.

WHERE TO EAT

The restaurants listed below are just a small sample of the 60 or so which are dotted around Grand Cayman. Styles and food choice vary and the selection is not necessarily a recommendation. Most require advance booking and several will issue a menu on request before you make your reservation. For anyone who wants pizzas, fried chicken and burgers there are several of these fast-food eateries.

Cracked Conch West Bay; tel 945–5217. Rustic, relaxed. Steaks, turtle, conch and lobster.

The Blue Parrot Coconut Harbour, South Church Street; tel 949–9094. By the ocean, relaxed local seafood a speciality, plus all-you-can-eat ribs.

Ristorante Bella Capri Pleasant House, West Bay Road; tel 945–4755. Friendly, casual dining, fine Italian cuisine and seafood.

DJ's Cafe Coconut Place; tel 945–4234. Casual and fun, with American-style menu of salads, steak, pasta, seafood.

Paradise Bar & Grill Waterfront on South Church Street; tel 945–1444. Cayman style/Tex-Mex, speciality is 'Cheeseburger in Paradise'. Great view of sunsets.

Marriott Beach Resort Seven Mile Beach; tel 949–0088. International cuisine, mixed choice and styles, alfresco, ocean front and terrace.

Hemingway's Hyatt Regency Hotel Seven Mile Beach; tel 945–5700. Caribbean cuisine, seafood specials, local fruit and vegetables, informal but elegant dining.

David's Restaurant at Morritt's Tortuga Club East End; tel 947–7449. International cuisine, smart casual dining, views overlooking the sea, good wine list.

Smuggler's Cove on the Waterfront, North Church Street; tel 949–6003. Caribbean and international cuisine, smart casual, seafood specialities, good wine list.

Casanova Cafe on the Waterfront, George Town; tel 949–7633. Italian and local specialities, romantic waterfront dining.

Benjamin's Roof Coconut Place, Off West Bay Rd; tel 947–4080. American and family style, casual and relaxed, including seafood and alligator on the menu.

Almond Tree North Church Street/Eastern Avenue; tel 949–2893. Caribbean cuisine, island-style thatched roof, excellent fish, served Cayman style. Casual dining.

The Lobster Pot Waterfront, George Town; tel 949–2736. Caribbean style, romantic ocean view and sunsets, lobster and conch, banana daiquiris.

Ristorante Pappagallo Barkers; tel 949–1119 or 949–3479. North Italian gourmet cuisine, romantic and elegant bamboo-thatched structure.

Lantana's West Bay Road; tel 945–5595. Caribbean and new American style, smart casual restaurant, interesting and varied menu.

Lone Star Bar & Grill West Bay Road; tel 945–5175. Tex-Mex, casual fun spot favoured by divers, all-you-can-eat specials, ribs, fajitas etc.

The Links at Safehaven Club House, West Bay Road; tel 949–5988. Continental and Caribbean flavour, with superb views over golf course and North Sound; friendly atmosphere.

Ottmars Grand Pavilion Hotel, West Bay Road; tel 945–5879. Local and continental cuisine, relaxed tropical, smart casual, fresh seafood specialities.

Hog Sty Bay Cafe Waterfront, North Church Street; tel 949–6163. Pub atmosphere, English beer and darts, patio overlooks harbour, specials available all week.

Grand Old House South Church Street; tel 949–9333. American/Caribbean, elegant mansion overlooking sea, smart casual, varied menu.

Golden Pagoda West Bay Road; tel 949–5475. Chinese, Hakka-style, No MSG used in cooking, takeaway; smart casual.

Lighthouse at Breakers; tel 947–2047. Fresh seafood, nautical feel on screened patio overlooking sea, great wine list.

Island Taste South Church St, Harbour Front; tel 949–4945. Seafood and continental, all-you-can-eat-shrimp every night; relaxed and friendly.

DIVE FACILITIES

All the dive centres, diving and snorkelling operations on Grand Cayman work to a very high standard of safety and instruction – they are all members of the Cayman Islands Watersports Operators Association – (CIWOA) .

The average cost for a two-tank dive excluding full rental equipment is in the region of $50–$70. A Full Open Water PADI Certification course including use of all equipment, text books etc. is generally about $450.

Other advanced courses and speciality courses can cost anything from $100 to $800 – depending on the level of skill required and the time available in which to complete the course.

It is always worth checking with the diving or snorkelling operation of your choice to find out whether there are any specials or discounts for a full rental package.

Live-Aboards

Cayman Aggressor 111 PO Box 1882 G, Biggie's Plaza, Airport Road, George Town; tel toll free 800–348–2628. (Admin tel 1–504–385–2628); tel 949–5551/fax 949–8729. Operates weekly from George Town, Grand Cayman. Extends to Bloody Bay Marine Park on Little Cayman Island.

Little Cayman Diver 11 PO Box 280058, Tampa, Florida 33682–0058, USA; tel toll free 800–458–BRAC, tel 1–813–932–1993/fax 1–813–935–2250. Operates weekly from Cayman Brac. All week on Little Cayman Island, Bloody Bay Marine Park.

Soto's Cruises Ltd PO Box 30192 SMB, Snug Harbour, West Bay Road, Seven Mile Beach; tel 945–4576/fax 945–1527. Weekly out of Grand Cayman: maximum 6 divers.

The Indies Suites offer good diving services (see page 96 for contact details).

Diving Operations
(all offer snorkelling)
Ambassador Divers PO Box 1789 G, South Church Street, George Town; tel/fax 949–8839.

Aquanauts Diving PO Box 30147 SMB, Regency Court Building, Seven Mile Beach; tel 945–1990/fax 945–1991.

Beach Club Divers PO Box 903 G, West Bay Road, Seven Mile Beach; tel 949–8100/fax 945–5167.

Bob Soto's Diving Ltd PO Box 1801 G, North Church Street, George Town; tel toll free 800–BOB–SOTO, tel 949–2022/fax 949–8731.

BSAC #360 (Cayman Island Divers/Decompression Chamber) PO Box 1515 G, George Town; tel 949–2989/0685/fax 945–5024.

Cayman Dive College PO Box 30780 SMB, Seaview Hotel, South Church Street; tel/fax 949–4125.

Cayman Diving Lodge PO Box 11 EE, East End; tel 947–7555/fax 947–7560.

Cayman Marine Laboratory (Personalised Marine Biological Tours) PO Box 30548 SMB, North West Point; tel 916–0849/fax 945–5586.

Dive Inn Ltd PO Box 1882 G, Sleep Inn, West Bay Road, George Town; tel 949–0321/fax 949–8729.

Dive N' Stuff PO Box 185, North Side; tel 949–6033/fax 945–9207.

Divers Supply PO Box 1995 G, West Shore Centre, West Bay Road, George Town; tel 949–7621/fax 949–7616.

Divers World Ltd. Of Cayman PO Box 917 G, Seven Mile Shops, West Bay Road, Seven Mile Beach; tel 949–8128/fax 949–7178.

Don Foster's Dive Cayman Ltd PO Box 31486 SMB, Seven Mile Beach; tel toll free 800–83–DIVER, other tel nos: West Bay Rd: 945–5132, fax 945–5133.

Eden Rock Diving Centre Ltd PO Box 1907 G, South Church Street, George Town; tel 949–7243/fax 949–0842.

Fisheye Diving, Photography and Video PO Box 30076 SMB, Cayman Falls, West Bay Road, Seven Mile Beach; tel toll free 800–887–8569, tel 945–4209/fax 945–4208.

Indies Divers PO Box 2070 G, Foster's Drive, Seven Mile Beach; toll free 800–654–3130; tel 945–5025/fax 945–5024.

Off The Wall Divers PO Box 30176 SMB, Breezy Pines Apartments, South Sound; tel 947–7790/fax 947–7790.

Parrots Landing Watersports Park PO Box 1995 G, South Church Street, George Town; tel 949–7884/fax 949–0294.

Peter Milburn's Dive Cayman Ltd PO Box 596 G, George Town; tel 945–5770/945–4341/fax 945–5786.

Quabo Dives PO Box 157G, Watercourse Road; tel 945–4769/fax 945–4978.

Red Sail Sports PO Box 1588 G, Hyatt Regency, Seven Mile Beach; tel toll free 800–255–6425, tel 945–5965/fax 945–5808; also located at Grand Cayman Marriott.

The live-aboard dive boat Cayman Aggressor III.

Sunset Divers PO Box 479 G, South Church Street, George Town; tel toll free 800–854–4767, tel 949–7111/fax 949–7101.

Surfside Watersports PO Box 891G, Watler Building, North Church Street, George Town; tel 949–7330/fax 949–8639.

Tortuga Surfside Divers PO Box 496 G, East End; tel 947–2097/fax 947–9486.

Treasure Island Divers & Watersports PO Box 1817 G, Seven Mile Beach; tel toll free 800–872–7552, tel 949–4456/fax 949–7125.

Non-Diving Affiliate Member of CIWOA
Atlantis Submarine PO Box 1043 G, South Church Street, George Town; tel toll free 800–253–0493, tel 949–7700/fax 949–8574.

Dive Centres and Operators Not Affiliated to the CIWOA
Ashton's Scuba View PO Box 218 WB, North Church Street; tel 949–4107/949–4142/fax 949–2549.

Bayside Watersports Ltd PO Box 30470 SMB, Morgan's Harbour Marina West; tel 949–3200/fax 949–3700.

Captain Marvin's North Sound Excursions PO Box 413 WB, West Bay Road; tel 945–4590/fax 945–5673.

Cayman Diving School PO Box 1308 G, South Church Street, George Town; tel 949–4729.

Clint Ebanks Scuba Cayman PO Box 746 G, Public Beach, George Town; tel 949–3873/fax 949–6244.

Japan Cayman Services Ltd PO Box 30780 SMB, Seven Mile Beach; tel 945–1983/947–0726/fax 945–1983.

Kirk's Sea Tours PO Box 2014 G, On the beach at Treasure Island Resort; tel 949–6986/fax 949–4595.

Ollen Miller's Sun Divers PO Box 30181 SMB, Birch Avenue, Spotts; tel 947–6606/fax 947–6706.

Neptune's Realm Divers PO Box 30520 SMB, North Church Street, George Town; tel 949–4610/fax 949–4417.

Rivers Sports Ltd PO Box 374 WB, Coconut Place, West Bay Road, Seven Mile Beach; tel 949–1181/fax 949–1296.

Seasports PO Box 431 WB, Town Hall Crescent, West Bay; tel 949–3965.

Snorkelling Operators
Bayside Watersports Ltd PO Box 30470 SMB, Morgan's Harbour Marina West; tel 949–3200/fax 949–3700.

Cali Wreck PO Box 920 G, The Jamin Building, Harbour Drive, George Town; tel 949–6161/fax 949–4358.

Captain Marvin's North Sound Excursions PO Box 413, Coconut Place, West Bay Road; tel 945–4590/fax 945–5673.

Cayman Delight Cruises PO Box 277 WB, Opp. Marriott, Seven Mile Beach; tel 949–6738/8111/fax 949–8385.

Cayman Mermaid Beach Club Hotel PO Box 903 G, Seven Mile Beach; tel 949–8100/fax 945–5167.

Charter Boat Headquarters PO Box 2005 G, Coconut Place, West Bay Road, Seven Mile Beach; tel 945–4340/fax 945–5531.

The Cockatoo PO Box 1995 G, South Church Street, George Town; tel 949–7884/fax 949–0294.

Divers Supply PO Box 1995 G, West Shore Centre, West Bay Road, Seven Mile Beach; tel 949–7621/fax 949–0294.

Fantasea Tours PO Box 30654 SMB, Oceanside Plantation, West Bay; tel 949–2182/fax 949–5459.

Kirk's Sea Tours (Reef Teach Ecotour Programme) PO Box 2014 G. On the Beach at Treasure Island; tel 949–6986/fax 949–4595.

Parrots Landing Watersports Park PO Box 1995 G, South Church Street, George Town; tel toll free 800–448–0428, tel 949–7884/fax 949–0294.

Seasports PO Box 431 WB, Town Hall Crescent, West Bay; tel 949–3965.

FILM PROCESSING

Many of the larger diving operations have underwater stills photographic equipment and video equipment for hire. Some will even produce a video of your holiday with you as the star. A 35mm Nikonos V camera plus lens and flash will cost from $35 for a half day's hire and video from $50 for a half day, which will include tape.

For instruction, there are four preferred centres in Grand Cayman; the two oldest and most established are Sunset and Fisheye, see addresses below.

Cathy Church at the Sunset Underwater Photo Centre and Gallery Sunset House Hotel, South Church Street, PO Box 479; tel 949–7415/fax 949–9770.

Martin Sutton at Fisheye Diving Photography & Video Cayman Falls, West Bay Road, PO Box 30076; tel 945–4209/fax 945–4208.

Ocean Photo Centre Seven Mile Beach, PO Box 30240; tel 949–6607/fax 949–8129

Parrot's Landing Photo Centre South Church Street, PO Box 1995; tel 949–7884/fax 949–0294. Instruction is aimed at all levels and costs from around $100 per day including film and equipment. A PADI Certification course is available over four days and costs from $350.

Full E-6 film processing and Ilfachrome printing is available at:
Sunset Underwater Photo Centre and Gallery, Fisheye Diving, Photography and Video, Ocean Photo Centre (addresses, tel and fax as above), and at **Cayman Camera Ltd** PO Box 2172, George Town; tel 949–8359/fax 949–7479.

Other Print & Processing Services
Action Photo Ltd Regency Plaza, West Bay Road, PO Box 655; tel 945–4779.

Foto Fast L Thompson Building, The Village, PO Box 1501; tel 949–0997.

Instant Print & Photography PO Box 173, George Town; tel 949–2662.

The Photo Centre Bush Centre, North Church Street, PO Box 1045; tel 949–0030/fax 949–6577.

Photo Kingdom Seven Mile Shop, PO Box 17BT; tel 945–1919/fax 945–1920.

Photo Plus Photo-Pharm Centre, Walker Road, PO Box 951; tel 949–2420/fax 949–4240.

Rainbow Photo Stanwick Plaza, Sheddon Road, PO Box 30759; tel 945–2046.

Rapid Photo Ltd. Merren's Shopping Centre, PO Box 1566; tel 949–7514/fax 949–8643.

Ray's One Hour Photo Dolphin Centre, Eastern Avenue, PO Box 971; tel 949–6002.

EMERGENCY NUMBERS

Recompression chamber:
PO Box 1551 G, George Town; tel 949–2989. Emergency: 555. The chamber also operates a medical alert flight with Island Air if there are any problems on the Island. DAN – the Divers Alert Network – are also consulted when necessary, for help.

Hospital:
George Town Hospital tel 949–8600. Out patients: tel 949–8601.

Air Ambulance:
Aero Care toll free 800–627–2376, tel 747–8923. Operated by Aero Care based in Lubbock, Texas, USA, this jet service will take you back to the USA if necessary.

Island Air offer a 30-minute response time with a full 24-hour Learjet service with professional medical care; toll free 800–922–9626, tel 949–5252.

Executive Air Services tel 949–7775/fax 945–5732 transport patients from George Town Hospital. Offer a full 24-hour service with registered doctors, nurses and trauma physicians.

National Air Ambulance, operating out of Fort Lauderdale in Florida, offer a worldwide capability with a bedside-to-bedside service; tel 1–305–358–9900/fax 1–305–359–0039.

Critical Air direct from Grand Cayman, with Cayman medical staff by Learjet; tel toll free 800–247–8326, tel 1–619–571–0432/fax 1–305–253–9641.

LOCAL HIGHLIGHTS

In April 1995, the National Trust for the Cayman Islands (tel 949–0121/fax 949–7494) opened its newest attraction: the **Mastic Trail** – a 3-km (2-mile) nature trail through a splendid variety of Grand Cayman's wilderness ecosystems. Qualified guides lead small groups and give a very informative talk on each of the habitats.

The National Trust for the Cayman Islands played a central role in founding the first botanic park, the **Queen Elizabeth II Botanic Park**, which was officially opened by the Queen in February 1994 and has been expanded since. This 24-hectare (60-acre) park is the showcase for the indigenous and endemic flora and fauna of the Caymans. The park features a fern swamp, a crocodile hole, a buttonwood swamp, a pond, various garden displays, the Queen Elizabeth II Monument and picnic area, and a captive breeding programme for the endangered Cayman blue iguana. A new visitor centre was opened in 1997. The Botanic Park is off Frank Sound Road, on North Side, open daily from sunrise to sunset; tel 947–9462/fax 947–7873.

Grand Cayman has two museums, both located in George Town: the **Cayman Islands National Museum**; tel 949–8368/fax 949–0309 and the **Cayman Maritime and Treasure Museum**; tel 945–5033. Both display various artefacts from the Cayman Islands.

The **Conch Shell House** is a charming little Cayman house located on North Sound Road. Both the house and the garden are constructed and decorated with thousands of conch shells. Although the house is privately owned, the owners do not mind the photographic intrusion but draw the line at people camping on their lawn – which has been known.

The **Cayman Turtle Farm** is the only one of its kind in the world and is able to offer opportunities to hold and photograph green sea turtles. Although the farm is quite a tourist attraction, it is principally a centre for research, conservation and breeding programmes.

Hell is an aptly named area of old ironstone rock formations in the West Bay district. The ironstone has eroded over the centuries and the area resembles a scene of petrified flames rising up from hell. There is a post office next to this rugged pit and you can send a postcard which is postmarked 'Hell, Grand Cayman'.

Car Hire
It is sensible to hire a car for at least part of your holiday. Cayman Islands temporary driving permits are mandatory. These cost $7.50 and are available from any police station or from the car hire companies; you must be 21 or over to obtain one. There is a wide range of vehicles and by far the most popular is the 4x4 jeep. This will cost around $50 per day or $300 per week. Saloon cars cost about the same. Most companies offer corporate rates and will also offer seven days for the price of six. Collision waver insurance is recommended.

It takes at least a full day to explore around Grand Cayman and if you want to see anything of Little Cayman and Cayman Brac without getting too badly sunburned you will need to rent a car. (The sun really is too hot to go exploring on foot – so be warned.) Jeeps are fine but are lacking in security. However, they are ideal for transporting your diving gear between locations and for visiting any of the shore diving sites. If you have a saloon car, it would be appropriate to use waterproof bags to store gear. Remember to drive on the left-hand side of the road.

Andy's Rent a Car Marriott, PO Box 277; tel 949–8111/6738/fax 949–8385.

Avis Cico Rent a Car Airport Road, PO Box 400; tel toll free 800–331–1084, tel 949–2468/fax 949–7127, Holiday Inn Booth: tel 945–4044, Hyatt Regency Booth: tel 949–8468.

Budget Rent a Car Walkers Road, PO Box 686; tel toll free 800–527–0700, tel 949–5605/fax 949–2224.

Cayman Auto Rentals North Church Street, PO Box 103; tel 949–6408/6500/fax 949–6500.

Coconut Car Rentals Nissan Building, Crewe Road, PO Box 681; tel toll free 888–227–0654 tel 949–4377/4037; Airport office: 949–7703/fax 949–7786.

Conmac Car Rental Airport Road, PO Box 16EE; tel 949–6955/fax 949–6955.

Dollar Rent a Car Rankin's Airport Centre, PO Box 31366; tel 949–4790/0700/fax 949–8484.

E Scott Rent a Car Airport Centre, PO Box 1322; tel 949–8867/fax 949–8185.

Economy Car Rental Biggies Plaza, Airport Road, PO Box 1570; tel 949–9550/fax 949–1003.

Hertz Rent a Car Airport Plaza, PO Box 53G; tel toll free 800–654–3131, tel 949–2280/7861/fax 949–0572. Industrial Park: 949–2932. Beach Club Office tel 945–5621. Radisson Hotel office tel 949–8147.

Island Paradise Rent-a-Car North Sound Road, PO Box 2035G; tel 949–5831/fax 945–1240.

Just Jeeps North Church Street, PO Box 58; tel 949–7263/fax 949–0216.

Marshall's Rent-a-Car Turtle Beach Villas, PO Box 1754G; tel 949–2127/7821/fax 949–6435.

Soto's 4X4 West Bay Road, PO Box 2176G; tel 945–2424/fax 945–2425.

Motorcycle and Scooter Rentals
Motorcycle rentals cost in the region of US$20–25 a day (US$150.00 a week) and you must also obtain a Cayman Licence, which is the same as a car licence, from any police station or from the rental company concerned. All the companies also have bicycles for hire at US$10.00–US$16.00 a day, or approximately US$90.00 a week.

Cayman Cycle Rentals Coconut Plaza, West Bay Road, PO Box 31219SMB, Grand Cayman Is; tel 945–4021/4031/fax 945–8596.

Eagles' Nest Cycles Watler's Square, North Church Street, PO Box 30609, Grand Cayman Is; tel 949–4866.

Soto's Scooters Soto's Plaza, Coconut Place, West Bay Road, PO Box 1081G, Grand Cayman Is; tel 945–4652/fax 945–4465.

PEDRO ST JAMES' CASTLE

Pedro's Castle lays claim to being the oldest structure on Grand Cayman. It was built around 1780 by William Eden and survived the hurricane of 1785 which destroyed every other structure on the Cayman Islands. This former great house, officially known as Pedro St James Castle, was a remarkable building for its time, considering that the population on the Islands was only 400, of whom 200 were slaves. Pedro's Castle is now known as the Birthplace of Democracy in the Cayman Islands, commemorating the location where on 5 December 1831, the decision was made to establish the first legislative assembly in the Cayman Islands.

The castle now includes a visitors' reception area and the land has been developed as a national park. This major historic landmark and tourist attraction is definitely worth a visit.

Morritt's Tortuga Club offers a wide range of water sports (see page 94 for contact details).

Grand Cayman is home to a legendary dive location – Stingray City, quite possibly one of the most popular and spectacular dive locations in the world. Dubbed as 'the world's greatest 12 foot dive' it is located inside the barrier reef along the Northshore of Grand Cayman Island where the waters are virtually always sheltered and calm. The stingrays are the southern stingray (*Dasyatis americana*) and there are approximately 250 of the creatures which swoop in and envelop you in their search for a free meal. Stingray City and its counterpart, the Sandbar, have been featured in National Geographic and promoted throughout the world in film, video and magazine articles.

The Sandbar on the eastern side of the deeper channel is much shallower. On the main sandbar, the white sands of the inner lagoon shelve up to only 1m (3ft) in some parts, making this site the preferred location for children and snorkelling. You can also dive this area again and again, the dive is in only 4m (13ft).

As you can imagine, this area is extremely popular with charter boats and care must be taken whilst in the water in not being run over by a boat, not rising too quickly under a dive boat and making certain that you swim back to the same dive boat you came out on!

Local fishermen used to come to these sheltered waters inside the fringing reef of North Sound to clean all the fish they had caught before sailing in to market. The Stingrays, being bottom feeders, were soon attracted to this additional source of a free meal. Over the years, the number of rays has increased and they appear to be totally unafraid of humans.

The surge of excitement is incredible as these trusting beasts zoom in on you from the outer reef and envelop you in their 'wings'. The dive guides accompanying you tend to handle the food (frozen squid) in a sealed container and feed the stingrays individually.

If you are given the chance of feeding the stingrays, hold the squid in the palm of your hand. The sensation is similar to feeding a horse – underwater. The mouth–parts of the stingray are located underneath the body: they do not have teeth as such, but have a series of rasping plates with which they crush and grind the molluscs and crustaceans which are their normal food.

This dive becomes very much like a feeding frenzy, the water visibility drops and

once the food has all been eaten, the stingrays get bored with our antics and either go off in search of other diver/feeding groups or return to their normal foraging on the sandflats.

You must wear a protective suit of some kind to avoid the stingrays giving you a nasty suck (something like a 'love-bite' or 'hicky')

Gloves should not be worn as the fabric can remove the protective mucus on the stingrays' leathery skin. If this protective mucus is removed, infection can quickly set in, and disease and death may follow. When handling the stingrays, do not try and ride them or grab them by the tail. Remember, these are wild animals and if they feel threatened in any way, their defensive mechanism is designed to sting, just as their name implies.

Pliny, describing the stingray, wrote in the Historia Naturalis: ' So venomous it is, that if it be struchen into the root of a tree, it killeth it: it is able to pierce a good cuirace or jacke of buffe, or such like, as if it were an arrow shot or a dart launched: but besides the force and power that it hath that way answerable to iron and steele, the wound that it maketh, it is therewith poisoned.'

Some of the best photographs can be taken of these creatures immediately after the feeding session. The stingrays are quite docile and they can be approached and observed feeding naturally. They settle on the seabed and flap their 'wings' in a downwards motion in order to remove the top layers of sand to expose marine molluscs, crustaceans and worms.

Stingray City and the Sandbar are amazing, and simply nothing can prepare you for that first rush of adrenaline. This balance of nature and enterprise is a curious mix and experiencing it at first hand is a rare treat. Several hundred thousand tourists have already enjoyed the delights of the interaction, and there is no reason to doubt that many more will continue to do so for many years to come.

Opposite left: *Snorkellers enjoying the stingray experience at the Sandbar.*
Opposite right and below: *Visibility is reduced when the sand becomes churned up by the feeding frenzy. When all the food has been eaten, the stingrays lose interest and move on to the next group of divers.*

CAYMAN BRAC

Cayman Brac, one of Grand Cayman's sister islands used to be known affectionately as 'the island that time forgot'; now the word 'almost' can be added to the phrase. Whilst the diving here is similar to Grand Cayman, the isolation of the island has served it well.

Situated 145km (90m) northeast from Grand Cayman Island, Cayman Brac is 20km (12m) long by just over 1.6km (1m) wide. It is roughly split into two: the flat area to the west of the island where the airport is located, and the steep bluff with its remarkable ancient coral limestone cliff and caves to the east.

The Cayman Brac Airport has a tarmac runway, unlike Little Cayman, and it even has its own airport buildings! The island is served regularly each day by Island Air and Cayman Airways. The 70 minute flight from Grand Cayman is well worth the time, if only to view the glorious colours of the sea and reefs from the air.

The island now has a resident population of around 2000. There are 12 churches, one hospital – Faith Hospital – and over the past 30 years, the old one-room school house has expanded to the needs of the rising local population. There are now three primary schools, a secondary school and a community college.

During the 1932 hurricane which devastated the Caribbean, 109 lives were lost and 95 per cent of all the homes on the island were destroyed. Today, Cayman Brac has two small resorts and there are several villages dotted around the island.

The two main roads run each side of the island but are unable to go all the way round because of the height of the rugged bluff at North East Point which rises to 42m (140ft). The numerous caves here are still used as hurricane shelters and these are well worth exploring. The caves were reputed to have been used by Edward Teach (Blackbeard) to hide his ill-gotten gains plundered from the ships of the Spanish Main. The road on the northern side of the island ends at Spot Bay and the southern road ends at Pollard Bay. The latter is more splendid because of the size of the vertical cliff and the contrasting colours of the sea as you drive along. From Pollard Bay you can walk to the edge of the bluff, where the ironstone shore terminates; this is incredibly dramatic and there are several blowholes.

Opposite: *The ancient coral limestone cliff of the bluff, Cayman Brac.*
Above: *The marine park reserves around the Cayman islands are protected by law.*

You can rent a small car or scooter (both of which cost about the same) to explore the island at your leisure.

The Cayman Brac Chapter of the National Trust has recently declared a 40.5-hectare, 100-acre parrot reserve out on The Bluff and the Conservation Society has already earmarked more land as an orchid preserve. The parrot reserve can be reached along the dirt road which starts from the cross-island road and continues all the way up to the lighthouse tower.

There is little else to do but dive on the island – with three dive centres, a couple of hotels and a number of condominiums to suit all tastes and purses. Each of the major families has a provisions store of some sort and all will sell home-made jams and chutneys as well as the usual goods. The local residents are some of the friendliest people I have come across.

Whilst the diving is similar to Grand Cayman, there are far fewer divers here. As a result the corals are in good condition and there is a huge variety of marine life around its shores, as well as four wrecks.

BRAC

Brac is the Gaelic word for 'bluff' and aptly identifies the main feature of Cayman Brac. This rugged limestone cliff forms half of the island and soars to a massive 42m (140ft) at the eastern point of the island. There are a number of large caves, some of which are still used for hurricane protection.

BRAC SEAMEN AND BOAT BUILDERS

The seamen and boat builders of Cayman Brac have long been regarded as some of the best seamen in the world and their travels and exploits are well documented. Local ship builders are still very much in demand and their traditional skills are passed down from generation to generation.

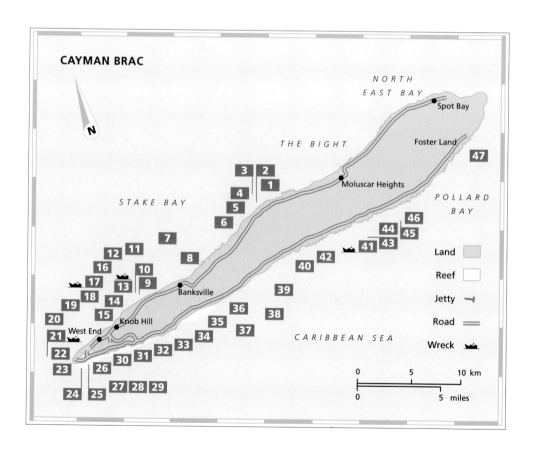

In addition to the 47 dive sites registered with the Department of the Environment Marine Resources Unit and the Cayman Islands Watersports Operators Association, the newly sunk Russian Destroyer 356, renamed the *M.V. Captain Keith Tibbetts*, has three permanent mooring buoys on her and is suitable as a snorkel dive or a deep dive for experienced divers. She sank at 5.30pm on 17 September 1996, with Jean-Michel Cousteau "riding" her as she went down. Only dive sites with permanent moorings on Cayman Brac are used by the local operators to avoid coral damage, and more buoys are scheduled to relieve pressure on existing sites. The conservation-conscious local dive operators hope that once all the mooring buoys are in place around Cayman Brac, they will be able to institute a voluntary ban on certain areas by removing selected mooring buoys to allow for coral growth and fish stock regeneration.

Snorkelling is best in the lagoon between the island's south shore and the fringing reef. Several areas have sandy beaches, but some are old coral limestone or ironstone and protective footwear should be worn. The western shore has a small coral rubble beach where flotsam and jetsam is washed up. The more exposed north shore may be hard to snorkel in winter.

The dives listed are used commonly by local dive operators, but many other, more distant sites, such as Bert Brothers Boulders at the northeast end of the island, are dived when the weather is suitable for longer boat rides. The same operators dive the nearby Little Cayman as often as they can – though the journey is usually uncomfortable and wet. When conditions are right visit the *M.V. Capt. Keith Tibbetts* near the Buccaneer Inn (see page 112).

North Shore

1 JAN'S REEF

★★★★☆☆☆☆

Location: Shallow dive. Midway along north shore, opposite Mollusca Heights. Single pin mooring buoy. See map page 104.
Access: Boat or from the shore (shore is difficult).
Conditions: Weather dependent, can be exposed on this stretch of coast, with a moderate current.
Minimum depth: 7m (25ft)
Maximum depth: 15m (50ft)
Similar to Site 2.

2 GREENHOUSE REEF

★★★★☆☆☆☆

Location: Shallow dive. Midway along north shore, opposite Mollusca Heights. Single pin mooring buoy. See map page 104.
Access: Boat or from the shore (shore is difficult)
Conditions: Weather dependent, can be exposed on this stretch of coast, with a moderate current.
Minimum depth: 7m (25ft)
Maximum depth: 15m (50ft)
This is a typical spur and groove reef system running perpendicular to the shore. Angelfish and butterfly fish in abundance and the occasional ray swimming by. I saw a juvenile green turtle along this stretch of reef. The entire length of the reef seemed a little sparse at first and some of the corals in bad shape, but this was due to storm damage and not diver damage. The gullies and overhangs, however, have a tremendous amount of marine life and a rich fish population.

3 GREENHOUSE WALL

★★★★

Location: Deep dive. Opposite Bamboo Bay, northwest of Greenhouse Reef to the edge of the wall. See map page 104.
Access: Boat.
Conditions: Weather dependent. Surface conditions can be choppy at best.
Minimum depth: 20m (66ft)
Maximum depth: Beyond 30m (100ft)
This wall as always is indeed dramatic and very reminiscent of the North Wall of Grand Cayman. It is deeply incised where the spur and grooves become the reef crest.

Large canyons cut into the reef crest which is topped by a wide sandy plain. You can virtually always find garden eels on these plains as well as numerous rays and molluscs.

4 JEFF'S REEF (PLYMOUTH ROCK)
★★★★★★★★★

Location: Shallow dive. Single pin mooring buoy. See map page 104.
Access: Boat. Can be done from the shore, but difficult.
Conditions: Fairly sheltered and calm amongst reef system.
Minimum depth: 8m (30ft)
Maximum depth: 15m (50ft)
Similar to Site 6.

5 RADAR REEF
★★★★★★★★★

Location: Shallow dive. Single pin mooring buoy. See map page 104.
Access: Boat. Can be done from the shore, but difficult.
Conditions: Fairly sheltered and calm amongst reef system.
Minimum depth: 8m (30ft)
Maximum depth: 15m (50ft)
Similar to Site 6.

6 SNAPPER REEF (DUPPY'S REEF)
★★★★★★★★★

Location: Shallow dive. Near the southwest end of Stake Bay at The Rock. Single pin mooring buoy. See map page 104.
Access: Boat. Can be done from the shore, but difficult.
Conditions: Fairly sheltered and calm amongst reef system.
Minimum depth: 8m (30ft)
Maximum depth: 15m (50ft)
Again, this is a wide spur and groove reef topped with sea fans and sea plumes. Reef-dwellers include large numbers of wrasse and parrotfish and, as the name suggests, lots of over-friendly yellow snapper which get in the way of your photographs.

7 SCHOOLHOUSE WALL
★★★★

Location: Deep dive. Northwest of Snapper Reef (Site 6) to outer reef crest on the wall. Single pin mooring buoy. See map page 104.
Access: Boat.
Conditions: Weather dependent.
Minimum depth: 25m (82ft)

Maximum depth: Beyond 30m (100ft)
This location has a deep open water drop to the reef crest where the wall starts. Steep sand chutes run over the crest from the wide sand plain. Large pelagics, such as barracuda, wahoo, sharks and tuna swim by here and can be seen occasionally. Unfortunately, diving at these depths allows for little exploration and you can only have a general look at the location. The reef here is more gradually sloping (not vertical as in many of the other locations) and features large barrel sponges, strawberry sponges and angelfish.

8 GRUNT VALLEY
★★★★★★★★★

Location: Shallow dive. Opposite the school along Cotton Tree Bay. Single pin mooring buoy. See map page 104.
Access: Boat. Can be done from shore. Inner fringing reef system.
Conditions: Weather dependent.
Minimum depth: 8m (30ft)
Maximum depth: 15m (50ft)
Similar to Site 10.

9 PATCH REEF
★★★★

Location: Shallow dive. Opposite the school along Cotton tree Bay. Single pin mooring buoy. See map page 104.
Access: Boat. Can be done from shore. Inner fringing reef system.
Conditions: Weather dependent.
Minimum depth: 8m (30ft)
Maximum depth: 15m (50ft)
Similar to Site 10.

10 CHARLIE'S REEF
★★★★

Location: Shallow dive. Opposite the school along Cotton Tree Bay. Single pin mooring buoy. See map page 104.
Access: Boat. Can be done from shore. Inner fringing reef system.
Conditions: Weather dependent.
Minimum depth: 8m (30ft)
Maximum depth: 15m (50ft)
The inner reefs seem a bit battered sometimes, especially the sea fans – the damage is from the infrequent but

powerful storms which catch this end of the island. Large elkhorn and staghorn coral can be found with small schools of snapper and white margate beneath.

PIPERS WALL
★★★★

Location: Deep dive. North end of White Bay. Single pin mooring buoy. See map page 104.
Access: Boat.
Conditions: Weather dependent. Can be rather rough at times, making for an uncomfortable boat ride.
Minimum depth: 20m (66ft)
Maximum depth: Beyond 30m (100ft)
The reef crest tops at around 14m (50ft) and seems to 'fold' over into the depths below. The reef has numerous large canyons with nice sea fans and black coral, as well as large tube sponges dotted around with pairs of angelfish in attendance.

12 CEMETERY WALL
★★★★

Location: Deep dive. Northwest off Cotton Tree Bay opposite the cemetery. Single pin mooring buoy. See map page 104.
Access: Boat.
Conditions: Weather dependent, can be rather exposed.

Minimum depth: 14m (45ft)
Maximum depth: Beyond 30m (100ft)
The reef crest is at 14m (45ft), which is unusual for the Brac. There are large star coral, the basic coral reef builders. Black coral can be found over the ledges and there are numerous pairs of angelfish and butterflyfish. The deep fissure is virtually overgrown with superb coral growth, almost forming a tunnel into the depths.

13 KISSIMEE (WRECK)
★★★★

Location: Shallow dive. North end of Stake Bay. Single pin mooring buoy. See map page 104.
Access: Boat. Can be done from the shore 90m (300ft).
Conditions: Fairly calm with little current, choppy surface conditions.
Minimum depth: 14m (45ft)
Maximum depth: 20m (66ft)
This retired tug boat was deliberately sunk in 1982 as an addition to the reef system and to provide an interesting second dive location for avid wreck explorers. She is 18m (60ft) long and now rests on her port side, surrounded by good quality reef. The wreck is a favourite site for photographers and, during the summer months, large numbers of rays can be seen.

The Giant Netted Barrel sponge, Verongula gigantea, is more fragile than it looks so divers should resist the temptation to climb inside.

14 BUCCANEER

★★★★

Location: Shallow dive. North end of Stake Bay. Single pin mooring buoy. See map page 104.
Access: Boat. Can be done from the shore 90m (300ft).
Conditions: Fairly calm with little current, choppy surface conditions.
Minimum depth: 14m (45ft)
Maximum depth: 20m (66ft)
Similar to Kissimee (Site 13) reef area. Also good snorkelling to be enjoyed here.

15 STRAWBERRY SPONGE WALL

★★★★

Location: Deep dive. Along the drop-off of northwest area of White Bay. Single pin mooring buoy. See map page 104.
Access: Boat.
Conditions: Weather dependent. Choppy surface conditions.
Minimum depth: 23m (75ft)
Maximum depth: Beyond 30m (100ft)
This is very similar to the North Wall of Grand Cayman, but you would expect it to be so, because they were formed at the same time by the same forces. It is a lovely reef wall cut by fissures and overhangs, festooned with sponges, particularly the strawberry vase sponge. Look inside these sponges, because you can often find brittle starfish and the coral banded shrimp. The location is well known for the thousands of garden eels.

16 GARDEN EEL WALL

★★★★

Location: Deep dive. Further southwest along same wall. Single pin mooring buoy. See map page 104.
Access: Boat.
Conditions: Weather dependent. Choppy surface conditions.
Minimum depth: 20m (66ft)
Maximum depth: Beyond 30m (100ft)
As the name implies there is a large colony of garden eels on the sand plateau at the top of the reef and running into the grooves. These eels actually belong to the conger eel family and will retreat into their holes, tail first as you approach them. Continue to swim southwest along the sand plateau and you will eventually come to East Chute (Site 19).

17 EAST CHUTE (WRECK)

★★★★★

Location: Deep dive. Out from White Bay to the edge of the drop-off. Single pin mooring buoy. See map 104.
Access: Boat.
Conditions: Sometimes ocean swell here and it can be difficult to get in and out of the small day boat.
Minimum depth: 20m (66ft)
Maximum depth: Beyond 30m (100ft)
This steel tug boat, the 20m (66ft) *Cayman Mariner*, sits upright with the bow facing the ridge of the wall. The

Signposts at Brac reef resort lead the way.

workboat was originally operated by Cayman Energy Ltd and was purchased by Brac Aquatics and deliberately sunk in September of 1986. There is a wide sandy plateau along the top and you can regularly see rays and barracuda. The reef crest in this location is cut by numerous deep fissures and it is very easy to overstay your welcome and find yourself too deep. Very good dive and popular amongst the dive operators, given the combination of deep wreck and reef wall.

18 MIDDLE CHUTE

★★★★★

Location: Further southwest along same stretch of wall. Single pin mooring buoy. See map page 104.
Access: Boat.
Conditions: Weather dependent. Similar conditions to Site 17.
Minimum depth: 20m (66ft)
Maximum depth: Beyond 30m (100ft)
Similar to Site 19. Deep dive.

19 WEST CHUTE

★★★★★

Location: Deep dive. Further southwest along same stretch of wall. Single pin mooring buoy. See map 104.
Access: Boat.
Conditions: Weather dependent. Similar to Site 17.
Minimum depth: 20m (66ft)

Maximum depth: Beyond 30m (100ft)
A similar dive to Site 17 but without the wreck. There are some very steep sand chutes all the way along this area of reef wall. The top of the reef crest is deep, but the clarity of water and abundance of sponges and corals on the wall more than makes up for it. There are some huge barrel sponges and a large number of hermit crabs around, and squirrel fish and bigeye can be seen lurking in the shadows of the crevices. It is always important to remember when diving in exposed reef wall areas to keep a check on your depth and your location in relation to the dive boat. Fortunately these waters are generally so clear that you should always be able to see where the boat and mooring buoy are.

20 AIRPORT WALL

★★★★★

Location: Deep dive, west to northwest of the end of the airport runway. Single pin mooring buoy. See map page 104.
Access: Boat.
Conditions: Very exposed on corner, choppy surface conditions and moderate to strong current.
Minimum depth: 20m (66ft)
Maximum depth: Beyond 30m (100ft)
Similar to Site 21.

Giant anemone, Condylactis gigantea, perhaps the most common anemone on the outer reef.

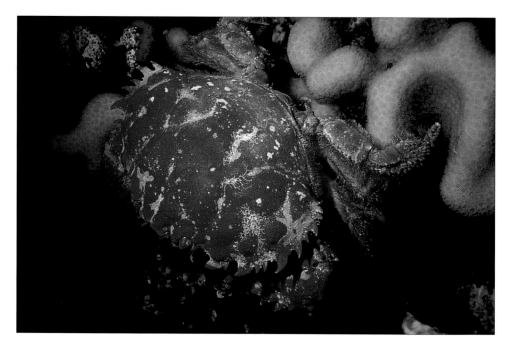

21 DOUBLE WALL (END OF ISLAND WALL)
★★★★★

Location: Deep dive, west to northwest of the end of the airport runway. Single pin mooring buoy. See map page 104.
Access: Boat.
Conditions: Very exposed on corner, choppy surface conditions and moderate to strong current.
Minimum depth: 20m (66ft)
Maximum depth: Beyond 30m (100ft)
Here, a steeply fissured reef crest at 14m (50ft) 'folds' over into the depths; a secondary small ledge has formed in some areas due to the accumulation of sand. Extremely good coral growth out into the canyons, as you would expect from an exposed location. Lots of fish life and a profuse growth of sponges. Very good area. The very old remains of what could be a pirate wreck have been discovered here: a large mound of ballast stones has been found.

22 AIRPORT REEF
★★★★★★★

Location: Shallow dive. See map page 104.
Access: Boat.
Conditions: Weather dependent. You can still encounter current on this exposed site.
Minimum depth: 4m (15ft)
Maximum depth: 15m (50ft)
This is a spur and groove reef which has suffered in the past from the construction of the runway, however, it is now recovering nicely and is teeming with fish life. There are lots of sea fans and plumes and also quite a lot of fire coral. (Care should be taken as always to avoid touching the coral).

23 FISHERY
★★★★★★★★★★★

Location: Shallow dive. Turning the corner next to Airport Reef. See map page 104.
Access: Boat. Can be done from the shore, but a long swim.
Conditions: Weather dependent. You can still encounter current on this exposed site.
Minimum depth: 4m (15ft)
Maximum depth: 15m (50ft)
This site is a large spur and groove system and is still relatively undived big schools of grunt and snapper and large anemones with cleaner shrimps can be found as well as several cleaning stations. The grouper are cleaned by small blennies and not the more regularly associated cleaner wrasse.

Above: *Red-ridged clinging crab, Mithrax forceps.*

Above: *The delicate structure of the feeding fans of this tube worm are vibrantly coloured.*
Below: *Sponge brittle stars,* Ophiothrix suensonii, *live on sponges, fire coral and occasionally on Gorgonian sea fans. Hiding during the day, they are more readily observed at night.*

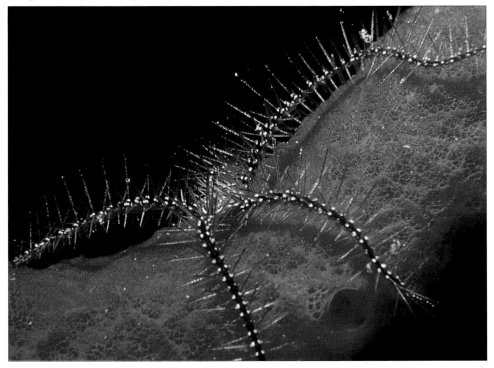

In 1996, amid much publicity, a large decommissioned Russian destroyer was sunk off the north shore of Cayman Brac. This one-time vessel of destruction is now set to become a flagship of marine conservation.

Built in 1984 at Nakhodka in the former USSR at a cost of US$30 million, the ship is a Brigadier Type II Class Frigate. She measures 95m (330ft) in length with a beam of 12.8m (42.6ft), and weighs 1590 metric tons. Part of the old Soviet fleet stationed in Cuba during the Cold War and known as Patrol Vessel 356, the vessel never actually saw military conflict. When the USSR dissolved in 1992, the newly created Russian Republic took over operational control of the base, but was unable to continue its financial support due to economic upheavals in Russia. So in 1993 the base and all the ships stationed in the Caribbean were removed from active duty. Patrol Vessel 356's complement of 11 officers and 99 enlisted personnel were all repatriated to Russia.

In 1996 the Cayman Islands Government acquired the ship. A location for her sinking was thoroughly examined by local diving operators aided by the Cayman Islands Department of the Environment, who carried out a further, on-board inspection of the

destroyer to determine her suitability as a dive site and to check there were no harmful elements still on board, such as radioactivity. The location was carefully chosen to ensure minimal environmental impact: inside the drop-off along the north wall of Cayman Brac, a few hundred metres west of the old Buccaneer Inn at West End, in depths of 20-30m (65-100ft). There was no coral in the impact zone and divers from the Department of Environment managed to relocate as much other marine life as possible.

In front of a packed and excited crowd, the ship was renamed the *M.V. Captain Keith Tibbetts* by the wife of the Cayman Islands Governor, his Excellency John Owen M.B.E. Then the Governor, the Hon. Thomas Jefferson and Jean-Michel Cousteau related the story of the acquisition of the destroyer and their hopes for the future of Cayman Brac.

Whilst the ship was moored at Creek Dock at Cayman Brac, we had been given the opportunity to dive beneath the hull as the ship was made 'diver-safe'. We had found that, because the ship had sat still for over ten years, there was already a large concentration of marine growth along the hull and propellors. As Jean-Michel Cousteau noted at the time, 'This will greatly speed up the colonisation of other marine growths on to the steel hull.'

Preparations for the sinking began in the early hours of Tuesday 17 September, when 8,500 gallons were pumped into each of the sealed areas which would remain unaffected by the opening of the sea-cocks. This was done by the Cuban tug-boat *Rigel*, which had first towed the ship to Cayman Brac. The *Rigel* crew had already carried out the controlled sinking of 64 other vessels for dive sites around the coast of Cuba.

Even with the sea-cocks open, the process of sinking was very slow, since the ship's three anchors had to be placed securely and well away from any coral. As the ship started to sink, the tug kept a constant strain on the bow of the ship to ensure that she would land properly in the sand chute.

In an act of bravery, Jean-Michel Cousteau chose to remain on board the ship as she sank. At 5.20pm the newly named *Captain Keith Tibbetts* finally plunged beneath the waves to a resounding cheer from on-lookers and a blast of the tug's steam whistle. Such sounds were almost drowned out by the noise from the ship itself as air was forced out of the companionways and engine room. We watched Jean-Michel Cousteau, in full SCUBA gear, cling to the guard rail as the ship vanished from sight.

Later that night, after we had completed filming, Cousteau said, 'Fear did not come into it – this is something I always wanted to do, and the preparations beforehand to ensure that there would be no accidents were meticulous', though, he admitted, 'what did cause a moment of anxiety was when the aluminium superstructure cracked open in two places, splitting the living quarters with a resounding crack.'

In its new resting place, the ship appears simply massive. She lists only slightly to starboard, otherwise perfectly placed in a sand-chute which plunges over the wall off the north shore of Cayman Brac. On either side of her are healthy sections of coral reef carpeted with huge barrel sponges. Under the bow at 25m (83ft) is a field of garden eels, and under the stern the rudders and propellors keep the hull clear of the bottom. To our amazement, we found fish around the ship almost immediately after she sank. The *Captain Keith Tibbetts* is clearly destined to become an integral part of reef life in the Cayman Islands.

Opposite: *Her bow restrained by a tug, the* Captain Keith Tibbetts *starts the final plunge.*
Below left: *A diver explores the mid-section.*
Below right: *The Cousteau dive team examine intact radar heads.*

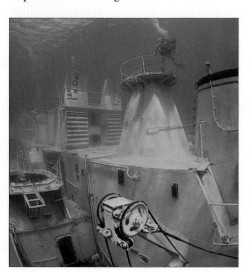

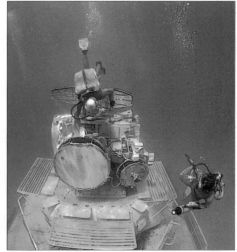

South Shore

The southern sites on Cayman Brac resemble those on Grand Cayman. The spur and groove reef system is more pronounced and the wall starts around 20m (66ft). The wall is more gently sloping in this area and starts much further out from the shore. This means that there are large areas of sand flats with small but very good quality coral growths on the lower slopes including lots of elkhorn coral and numerous large sponges. A lot of people still, however, prefer to cross the short distance to Little Cayman, leaving the southern shore relatively underdived. Its coastline also suffered during Hurricane Gilbert, although the reefs are now recovering nicely.

24 TARPON REEF
★★★★

Location: Shallow dive. South of the Ledges and Channel Bay. Double pin mooring buoy. See page 104.
Access: Boat. Opposite Brac Aquatics to the left of the channel.
Conditions: Weather dependent. Generally calm with good light.
Minimum depth: 8m (30ft)
Maximum depth: 15m (50ft)
Similar to Site 26.

25 LIGHTHOUSE REEF
★★★★

Location: Shallow dive. South of the Ledges and Channel Bay. Double pin mooring buoy. See map page 104.
Access: Boat. Opposite Brac Aquatics to the left of the channel.
Conditions: Weather dependent. Generally calm with good light.
Minimum depth: 8m (30ft)
Maximum depth: 15m (50ft)
Similar to Site 26.

26 SERGEANT MAJOR REEF
★★★★

Location: Shallow dive. South of the Ledges and Channel Bay. Double pin mooring buoy. See map page 104.
Access: Boat. Opposite Brac Aquatics to the left of the channel.
Conditions: Weather dependent. Generally calm with good light.
Minimum depth: 8m (30ft)

Maximum depth: 15m (50ft)
This is a spur and groove reef with numerous gullies, canyons and swim-throughs. Elkhorn coral and star coral, vase and tube sponges, cowfish, trumpetfish and snapper abound. Good for invertebrates too. Tarpon can be found at the top of the gullies and the whole area is very reminiscent of the similar Tarpon Alley on the southwest shore of Grand Cayman. Excellent night dive with a profuse amount of invertebrate life, particularly the red night shrimp and small squid.

27 ANCHOR WALL
★★★★

Location: Deep dive. South of the Ledges and Channel buoy. Single pin mooring buoy. See map page 104.
Access: Boat. Through channel to east of Divi Tiara.
Conditions: Weather dependent. Generally calm with good light.
Minimum depth: 20m (66ft)
Maximum depth: Beyond 30m (100ft)
Similar to Site 28.

28 ORANGE CANYON
★★★★

Location: Deep dive. South of the Ledges and Channel buoy. Single pin mooring buoy. See map page 104.
Access: Boat. Through channel to east of Divi Tiara, diving centre.
Conditions: Weather dependent. Generally calm with good light.
Minimum depth: 20m (66ft)
Maximum depth: Beyond 30m (100ft)
A spur and groove reef with numerous gullies, canyons and swimthroughs. The predominant feature is the three large tunnels which come out on the reef wall around

Opposite: *Superb visibility at 20m (65ft).*

the 25m (83ft) area. The mooring is placed between two of them, so they are very easy to find. Excellent wide angle photography in this area with large tube and barrel sponges.

29 SEAFEATHER WALL
★★★★

Location: Deep dive. South of Dennis Point and south east of Divi Tiara. Single pin mooring buoy. See map page 104.
Access: Boat.
Conditions: Generally sheltered area with moderate current.
Minimum depth: 20m (66ft)
Maximum depth: Beyond 30m (100ft)
Sometimes it's hard to remember which island you are diving on: as these names imply, these sites have their counterparts on Grand Cayman and the similarities are astonishing. This is, however, only to be expected since the reefs are of the same age, in the same geographical location and have been shaped by the same forces of nature into their present-day condition. Seafeather Wall has lots of gullies, caves and fissures covered in sponges, black corals and sea fans.

30 BUTTERFLY REEF
★★★★

Location: Shallow dive. South of the Ledges along Dick Sessinger's Bay. Single pin mooring buoy. See map page 104.
Access: Boat.
Conditions: Weather dependent. Generally calm with good light.
Minimum depth: 8m (30ft)
Maximum depth: 13m (45ft)
Similar to Site 31.

31 ELKHORN REEF
★★★★

Location: Shallow dive. South of the Ledges along Dick Sessinger's Bay. Single pin mooring buoy. See map page 104.
Access: Boat.
Conditions: Weather dependent. Generally calm with good light.
Minimum depth: 8m (30ft)
Maximum depth: 13m (45ft)
Elkhorn reef comprises four ridges of the spur and

groove reef with numerous gullies, canyons and swimthroughs. As well as elkhorn coral and star coral, vase and tube sponges, there is a huge brain coral near the mooring buoy. It is common to see large barracuda in this area as well as many sergeant majors, damsel fish and coney.

32 CRAB VALLEY
★★★★

Location: Deep dive. South east to the reef crest. Single pin mooring buoy. See map page 104.
Access: Boat.
Conditions: Weather dependent. Slightly more exposed to surface chop and wind.
Minimum depth: 20m (66ft)
Maximum depth: Beyond 30m (100ft)
This deep fissure cuts through from the reef crest and plummets into the depths.

There are numerous overhangs covered in rope sponges and the recesses have large coral crabs and lobster. Lots of hermit crabs lumbering around in their mobile mollusc shell homes and small wrasse and gobies seem to be everywhere.

33 PILLAR CORAL REEF (ELKHORN FOREST)
★★★★★★★★

Location: Shallow dive. Off Salt Water Point. Single pin mooring buoy. See map page 104.
Access: Boat. Could be a shore dive with a 200m (660ft) swim.
Conditions: Weather dependent, moderate current. Good light.
Minimum depth: 8m (30ft)
Maximum depth: 15m (50ft)
Similar to Site 35.

34 HEDDY'S REEF
★★★★★★★★

Location: Shallow dive. Off Salt Water Point. Single pin mooring buoy. See map page 104.
Access: Boat. Could be a shore dive with a 200m (660ft) swim.
Conditions: Weather dependent, moderate current. Good light.
Minimum depth: 8m (30ft)
Maximum depth: 15m (50ft)
Similar to Site 35.

Above: *French angelfish are usually seen in pairs and seem to be unafraid of divers.*
Below: *Silversides group together for protection in huge shoals amongst gullies and caves.*

35 FRY CAVE

★★★★☆☆☆☆☆

Location: Shallow dive. Off Salt Water Point. Single pin mooring buoy. See map page 104.
Access: Boat. Could be a shore dive. 200m (660ft) swim.
Conditions: Weather dependent, moderate current. Good light.
Minimum depth: 8m (30ft)
Maximum depth: 15m (50ft)

This is a typical rugged spur and groove reef and mini wall, cut by many different gullies and canyons. Lots of elkhorn and pillar corals in good structure and form make this a delightful dive. Snapper and sergeant majors make a nuisance of themselves. The sergeant majors become very aggressive and territorial when you approach their nesting sites. The fry of Fry Cave name are silverside minnows comprising four different species of juvenile fish which congregate together to make one huge mass of moving fish, found in the summer months. Good quality sponges and sea fans. Very interesting area for invertebrates including file clams, nudibranchs and arrow crabs. Pistol shrimp can be found amongst the coral rubble as well as jawfish and yellow sting rays. Very similar to The Meadows on Little Cayman.

36 ANGEL REEF

★★★★

Location: Deep dive. On outer fringing reef off South East Bay. Single pin mooring buoy. See map page 104.
Access: Boat.

Conditions: Weather dependent choppy surface conditions, can be current.
Minimum depth: 24m (80ft)
Maximum depth: Beyond 30m (100ft)

Named after the same manta ray that is now found off Little Cayman. She was first seen along this stretch of reef and still cruises this area during the winter months when Bloody Bay marine Reserve is at its least divable. This site has a huge long cave which cuts through the wall and the reef is horseshoe-shaped. There are many small holes and shafts in the reef crest where the light shines through, making it an excellent photographic site.

37 INSIDE OUT

★★★★

Location: Deep dive. Southeast of Saltwater Point on outer drop-off. Single pin mooring buoy. See map page 104.
Access: Boat.

Conditions: Weather dependent, more exposed to surface chop and current on the outer wall.
Minimum depth: 20m (66ft)
Maximum depth: Beyond 30m (100ft)

This is a spectacular section of wall with a large sand chute and cave system disappearing into the depths. It's very easy to find yourself too deep in this area. The wall has large sponges of all types and excellent coral growth. There are lots of tunnels and the site gets its name from a mini wall which is on the inside of what should be the main wall. This strip reef has more

The White speckled hermit crab, Paguristes punticeps, can grow to 12cm (5in).

dimension to its geography, with larger individual coral heads and deeply incised grooves. There is a good possibility of finding nurse sharks in the shallows. Giant hogfish can be spotted by their shadow, bar jacks and sailfin blennies can be found on the dead coral areas. Good variety of sponges and sea fans. Look for the juvenile filefish amongst the sea fans and sea lilies.

38 EDEN WALL
★★★★

Location: Deep dive. Opposite Beach Point on outer wall. Single pin mooring buoy. See map page 104.
Access: Boat.
Conditions: Weather dependent, more exposed on this corner of the wall. Moderate current.
Minimum depth: 12m (40ft)
Maximum depth: Beyond 30m (100ft)
Similar to Site 39.

39 CIO'S CRAIG (WILDERNESS WALL)
★★★★

Location: Deep dive. Opposite Beach Point on outer wall. Single pin mooring buoy. See map page 104.
Access: Boat.
Conditions: Weather dependent, more exposed on this corner of the wall. Moderate current.
Minimum depth: 12m (40ft)

Maximum depth: Beyond 30m (100ft)
This site has a very good reef crest with a wide sandy plateau on top sloping into the wall. The steep drop is cut by a deep fissure and the more exposed corner of the vertical spur has some excellent coral formations. This is very typical of the spur and groove reefs – it also has lots of chimneys cutting the vertical reef wall, running from the crest. Although the reef structure is the same as the rest of the area, you are able to recognise individual sites by the formations of the coral arches and canyons.

40 NORBERT'S REEF
★★★★

Location: Shallow dive. Out between Deep Wall and Tom Jennett's Bay. See map page 104.
Access: Boat.
Conditions: Weather dependent. Fairly sheltered due to the Bluff.
Minimum depth: 8m (30ft)
Maximum depth: 15m (50ft)
Norbert's Reef is a lovely little spur and groove system of coral gullies topped with pillar coral, elkhorn and star coral. The reef features sea fans and plumes and a few large anemones with lots of wrasse, parrotfish and snapper. There are some interesting swimthroughs and a few deeply incised cuts through the top of the reef crest.

Above: *The radioles of the Featherduster worm, Bispira brunnea, trap particles of food.*

41 PRINCE FREDERICK WRECK
★★★★☆☆☆☆

Location: Shallow dive. Out from Hawksbill Bay. See map page 104.
Access: Boat. You can snorkel dive this from the shore and ballast stones can be found.
Conditions: Weather dependent. More exposed to surface chop, makes for a difficult boat ride.
Minimum depth: 5m (20ft)
Maximum depth: 15 (50ft)
The *Prince Frederick* was a wooden-hulled, twin-masted schooner 33m (110ft) long. Powered by steam and sail she was said to have sunk in the late 1800s, although no accurate date is given. There is lots of scrap metal lying about the reef including the windlass, anchor and chains, cast iron masts and lots of copper nails and cladding. You can find many juvenile species of fish in and around the wreck.

42 BAT CAVE
★★★★

Location: Deep dive. Running east along the drop-off. Opposite Brac Haven Apartments. Single pin mooring buoy. See map page 104.
Access: Boat.

PROJECT OCEAN SEARCH

Renowned environmentalist Jean-Michel Cousteau chose Cayman Brac for the second location for Project Ocean Search, a unique educational dive adventure/environmental discovery programme.
Based at the Brac Reef Beach Resort, Cousteau headed a team of scientists and marine biologists to investigate and study the nature and diversity of the Caymans' marine life. Participants used snorkel and scuba to view the reefs and record information on the unique tropical ecology, the processes of nature and the way man interacts with the environment. A Nikon underwater photographer was also on hand to instruct in the use of the Nikonos V as a recording tool on the expedition.
Cousteau announced that he and his team would appear exclusively on the Aggressor Fleet worldwide, including the Cayman Islands. Guests on these accompanied Voyages L'Aventure with Cousteau have become acquainted with the life, work and vision of this legendary marine champion through diving, discussions, presentations or assisting with research and film production.
Further information can be obtained from PROJECT OCEAN SEARCH c/o Jean-Michel Cousteau Productions, 1933 Cliff Drive, Suite 4, Santa Barbara, CA 93109; tel 1–805–899–8899/fax 1–805–899–8898 or contact Aggressor Fleet Limited, PO Drawer K, Morgan City, LA 70381; tel toll free: 1–800–348–2628, tel 1–504–385–2628/fax 1–504–384–0817.

Conditions: Weather dependent. Can be exposed to current and choppy conditions.
Minimum depth: 14m (48ft)
Maximum depth: Beyond 30m (100ft)
Similar to Site 43.

43 FOSTER'S WALL
★★★★

Location: Deep dive. Running east along the drop-off. Opposite Brac Haven Apartments. Single pin mooring buoy. See map page 104.
Access: Boat.
Conditions: Weather dependent. Can be exposed to current and choppy conditions.
Minimum depth: 14m (48ft)
Maximum depth: Beyond 30m (100ft)
Foster's wall features a very good coral reef crest which curls over into the wall proper. Numerous fissures and deep gullies make for an interesting dive. Large sea fans and barrel sponges, queen angelfish and French angelfish can be found, with slipper lobster on the upper slopes. This is typical of the South Shore. Two large tunnels open out onto the main wall at about 28m (93ft). On the inside of the wall there is a very large sandy area with all kinds of rays and Sharptail moray eels. You must be very careful of the depth in this area, it is very easy to go beyond the safe diving limits.

Spotfin butterflyfish, Chaetodon ocellatus. Most species occur in shallow depths or on the reef.

44 ROCKMONSTER CHIMNEY
★★★★★

Location: Deep dive. Due south of Pollard Bay. See map page104.
Access: Boat.
Conditions: Weather dependent. Long boat ride can be uncomfortable.
Minimum depth: 20m (66ft)
Maximum depth: Beyond 30m (100ft)
Similar to Site 47.

45 SON OF ROCKMONSTER
★★★★★

Location: Deep dive. Due south of Pollard Bay. See map page 104.
Access: Boat.
Conditions: Weather dependent. Long boat ride can be uncomfortable.
Minimum depth: 20m (66ft)
Maximum depth: Beyond 30m (100ft)
Similar to Site 47.

Foureye butterflyfish, Chaetodon capistratus, have a large eye marking near the tail to confuse predators.

46 KEN'S MOUNTAIN
★★★★★

Location: Deep dive. Due south of Pollard Bay. See map page 104.
Access: Boat.
Conditions: Weather dependent. Long boat ride can be uncomfortable.
Minimum depth: 20m (66ft)
Maximum depth: Beyond 30m (100ft)
Similar to Site 47.

47 BLUFF WALL
★★★★★

Location: Due south of Pollard Bay. See map page 104.
Access: Boat.
Conditions: Weather dependent. Long boat ride.
Minimum depth: 20m (66ft)
Maximum depth: Beyond 30m (100ft)
Very dramatic wall. Steep to vertical with deep fissures which bisect it into the depths. Very good quality large sea fans and black coral, as well as arrow. Arrow blennies, hermit crabs, rope and pink vase sponges. Sharks are possible and rays and turtles are common. Although there isn't the profusion of tropical fish, the drama of this steeply vertical wall makes up for it..

How to Get There

By air: The Gerrard Smith International Airport, at the west end of Cayman Brac, has a tarmac runway, unlike Little Cayman which has a grass runway. The fairly new terminal building has a ticketing counter, security checks, a departure lounge, Immigration, Customs and a Cayman Airways office. Normal operating hours are 8:30–17:30 local time.

Both Cayman Airways and Island Air operate regular services to Cayman Brac from Little Cayman and Grand Cayman. The Island Air service runs twice daily and the Cayman Airways schedule should be checked in advance. Because the airport has been upgraded to International status, Cayman Brac is able to accept Cayman Airways flights from Miami, Tampa and Houston.

Cayman Airways, PO Box 1101G, Airport Road, George Town, Grand Cayman, toll free tel 800–G–CAYMAN, tel 949–7564/fax 949–0082. Cayman Brac residents tel 948–2535, Cayman Brac flight info tel 948–1221/fax 948–1286.

Island Air, PO Box 1991G, Island Air Hangar, Owen Roberts International Airport, George Town, Grand Cayman, toll free tel 800–9–CAYMAN, tel 949–0241/fax 949–7044.

Cayman Brac Air Terminal tel 948–1656.

Baggage allowance
You may check up to 20 kg (55 lb) of baggage per passenger free of charge. Excess baggage will be charged and is guaranteed to arrive at the destination within 24 hours of checking in. The Island Air planes are quite small and if they are operating with a full passenger load, you may think twice about bringing every bit of diving and photographic equipment with you. All the dive centres offer first-class equipment for rent, including wet suits, regulators, BCs, masks, fins and snorkels, and always keep ample supplies of air tanks and weight belts with weights.

Where to Stay

All the accommodation is similarly priced and styled. Apart from the individual self-catering apartments and villas, all the hotels have good restaurants, where meals are generally served buffet-style, but the food is cooked with little flair or imagination. There is plenty of it, however – more than enough for the active diver. Lunches tend to be a local spicy dish of fish or chicken, salad, french fries and a dessert of some kind, plus fruit and soft drinks. All the hotels and dive centres have the same rule: no alcohol until the day's diving is finished and no diving on your last day before flying off the Island.

Brac Apartments, contact Cornell Burke, PO Box 89, West End; tel 948–1499.

Brac Caribbean Beach Village, PO Box 4, Stake Bay, toll free tel: 800–791–7911; tel 948–2265/fax 948–2206. Overlooking the sea, modern, bright and airy. New swimming pool at entrance. Better to be here in a group as it can be impersonal.

Brac Haven Villas, PO Box 89, Stake Bay; tel 948–2473/fax 948–2329.

Brac Reef Beach Resort, PO Box 56, West End, toll free tel: 800–327–3835; tel 948–1323/fax 948–1207. Modern, open-plan, with meals taken outside. Comfortable, with a swimming pool and a raised deck area. Located on the beach and with its own dive centre situated next to the jetty. Well-stocked shop.

Divi Tiara Beach Resort, PO Box 238, Stake Bay, toll free tel: 800–367–3484, US res: 1–305–633–3484; tel 948–1553/fax 948–1316. PADI 5-Star Centre and hotel on two storeys. Located directly on the beach with a large swimming pool. Timeshare apartments are available. Bicycles supplied free to guests.

La Esperanza, PO Box 28, Stake Bay, tel 948–0591/fax 948–0525. With private beach.

Reefside Retreat, Brac Villa, c/o Cayman Villas, PO Box 681, toll free tel: 800–235–5888; tel 945–4144/fax 949–7471.

Walton's Mango Manor, PO Box 56, Stake Bay, tel/fax 948–0518. Elegant bed and breakfast.

Where to Eat

The Cayman Brac restaurants offer excellent value for money and a greater variety than the in-house restaurants. Most offer Caribbean-style cuisine with a relaxed and pleasant atmosphere. Casual dress can be worn, but preferably no shorts in the evenings.

Angie's Ice Cream & Subs, Tibbets Square, West End; tel 948–1566.

Aunt Sha's Kitchen, West End, Cayman Brac; tel 948–1581.

Edd's Place, West End, Cayman Brac; tel 948–1208.

The Dive Centre at Divi Tiara is attached to the beach resort, see opposite.

G & M Diner, West End, Cayman Brac; tel 948–1272.

La Esperanza Bar & Restaurant at the Creek, Stake Bay, Cayman Brac; tel 948–0531/fax 948–0525.

Sonia's Restaurant, White Bay, Cayman Brac; tel 948–1214.

Wallgreen Store & Restaurant, Spot Bay, Cayman Brac; tel 948–0222.

DIVE FACILITIES

Brac Aquatics Ltd, PO Box 89, West End, toll free tel: 800–544–BRAC; tel 948–1429/fax 264–2742. The oldest-established dive operation on Cayman Brac. Staff are very knowledgeable about whole reef system and ecology. Responsible for sinking of the wrecks/artificial reefs. Very conservation-minded. No-frills diving. Formerly attached to Brac Reef Resort, now independent.

Brac Reef Beach Resort Dive Centre (address, tel/fax as above). Located on the beach front next to the access road to the slipway, opposite Brac Aquatics.

Divi Tiara, PO Box 238, Stake Bay, toll free tel: 1–800–367–3484 ; tel 948–1553/fax 948–1316. PADI 5 Star Centre (Divi Tiara). Well-stocked shop and rental equipment in good order. Club atmosphere. Courses offered regularly to all levels. Attached to Tiara Beach Resort.

FILM PROCESSING

Photographic Services, Photo Tiara, PO Box 238, Stake Bay.
Toll free tel 800–367–3484; tel 948–7553/fax 948–7316.

Full E-6 slide processing and C-41 print processing. Same-day service is available if film is handed in before 13:30. Stills and video photographic rental are also available. All the equipment is the latest on the market and is well maintained. A video of your holiday can be put together with the adjoining hotel as part of your holiday package. Photo Tiara is also home to the Nikonos School of Photography and regular photographic 'shoot-outs' or competitions and instruction weeks are held during the year.

EMERGENCY NUMBERS

Hospital Faith Hospital, tel 948–2243/5.

Cayman Brac Day Care Centre Stake Bay, tel 948–2218.

Recompression Chamber, PO Box 1551G, George Town, Grand Cayman; tel 949–2989. Emergency tel 555. The chamber also operates a medical alert flight with Island Air if there are any problems on the Island. DAN – the Divers Alert Network – is also consulted, when necessary, for additional help.

Air Ambulance
Aero Care, toll free tel 800–627–2376, tel 747–8923. Operated by Aero Care based in Lubbock, Texas, this jet service will take you back to the USA if necessary.

Island Air, tel 949–5252. Island Air offer a 30-minute response time with a full 24-hour Learjet service with professional medical care.

Executive Air Services, tel 949–7775/fax 945–5732. Executive Air transport patients from George Town Hospital. Offer a full 24-hour service with registered doctors, nurses and trauma physicians.

National Air Ambulance
tel 1–305–358–9900/fax 1–305–359–0039. Operating out of Fort Lauderdale in Florida, this organization offers a world-wide capability with a bedside-to-bedside service.

LOCAL HIGHLIGHTS

People really only come to the island to dive, particularly on the new Russian Destroyer, the *M.V. Capt. Keith Tibbetts*, but if you are having a day's rest, visit the **Cayman Brac Museum**, Stake Bay; tel 948–2622 or the **Library**, Creek Post Office, Stake Bay, Cayman Brac; tel 948–0472.

Other local highlights include the view from the top of the Bluff at the Lighthouse, and exploring the many ancient limestone caves which used to serve as hurricane shelters for the locals.

Car Hire
It will only take you a day at the most to explore Cayman Brac, but it is well worth the effort. Costs are similar to those on Grand Cayman, at around $50 per day depending on the style and size of vehicle. Depending on the time of year, a car is also useful for transporting dive gear to shore destinations and for transfer to and from the airport.

Avis, Stake Bay; tel 948–2847/ 2516/2616 fax 948–1495. In front of airport terminal.

Hertz, PO Box 87, Stake Bay, tel 948–1514/1515/0277/fax 948–1380.

Four D's Car Rental, Kidco Building South side West end; tel 948–1599/0459.

B & S Motor Cycles Ventures, PO Box 48; tel 948–1546/fax 948–1576.

The idyllic Divi Tiara beach resort is modern and comfortable.

Night diving is an experience not to be missed – the true colours of the reef are shown in all their brilliant splendour, illuminated by torch-light.

Once you have chosen your location you should, if possible, familiarise yourself with the site by diving the area during the day. Diving at dusk and slowly acclimatising yourself to the change between ambient light and the artificial light of your dive torch is a good way to get used to night diving.

No special training is required, but divers and underwater photographers should be even more aware of their buoyancy control to avoid damaging the corals. If you need to steady yourself, choose an area of dead coral rock and only use one finger. Always dive with an experienced diver.

Nighttime is probably the best time to take marine life study photographs because many reef species are asleep and can be approached more easily. There are also fascinating nocturnal creatures to see such as octopus, lobster and a large variety of shrimps, crabs, squid, worms, anemones and fish.

Creatures which have been hiding in nooks and crannies and under boulders during the glare of the mid-day sun now crawl, slither and hop into the open. Hermit crabs joust with each other over possession of empty mollusc shells and sea urchins and featherstars crawl onto the reef top. Colourful cowrie shells and other dazzling molluscs such as nudibranchs or seaslugs actively browse amongst the algae which grows on dead corals.

Small blennies and shrimps which were impossible to photograph during the day seem to dare you to come closer at night Cayman reefs are home to the red night shrimp (*Rhynchocinetes rigens*), but be careful of their stinging hydroids (small hairs or feather-like formations) as the sting can be rather fierce. It is important to remember your buoyancy technique and stay well clear of the coral to avoid being stung.

The diamond-backed blenny (*Malacoctenus boehlkei*) will also show itself from under the protective embrace of the anemone's tentacles. Although relatively common in the Caribbean, it is still a joy to find them in the Cayman Islands. There are no true anemone fish or clown fish in the Caribbean and if you hear or see otherwise in books or in après dive bar lectures, someone is trying to dupe you!

Basket stars (*Astrophyton muricatum*) on the outer reef wall extend their multi-limbed body into the current to sift the plankton which rises each night from the depths. If you shine your dive light into them, many will curl up for protection. Using a flash is necessary, of course, and for many of the smaller fan worms, you may only get one chance at photographing them due to the intensity of the light output of the flash. Be patient and take your time over each photograph in case there's no second chance.

Pelagic or open water predators now move over the reef searching for an easy feast. Moray eels have bad eyesight, but they are able to sniff out their prey asleep in the reef. The scorpion fish which were so difficult to see during the day are also much more brightly coloured at night. Many other fish are also chameleon-like in their colour changes such as the blue fusilier which changes to red at night, as well as hogfish, damselfish and angelfish.

NIGHT-DIVING LOCATIONS

For shore diving at night I would recommend Eden Rock (Site 44, Grand Cayman). This site is well known for its caves, gulleys and inter-connected passageways, and is an ideal site as an introduction to night diving. Here you can find the diamond-backed blenny living under the anemone's tentacles, juvenile lobster only 3cm (1 in) long as well as octopus, squid and puffer fish. Perhaps the best night dive on Grand Cayman is the wreck of the Balboa just outside George Town harbour (Site 42)). You can find the rare orangeball anemone (Pseudocorynactis caribbeorum) on the wreck as well as sleeping parrotfish which have a protective mucus 'nest' secreted around them to ward off the free-swimming moral eels and snake eels which are active feeders at night.

The reef just seems to come alive at night so don't miss an opportunity for a night dive. Always check with the dive shop of your choice if they have anything organised. Some stores even have illustrated talks on the marine life at night and these should not be missed.

Top: *Red night shrimp, Rhynchocinetes rigens.*
Middle: *Red reef hermit crab, Paguristes cadenati.*
Bottom: *Spiny lobster, Panulirus argus.*

LITTLE CAYMAN

The Cayman Islands are undoubtedly a 'mecca' for divers and the wall off the North Shore of Grand Cayman is spectacular to say the least – until, that is, you have dived Little Cayman.

Lying 120km (75m) north of Grand Cayman, Little Cayman is the third and smallest of the Cayman Islands group. Located 11.2 km (7m) west across the channel from Cayman Brac, the island is only 14.4 km (9m) long and 1.6km (1 mile) at its widest point. Predominantly scrub, the island is almost completely flat, rising only 12m (40ft) above sea level. The Island has a unique charm which is enjoyed by the influx of divers and other tourists who relish the 'hideaway' feeling you get here.

Tarpon Lake, a large brackish pond, was flooded during Hurricane Gilbert in 1988 and the swampy regions are a haven for mosquitoes. (Little Cayman does not have the same mosquito control as Grand Cayman and precautions should be taken against mosquitoes and sand flies.) The lake itself now actually has a smaller sub-species of the common tarpon found around the reef crest.

Owen Island, a small islet, located along the south shore, is a bird sanctuary of about 4.5 hectares (11 acres) and has a glorious sandy beach and a blue lagoon. It used to be connected to Little Cayman by a sand spit – but this has long gone. You can snorkel out to the island which is about 200m (660ft) offshore. It looks very much as it must have done before any settlers arrived.

Little Cayman is served by a grass-strip runway with regular flights from Cayman Brac (15 minutes flight time), and Grand Cayman (about 45 minutes flight time). You get superb aerial views of the reefs on either of the flights. Virtually all the seats are window seats, but it is definitely first come, first served, so get there early to claim the best photographic seats. If one of the smaller service planes is being used, you may be able to sit up in the cockpit beside the pilot.

It is important to arrange your accommodation and transport well in advance because there are no taxis and you may have to thumb a lift around the island. There is a very small

Opposite: *Coconut palms on an empty beach, Little Cayman.*
Above: *This house is owned by one of the few residents of Little Cayman.*

resident population, and even this is seasonal, with approximately 60 residents, 12 of whom are local Caymanian. There is one car hire company on the island located next to the airport along the 'main street'. If you want to explore the island, you can also generally hire a bicycle from any of the resorts at which you are staying.

The island also boasts a large colony of boobies and a special preserve is now protected by the Little Cayman division of the Cayman Islands National Trust and is a designated RAMSAR site. (RAMSAR is not an acronym, it is a city in Iran which hosted a convention on the protection of wetlands and wildfowl.) The site now has a new bird information tower and interpretive centre including a telescope as well as lecture and meeting rooms.

You can often catch sight of the endangered Cayman parrot, a sub-species of the Cuban parrot. Wild iguanas are plentiful and you can even find the Cayman orchid. Most of the undergrowth next to the shoreline is inhabited by a huge population of hermit crabs. The swampy interior is also a protected area and the island is rapidly now becoming famous for its terrestrial life.

Snorkelling is available all around the island and much of the inner shoreline is protected by a fringing reef but, even still, most of the snorkelling areas are weather dependent. Quite strong currents can be experienced at Point of Sands and care, as always, should be taken. It is advisable to wear strong booties with your fins but gloves should not be worn.

Bloody Bay Marine Park

Bloody Bay Marine Park along the north shore of Little Cayman has to be one of the most spectacular and varied dive locations in the world. The name Bloody Bay loosely refers to the bay between Jackson Point to the east and Spot Bay in the west. Bloody Bay Marine Park actually has two separate walls: to the east is Jackson Wall with Bloody Bay Wall to the west, but both are known as Bloody Bay Marine Park. Of the 56 listed dive sites which are recorded around this island, 18 of them are along Bloody Bay and Jackson Walls.

The new legislation regarding Bloody Bay Marine Park limits the number of boats which have access to the park and all dive operators must be licensed. Only two dive boats per operator per day are allowed into the marine park and each dive boat must have no more than twenty divers. Each dive operation must therefore limit the number of dive trips to only 14 in any week. This may prove difficult for some dive operations, because the diving is also weather dependent. The Natural Resources unit of the Department of the Environment is scheduling more mooring buoys around the rest of the island and insists that accurate log books are maintained by all of the dive boats.

There are no shore tank rentals as yet because this would involve unsupervised diving which is not recommended in the marine park. A new shore diving operation is in the planning stages and there is much concern over the safety of the reefs.

Virtually all of the dives are potentially deep dives, with the reef plummeting to 2000m (6000ft). But when the wall starts at only 6m (20ft), you can plan a variable profile dive and spend as much time as you want in the shallows. A few of the dives can be reached by a lengthy snorkel out over the fringing reef, but the preferred way to dive these sites is by either a fast day boat from the local dive centres or by live-aboard dive boat.

The potential for serious diving incidents is as high on Little Cayman as anywhere else around the islands, perhaps even more so. The unlimited depths along Bloody Bay Marine Park are indeed a temptation and dives should not be taken lightly or unsupervised. This is a superb location, but extra care must be maintained at all times. Suffering a decompression incident (apart from the obvious life-threatening effect) not only stops you from diving for the rest of your vacation, it may also cause a severe disruption to your fellow guests, dive masters and boats' captains.

DIVE SITES (ANTI-CLOCKWISE FROM EAST POINT)

Dive sites 1-8 along North Shore and east of Bloody Bay Marine Park are spectacular. Unlike Bloody Bay, which in some popular areas is overdived, these eight new sites are the least dived of all the Caymans and are absolutely pristine. It is strongly recommended to give Bloody Bay Marine Park a rest and dive these locations.

Similarly two other new sites are not be missed: to the west of Bloody Bay – Paradise Plunge and Sandcastle (Sites 31 and 36) and two locations along South Shore – Lighthouse Wall and Dynamite Drop Off (Sites 38 and 43).

Little Cayman has an enviable reputation as having the best diving in the Caribbean and these new sites designated by the Department of Environment simply underline the fact.

NITROGEN NARCOSIS

Diving in the Cayman Islands invariably involves deep diving. The possibility of being affected by nitrogen narcosis is therefore very high so great care should be taken. The effects of nitrogen narcosis (or 'Rapture of the Deep' as it is sometimes known), is a feeling akin to euphoria and drunkenness. This condition can obviously cause serious problems for divers so if you are planning to dive deep it is advisable to take a deep diving course. One of the most important things to remember is to make sure you increase your depth gradually, 3m (10ft) at a time.

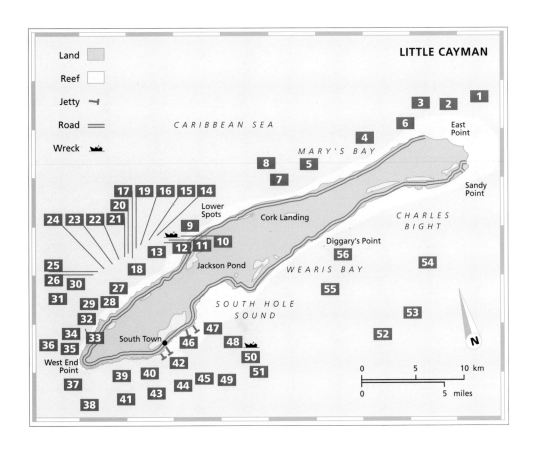

North Shore

1 BLACKTIP TUNNELS
★★★★★

Location: Shallow dive. North of East Point. Single pin mooring buoy. See map page 129.
Access: Boat.
Conditions: New dive site. Long boat ride can be uncomfortable, current on the corner, but sheltered in caves and tunnels.
Minimum depth: 15m (50ft)
Maximum depth: 20m (66ft)
With tunnels, swimthroughs and caves, the area is a riot of colour with many different species of hard corals and sea fans. Every part of the reef appears to be in virgin condition and it is an absolute delight to explore. This exposed area is also known for its turtle, barracuda and sharks. Excellent dive site and worth the journey.

2 PENGUINS LEAP
★★★★★

Location: Deep dive. Single pin mooring buoy. See map page 129.
Access: Boat. Down mooring line to 15m (50ft).
Conditions: Can be current and windy conditions. Visibility over 30m (100ft).
Minimum depth: 18m (60ft)
Maximum depth: Beyond 30m (100ft)
Similar to Site 5.

3 BOOBY PASS
★★★★★

Location: Deep dive. Single pin mooring buoy. See map page 129.
Access: Boat. Down mooring line to 15m (50ft).
Conditions: Can be current and windy conditions. Visibility over 30m (100ft).
Minimum depth: 18m (60ft)
Maximum depth: Beyond 30m (100ft)
Similar to Site 5.

4 THE BLUFFS
★★★★★

Location: Deep dive. Single pin mooring buoy. See map page 129.
Access: Boat. Down mooring line to 15m (50ft).

Conditions: Can be current and windy conditions. Visibility over 30m (100ft).
Minimum depth: 18m (60ft)
Maximum depth: Beyond 30m (100ft)
Similar to Site 5.

5 CRYSTAL PALACE WALL
★★★★★★

Location: Deep dive. North of Sparrowhawk Hill. Single pin mooring buoy. See map page 129.
Access: Boat. Down mooring line to 15m (50ft).
Conditions: Can be current and windy conditions. Visibility over 30m (100ft).
Minimum depth: 18m (60ft)
Maximum depth: Beyond 30m (100ft)
The wall is undercut to vertical in this section and the spur and groove system of reef structure is not really delineated. This is a fairly new site and a superb alternative to Bloody Bay Wall, even though it has a much deeper start to the wall and is more reminiscent of the North Wall of Grand Cayman. Excellent coral and sponge growth and large schools of fish.

6 SAILFIN REEF
★★★★★

Location: Shallow dive. Single pin mooring buoy. See map page 129.
Access: Boat. 12m (36ft) to bottom of mooring pin.
Conditions: Shallow dive, fairly sheltered, but seasonal.
Minimum depth: 13m (40ft)
Maximum depth: 20m (66ft)
Similar to Site 7.

7 SNAPSHOT
★★★★★

Location: Opposite house with blue roof. Single pin mooring buoy. See map page 129.
Access: Boat. 12m (36ft) to bottom of mooring pin.
Conditions: Shallow dive, fairly sheltered, but seasonal.
Minimum depth: 13m (40ft)
Maximum depth: 20m (66ft)

Opposite: *One of the major attractions of Little Cayman is Bloody Bay wall, a mile-deep vertical drop (page 128).*

Although the maximum depth is only listed as 20m (60ft) the reefs and sand chutes all trail off over the wall. This shallow to medium reef is of excellent quality, interspersed with sand patches where numerous rays can be found. In the old coral outcrops sailfin blennies are seen regularly and their comical swimming dance is always a delight to witness. It is recommended to dive this site shallow because of the profusion of fish and superb coral growth – a true photographers' paradise. An excellent alternative to Bloody Bay.

8 ROCK BOTTOM WALL
★★★★★

Location: Deep dive. North of Snapshot (Site 7) off Lower Spots. Single pin mooring buoy. See map page 129.
Access: Boat.
Conditions: Can be exposed with surface chop. Current on wall. Excellent visibility.
Minimum depth: 20m (66ft)

Maximum depth: Beyond 30m (100ft)
At 24m (80ft) looking west, the coral reef wall resembles a man's head. There are big barrel sponges and numerous interesting coral pinnacles and archways. Very good macro life on the top of the reef crest, with nudibranches and flat worms. Schools of Creole wrasse and some large anemones with cleaner shrimps are amongst the profusion of life found everywhere on this underdived site.

9 CASCADES
★★★★★

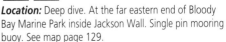

Location: Deep dive. At the far eastern end of Bloody Bay Marine Park inside Jackson Wall. Single pin mooring buoy. See map page 129.
Access: By boat, normally done by the faster day boats.
Conditions: Generally choppy due to its location and a strong current can run around the top corner. Visibility over 30m (100ft).
Minimum depth: Variable

Maximum depth: Variable, wall dive.

There are some spectacular sand chutes and very lovely corals on the outward reef wall. This dive is perhaps one of the least visited by the day boats due to its distance from the shore. The larger live-aboard boats also tend to limit their eastern dives at The Meadows (Site 13). You can quite often see larger pelagic fish in this area and the reefs are covered in all varieties of marine life.

In the shallower areas you will see a large number of conch shells and this is a major protected breeding area for the animals.

10 PAUL'S ANCHORS
★★★★

Location: Shallow dive. On Jackson Wall at far eastern end of the reef structure. Single pin mooring buoy. See map page 129.

Access: By boat and generally only by the much smaller and faster day boats.

Conditions: More sheltered than Cascades (Site 9), but the current can still run off the outer edge of the reef. Visibility around the 20m (66ft) mark in the shallows.

Minimum depth: 12m (40ft)

Maximum depth: Beyond 30m (100ft)

This site features large coral boulders giving way to the poorer fringing reef; this sand and old coral area is inhabited by jawfish as well as anemones and snapper shrimps.

Solitary barracuda cruise the shallows and nurse sharks are often seen resting on the inner edge of the reef. There are at least 12 anchors, dating back several centuries, embedded in the coral reef.

11 NANCY'S CUP OF TEA (MAGICAL ROUNDABOUT)
★★★★★★★★★★

Location: Shallow dive. Along the eastern edge of Jackson Wall. Double pin mooring buoy. See map page 129.

Access: Must be done by boat.

Conditions: This is on the outer edge of the wall and care must always be taken with your dive profile. Visibility over 30m (100ft).

Minimum depth: 7 m (23ft)

Maximum depth: Beyond 30m (100ft)

This dive is named after Nancy Sefton, one of the early pioneers of Bloody Bay Wall, who has contributed enormously to its popularity through her books and magazine articles.

It is an absolutely superb dive. The wall is vertical and boasts huge sponges, but the inner reef area is where there is the most enjoyment. Lots of coral heads and a

profusion of marine life. You can dive this area constantly and still see something different every time you enter the water.

The predominant feature is the single huge coral pinnacle on the outer wall separated by a very narrow canyon from the main reef. This canyon has at least three different varieties of black coral.

12 MIKE'S MOUNTAIN (JACKSON'S WINDOW)
★★★★★★★★★

Location: Very close to The Meadows (Site 13), but further east. Single pin mooring buoy. See map page 129.

Access: This can be done by a lengthy snorkel from shore, but it is recommended to dive the site by boat.

Conditions: Comfortable, shallow dive, little or no current. Visibility 20m (66ft).

Minimum depth: 6m (20ft)

Maximum depth: 15m (50ft)

This is a lovely easy dive where you can vary your dive profile by diving around the large coral block at various depths. This is also very good at night and you can see octopus fairly regularly. There are yellow-headed jawfish and sailfin blennies amidst the coral rubble, as well as many brightly coloured sponges.

13 THE MEADOWS (JACKSON CAVES)
★★★★★★★★★★

Location: Shallow dive. To the east of Eagle Ray Roundup (Site 14). Single pin mooring buoy. See map page 129.

Access: This can be dived from the shore, but it is rather exhausting. The easiest way is by any of the dive boats. The day boats use a mooring buoy very close to the site, but you have to swim approximately 75m (250ft) from the mooring buoy used by the much larger and heavier live-aboards.

Conditions: Visibility is clear about 13-18m (40-60ft), but can get stirred up by the sandy gullies and your dive-buddies! Very slight current, but not noticeable due to the numerous gullies. Very easy dive to suit all tastes.

Minimum depth: 6m (20ft)

Maximum depth: 15m (50ft)

These coral massifs are interspersed and cut by numerous gullies and canyons. There is a 'meadow' of garden eels nearby which may have given the site its name. This dive location is inexhaustible with something for everyone. The sand chutes which cut through the coral heads form gullies and canyons which can be passed through safely, without fear of touching and damaging the coral.

What makes this site so special is that at certain times of the year one of the gullies is absolutely filled with silverside minnows. (Silversides are juveniles of several species of fish which group together in large swarms for protection.) Literally thousands of these fish move as one around you. You can sit back and watch an 'aerial' display of jacks and barracuda attacking the silversides in squadron-like formation. Interestingly, the silversides all leave at night to feed on the outer wall and return each day to their protected gulley.

Yellow snapper are around as usual and the southern stingray (*Dasyatis americana*) is quite common. Amidst the coral rubble can be found sailfin blennies, snapper shrimp and jawfish.

A superb all-round site once you quickly become familiar with the coral outcrops.

14 EAGLE RAY ROUNDUP
★★★★★★★★★★

Location: Deep dive. To the west of Jackson Wall at the main mooring buoy used by the *Aggressor* live-aboard dive boat. Twin barrels mooring buoy. See map page 129.
Access: This can also be done as a shore dive, but preferably off the dive boat.
Conditions: No current. Visibility tends to be around 15-20m (50-70ft) owing to the shelter from the surrounding coral reef.
Minimum depth: 7m (23ft)
Maximum depth: 14m (46ft)
The lack of current and a gently sloping sand slope have formed a natural amphitheatre where stingrays glide by accompanied by barjacks, and large eagle rays forage in the sand.

This dive site has the usual yellow snappers and hogfish around, but in the late afternoon you get a preview of the night-time performance when a manta ray gracefully glides past.

Each night, during the summer months, under the boat's mooring buoy there is the most fantastic display I have ever witnessed. In fact, Little Cayman is the only location in the world where each night you can sit on the seabed, switch on your dive lights and sit in awe of a 3m (10ft) manta ray swooping in and performing barrel rolls in front of your eyes as the creature scoops up the plankton and krill (which have been attracted by the light from your torches) into its cavernous mouth.

Watching 'Molly the Manta' perform in this way would normally be a 'once-in-a-lifetime' experience, but it happens here every single night during the summer season, and has done for several years, (see feature Stingray City, page 134).

15 JACKSON'S BIGHT
★★★★★

Location: Deep dive. Southwest along Jackson Wall. Double pin mooring buoy. See map page 129.
Access: Boat.
Conditions: Moderate current on outer wall, more sheltered on inside of reef. Visibility over 25m (80ft).
Minimum depth: 15m (50ft)
Maximum depth: Beyond 30m (100ft)
This dive is typical of the whole Bloody Bay Marine Park. The crest is quite shallow, 6m (20ft), and it is deeply incised by a ravine which cuts the reef in two. Amongst other marine life, the reef features lots of gorgonian fan corals and rope sponges. The clarity of water on the outer reef is amazing. There is also a mini wall on the inside (which continues on to Blacktip Boulevard (Site 19)) and the area is well known for its squid and rainbow parrotfish.

16 CUMBERS CAVES
★★★★★

Location: Deep dive. Further southwest along the wall. Double pin mooring buoy. See map page 129.
Access: Boat.
Conditions: Little or no current on inner reef. Visibility over 30m (100ft).
Minimum depth: 10m (33ft)
Maximum depth: Beyond 30m (100ft)
The caves are actually a series of sand chutes which have cut through the coral aeons ago and the coral has then grown back over the ravines. To start this dive on the inner reef's sandy plain and descend out onto the wall is breathtaking. I experienced a real feeling of vertigo on this dive - a point to be remembered on all potentially bottomless wall dives. The area is also well known for its yellow-headed jawfish (the breeding season is April-May) and many juveniles of all species of fish can be seen.

17 SCHOOL BUS WALL (BUS STOP)
★★★★★

Location: Shallow dive. Continuing southwest. Single pin mooring buoy. See map page 129.
Access: Boat mainly, but can be done from the shore.
Conditions: Little or no current on inner reef. Visibility over 30m (100ft).
Minimum depth: 10m (33ft)
Maximum depth: Beyond 30m (100ft)

As an underwater photographer, I am constantly on the lookout for creatures I have never come across before and make a point of stopping and looking more closely at familiar animals which one would otherwise take for granted.

One of the prettiest reef fish found in the Caymans is the spotted drum (*Equetus punctatus*). The juveniles have a very long dorsal sail-like fin and a long tail. A black stripe runs from the tail to the fin and virtually bisects the fish. Often seen swimming in pairs, their comical dance attracts attention almost instantly.

When disturbed, they will dash under a nearby overhang, but will soon overcome their shyness and, if approached quietly, can be observed and photographed with ease.

Amongst some of the rarer fish species is the seahorse (*Hippocampus reidi*); the longsnout seahorse can be found along certain sections of Bloody Bay Wall in Little Cayman and fits in perfectly with the bright yellow sponges. It is also found on some mooring chains in more sheltered water and assumes a mottled-rust colour. The bony exoskeleton of this small fish (actually a member of the pipe-fish family) is very distinct as is its horse-shaped head.

Perhaps the rarest of all the fish encountered in Cayman waters ('rare' does not necessarily mean that there are few) is the frog fish. There is more than one species, but the best I have come across – although it is extremely rare to find such a fish – is the sargassum frogfish (*Histrio histrio*), a small fish perfectly suited to its life amidst the sargassum seaweed which drifts in clumps all over the Caribbean and Gulf Stream. The fish has numerous fleshy protruderances all over its body and its fins resemble small feet. It has a large mouth and feeds by lying in wait in the sargassum seaweed, then, when a prospective meal swims past, it opens its large mouth quickly, thus sucking in copious amounts of water and the prey along with it.

Another creature which visits the shores of the Cayman Islands is the sargassum nudibranch (*Scyllaea pelagica*). As its Latin name implies, it is a pelagic creature – a creature of the open oceans, always on the move. This tiny sea slug is only 1-2cm ($^1/_2$ - $^3/_4$in) long and is coloured the same as the sargassum seaweed, a semi-translucent olive brown. Its curious shape helps it to camouflage itself in the weed, where its main source of food can be found – a colonising hydroid. I found one of these creatures drifting in the slight current off Eden Rock during a night dive.

The arrow crab (*Stenorhynchus seticornis*) has a triangular-shaped body topped with a long pointed tip called a rostrum. The long spindly legs are finely striped and the tiny pair of claws are tipped with violet. These crabs are totally unafraid of divers, but will retreat if provoked. They make excellent photographic subjects.

The peacock flounder (*Bothus lunatus*) has blue rings and semi-circular markings all over its flattened body. It has an unusually long pectoral fin which is often erect and is able to change the overall colour of its skin dramatically. This species of fish has become specially adapted to living on the seabed and is quite a voracious feeder on small crustaceans and molluscs. The eyes of this flat fish are set diagonally and it inhabits the sandy plains surrounding patch reef systems.

Another unusual creature is the balloonfish or globefish (*Diodon holocanthus*). This species of pufferfish has very long spines on its head and the rest of its body, and it appears to have dusky bands of colour over its body. It is when this fish is threatened that the drama takes place. The fish will suck in rapidly large amounts of water until it has assumed the size of a soccer ball. When this takes place, the spines lying across the body are extended and point outwards.

This action renders the fish incapable of escape, but it is also such threatening behaviour that it is generally left well alone. If another fish tries to eat the Balloonfish, you can imagine the result.

However tempting it may be to handle any

of these fascinating creatures, you must not do so. Their skin is covered by protective mucus which can be easily rubbed off when touched – thus leaving them vulnerable to infection and death. Besides, any human touch causes great stress to any marine creatures and should be avoided at all times.

Top left: *Peacock flounder, Bothus lunatus.*
Top right: *Arrow crab, Stenarhynchus seticornis.*
Bottom left: *Sargassum frogfish, Histrio histrio.*
Bottom right: *Balloonfish, Diodon holocanthus.*

The reef crest here is beautiful, with all manner of corals and brightly coloured fish. As you descend over the crest, the wall is vertical with large coral promontories; long twisting rope sponges predominate, with Creole wrasse and blue chromis forming a cloud against the sky of the surface. Very lovely dive and excellent photographically.

18 SARAH'S SET
★★★★★

Location: Shallow dive. Further southwest down Jackson Wall. Double pin mooring buoy. See map page 129.
Access: Boat.
Conditions: Little or no current on inner reef. Visibility over 30m (100ft).
Minimum depth: 10m (33ft)
Maximum depth: Beyond 30m (100ft)
The dive on the inside of the reef crest is shallow and sheltered, but all dives along this wall are potentially deep dives, so care must be taken with your dive profile at all times, particularly on second or third dives of the day. The name derives from a 'set' of coral buttresses situated close together, however each has a special look of its own. Pairs of foureye butterflyfish shadow each other over the reef and groups of juvenile wrasse are forever moving around the base of the large sea fans and sea plumes. A very colourful dive.

19 BLACKTIP BOULEVARD
★★★★★

Location: Deep dive. Continuing west along the wall crest. See map page 129.
Access: Boat.
Conditions: Little or no current on inner reef. Visibility over 30m (100ft).
Minimum depth: 20m (66ft)
Maximum depth: Beyond 30m (100ft)
This is wall diving to dream about. It is a vertical coral drop-off with a deep cut running down into the blue. The name possibly refers to blacktip sharks which have occasion to swim past the reef: however, you are not supposed to get blacktip sharks in the Caribbean.

Very good quality sponges of large size stretch out into the current. Squirrelfish and bigeye inhabit some of the deeper crevices. Lobsters' antennae can be seen waving perpetually and there are large numbers of shrimps, hermit crabs, blennies and gobies.

Opposite: *Silverside minnows surround a diver.*

20 THREE FATHOM WALL (MIXING BOWL)
★★★★★

Location: Deep dive. This is the start of Bloody Bay Wall, southwest to next double pin mooring buoy. See map page 129.
Access: Boat.
Conditions: Little or no current on inner reef. Variable on outer reef. Visibility over 30m (100ft).
Minimum depth: 5.5m (18ft)
Maximum depth: Beyond 30m (100ft)
Featuring pristine corals and sponges, the name of this site refers to the depth of the reef crest – three fathoms or 18ft (5.5m). This is a large site with a deeply scarred spur and groove reef to the east and a vertical wall to the west of a wide sand chute that dissects the reef. The sand plain above has a number of coral heads with lots of attendant fish. There is a large fearsome looking barracuda which lies in wait under the boat.

Numerous fissures and swimthroughs add to the interest as well as the profusion of marine life which can be found here. This is one of those dive sites which can be enjoyed by everyone, no matter what the level of diving or photographic expertise.

21 MARILYN'S CUT (HOLE IN THE WALL)
★★★★★

Location: Midway along Bloody Bay Wall, an open passageway through the fringing reef is cut by a large gulley. Double pin mooring buoy. See map page 129.
Access: Direct from dive boat swim towards outer reef wall, descend and swim in an easterly direction.
Conditions: There can be a strong current in this area so care should be taken. There may also be more surface 'chop' so you should dive down immediately on entering the water. Follow the mooring line until comfortable. Visibility over 30m (100ft).
Minimum depth: Very deep wall, so take care.
Maximum depth: Dive guides will conduct calculations for you. The wall in this location is sheer and undercut in many areas, and is renowned for its gigantic barrel sponges and rope sponges. Please do not climb into the sponges because they can easily be permanently damaged. Spotted drum can be found in the shallows under the mooring as well as a large barracuda (see Site 20) which seems to have a permanent station under the hull of the boat. Large pelagics are common at this site. As you cross the reef top there also appears to be a large number of hermit crabs in a variety mollusc shells. This is a beautiful site, but care must be exercised due to the extreme depth of the locality.

22 DONNA'S DELIGHT (ON THE ROCKS)
★★★★★

Location: Shallow dive. West along the wall. Single pin mooring buoy. See map page 129.
Access: Boat.
Conditions: Little or no current. Visibility over 30m (100ft).
Minimum depth: 10m (33ft)
Maximum depth: Beyond 30m (100ft)
All of these shallow dives can be deep dives. The inner reef crest and patch reef are all in excellent condition with profuse marine life due to their sheltered habitat. Sailfin blennies can be found on the coral rubble as well as jawfish; you may be lucky to see the male jawfish protecting its eggs inside his mouth. The sandy plain generally has a few southern stingrays being shadowed by bar jacks which turn an opaque black when exhibiting this close feeding behaviour.

23 RANDY'S GAZEBO (THE ARCH) (THE CHIMNEYS)
★★★★★

Location: Deep dive. Opposite a rocky reef on shore. Double pin mooring buoy. See map page 129.
Access: Boat.
Conditions: Little or no current on inner reef. Visibility over 30m (100ft).
Minimum depth: 10m (33ft)
Maximum depth: Beyond 30m (100ft)
This is very similar to Three Fathom Wall (Site 20) and the different names accorded to the location are testimony to its diversity. There is a deep cleft at the top of the wall under the mooring line and if you travel west you will come across a chimney which drops down to 30m (100ft). Continuing back east you will come to a series of deep spur and grooves with caves and swimthroughs.

24 GREAT WALL EAST
★★★★★

Location: Deep dive. Single pin mooring buoy. See map page 129.
Access: Boat.
Conditions: Little or no current on inner reef. Visibility over 30m (100ft).
Minimum depth: 10m (33ft)
Maximum depth: Beyond 30m (100ft)
Similar to Site 25.

25 GREAT WALL WEST (SHEAR WALL) (TO RINGER) (ANGEL REEF)
★★★★★

Location: Deep dive. West along Bloody Bay Wall. Single pin mooring buoy. See map page 129.
Access: Boat.
Conditions: Little or no current on inner reef. Visibility over 30m (100ft).
Minimum depth: 10m (33ft)
Maximum depth: Beyond 30m (100ft)
The majesty of this absolutely flat vertical wall is superb. Yellow sea horses (*Hippocampus reidi*) and lettuce leaf nudibranches (*Tridachia crispata*) are amongst the many reef dwellers on what has to be one of the best dives along Bloody Bay. The reef top is a deeply grooved spur and groove system all neatly in a row. This just seems to stop at the edge of the wall and you can 'sail' over the edge.
Great care should be taken with both your depth and time in this location.

26 LEA LEA'S LOOKOUT (JACK'S JUMP) (BLOODY BAY RAVINE)
★★★★★

Location: Deep dive. West along Bloody Bay. Double pin mooring buoy. See map page 129.
Access: Boat.
Conditions: Little or no current on inner reef.
Minimum depth: 10m (33ft)
Maximum depth: Beyond 30m (100ft)
The whole of Bloody Bay Wall is superb. This area is deeply cut by spectacular ravines with lush coral and sponge growth.
Each dive site is only a few hundred metres from the next, and they are all similar to one another but with distinctly separate characters.

27 COCONUT WALL (COCO GROVE) (COCONUT WALK)
★★★★★

Location: Shallow dive. Single pin mooring buoy. See map page 129.
Access: Boat.
Conditions: Little or no current on inner reef. Visibility over 30m (100ft).
Minimum depth: 14m (48ft)
Maximum depth: Beyond 30m (100ft)
Similar to Site 31.

28 BARRACUDA BIGHT
★★★★★

Location: Shallow dive. Single pin mooring buoy. See map page 129.
Access: Boat.
Conditions: Little or no current on inner reef. Visibility over 30m (100ft).
Minimum depth: 14m (48ft)
Maximum depth: Beyond 30m (100ft)
Similar to Site 31.

29 JOY'S JOY
★★★★★

Location: Shallow dive. Single pin mooring buoy. See map page 129.
Access: Boat.
Conditions: Little or no current on inner reef. Visibility over 30m (100ft).
Minimum depth: 14m (48ft)
Maximum depth: Beyond 30m (100ft)
Similar to Site 31.

30 MCCOY'S WALL (CORAL CAY)
★★★★★

Location: Shallow dive. Single pin mooring buoy. See map page 129.
Access: Boat.
Conditions: Little or no current on inner reef. Visibility over 30m (100ft).
Minimum depth: 14m (48ft)
Maximum depth: Beyond 30m (100ft)
Similar to Site 31.

31 PARADISE PLUNGE
★★★★★

Location: Continuing west from Bloody Bay Wall. Single pin mooring buoy. See map page 129.
Access: Boat.
Conditions: Little or no current on inner reef. Visibility over 30m (100ft).
Minimum depth: 14m (48ft)
Maximum depth: Beyond 30m (100ft)
It is 14m (48ft) to the mooring pin at this new dive site. The wall plummets vertically with a series of overhangs

A well-equipped dive boat, Little Cayman.

covered in long rope sponges and pink vase sponges. Long sea whips (*Ellisella elongata*) are found deeper down the wall as is the devil's sea whip (*Ellisella barbadensis*). Small clumps of star coral are evident as is the almost neon disk coral (*Scolymia wellsi*). An absolutely superb dive.

32 JIGSAW PUZZLE
★★★★

Location: Shallow dive. Single pin mooring buoy. See map page 129.
Access: Boat.
Conditions: Exposed corner for wind and current, seasonal dive.
Minimum depth: 12m (40ft)
Maximum depth: 15m (50ft)
Similar to Site 34.

33 FISHEYE FANTASY
★★★★

Location: Shallow dive. Single pin mooring buoy. See map page 129.
Access: Boat.
Conditions: Exposed corner for wind and current, seasonal dive.
Minimum depth: 12m (40ft)
Maximum depth: 15m (50ft)
Similar to Site 34.

34 SALT ROCKS
★★★★

Location: Shallow dive off Salt Rocks headland. Single pin mooring buoy. See map page 129.
Access: Boat.
Conditions: Exposed corner for wind and current, seasonal dive.
Minimum depth: 12m (40ft)
Maximum depth: 15m (50ft)
Excellent shallow dive often neglected by dive operators in favour of Bloody Bay. It is well worth the effort to dive this end of the island as all of the locations are underdived and therefore in much better condition. Good corals, and a good variety of moray eels, pufferfish, angelfish and butterflyfish.

The unusual Green mermaids wine glass, Acetabularia calyculus.

35 BUSH GARDENS
★★★★★

Location: Deep dive. Single pin mooring buoy. See map page 129.
Access: Boat.
Conditions: Little or no current on inner reef. Visibility over 25m (80ft).
Minimum depth: 16m (55ft)
Maximum depth: Beyond 30m (100ft)
Similar to Site 36.

36 SANDCASTLE
★★★★★

Location: Deep dive. West of West End Point. Single pin mooring buoy. See map page 129.
Access: Boat.
Conditions: Little or no current on inner reef. Visibility over 25m (80ft).
Minimum depth: 16m (55ft)
Maximum depth: Beyond 30m (100ft)
This new dive site is still pristine and very few divers ever see it. The reef system at this end of the island becomes more complex as the vertical wall ends and a more recognisable spur and groove formation occurs. This is quite an exposed headland and can be reached from the small jetty, weather permitting. Lots of parrotfish and wrasse, but better known for the invertebrate life. This site is an excellent night dive.

South Shore

The southside topography differs in that there are a lot more soft corals and elkhorn coral. The wall starts much deeper, around 18m (60ft) and is very reminiscent of the south side of Cayman Brac and Grand Cayman. Sites are relatively undived and therefore tend to have more fish life and better quality corals.

37 WEST POINT (END OF THE ISLAND)
★★★★★

Location: Deep dive. Single pin mooring buoy. See map page 129.
Access: Boat.
Conditions: Exposed site, wind and choppy surface conditions on top, can be current below.
Minimum depth: 18m (60ft)
Maximum depth: Beyond 30m (100ft)
Similar to Site 38.

38 LIGHTHOUSE WALL
★★★★★

Location: South of West Point. Single pin mooring buoy. See map page 129.
Access: Boat.
Conditions: Exposed site, wind and choppy surface conditions on top, can be current below.
Minimum depth: 18m (60ft)
Maximum depth: Beyond 30m (100ft)
One of the newer dive sites on Little Cayman. As always, these exposed locations are weather dependent and can be seasonal. With the additional mooring buoys placed around the island, there should be an easing of the pressure along Bloody Bay and Jackson Walls. Very good quality corals on the reef crest; and lots of chromis and small parrotfish. Gorgonian fan corals and black corals abound as well as wire coral (*Cirrhipathes leutkeni*). An excellent dive.

39 PIRATE'S REEF
★★★★★

Location: Shallow dive. Single pin mooring buoy. See map page 129.
Access: Boat.
Conditions: Little or no current on inner reef.
Minimum depth: 20m (66ft)
Maximum depth: Beyond 30m (100ft)
Similar to Site 43.

40 RICHARD'S REEF
★★★★★

Location: Shallow dive. Single pin mooring buoy. See map page 129.
Access: Boat.
Conditions: Little or no current on inner reef.
Minimum depth: 20m (66ft)
Maximum depth: Beyond 30m (100ft)
Similar to Site 43.

41 PATTY'S POINT (PATTY'S PLACE)
★★★★★

Location: Shallow dive. Single pin mooring buoy. See map page 129.
Access: Boat.
Conditions: Little or no current on inner reef.
Minimum depth: 20m (66ft)
Maximum depth: Beyond 30m (100ft)
Similar to Site 43.

42 GAY'S REEF (JAY'S REEF)
★★★★★

Location: Shallow dive. Single pin mooring buoy. See map page 129.
Access: Boat.
Conditions: Little or no current on inner reef.
Minimum depth: 20m (66ft)
Maximum depth: Beyond 30m (100ft)
Similar to Site 43.

43 DYNAMITE DROP OFF
★★★★★

Location: South of Preston Bay. Single pin mooring buoy. See map page 129.
Access: Boat.
Conditions: Little or no current on inner reef.
Minimum depth: 20m (66ft)

Maximum depth: Beyond 30m (100ft)
Another new dive site. The reef running along the southern shore is much more like the structure of the spur and groove formations found along Cayman Brac. Lots of jawfish around as well as finger and elkhorn coral. There are large concentrations of small schools of snapper, grunts, margate and solitary porkfish (*Anisotremus virginicus*). There is everything in a dive you could want here. A dynamite dive!

CHARLIE'S CHIMNEY
★★★★★

Location: Shallow dive. Single pin mooring buoy. See map page 129.
Access: Boat.
Conditions: Little or no current on inner reef. Visibility over 25m (80ft).
Minimum depth: 20m (66ft)
Maximum depth: Beyond 30m (100ft)
Similar to Site 45.

45 BLACK HOLE
★★★★★

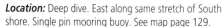

Location: Deep dive. East along same stretch of South shore. Single pin mooring buoy. See map page 129.

Access: Boat.
Conditions: Little or no current on inner reef. Visibility over 25m (80ft).
Minimum depth: 20m (66ft)
Maximum depth: Beyond 30m (100ft)
As the name implies, this is a chimney down through the spur and groove reef, with large cuts in the reef and numerous tunnels and fissures. Lots of gorgonian sea fans, black coral, plate coral, rope and encrusting sponges and very good for invertebrate life. Shoals of Creole wrasse and blue chromis above the reef crest and many species of parrotfish. Good chance to see barracuda here.

WINDSOCK REEF (WINDSTOCK)
★★★★

Location: Deep dive. Along inner reef along South Shore opposite the eastern end of the airstrip. Single pin mooring buoy. See·map page 129.
Access: Boat.
Conditions: Little or no current on inner reef. This can be quite an exposed site with surface chop. Visibility over 30m (100ft).
Minimum depth: 10m (33ft)
Maximum depth: Beyond 30m (100ft)

Below: *Fire worm, Hermodice carunculata.*

Very nice coral formations: most of these locations are underdived. Nice overhangs of plate coral and wire coral. There is an old cannon close to the mooring and bits of old wreckage all over the place. The site is also well known for its stingrays and nurse sharks, and you can always find bigeye and soldierfish in the recesses. The stony corals are absolutely covered in numerous species of blenny and goby.

47 GRUNDY'S GARDENS

★★★★★

Location: Deep dive. Southwest of Main Channel. Double pin mooring buoy. See map page 129.
Access: Boat.
Conditions: Little or no current on inner reef, more exposed outside. Good light for photography and excellent visibility.
Minimum depth: 20m (66ft)
Maximum depth: Beyond 30m (100ft)
Named after Mike Grundy of the Cayman Islands Marine Conservation Unit, these coral buttresses really are a veritable garden of all different species cascading over the wall. Large hermit crabs can be seen jousting for position on the reef crest. Barracuda, Bermuda crab and halfbeaks (*Tylosurus crocodilus*) can be seen cruising the reef and in the sandy areas mojarra (*Gerres cinereus*) forage in the sand for marine worms.

48 SOTO TRADER

★★★★★

Location: Shallow dive. Wreck opposite Main Channel. Two mooring buoys. See map page 129.
Access: Boat.
Conditions: Moderate current. Visibility over 25m (80ft).
Minimum depth: 20m (66ft)
Maximum depth: Beyond 30m (100ft)
The *Soto Trader* tragically caught fire and sank in April 1975. Thirty-six metres (120ft) long by 9m (30ft) wide she now rests in 18m (60ft) of water intact and upright in the southwest of Little Cayman in an area called The Flats. This is an underdived site due to the distance from the dive shops and the popularity of Bloody Bay Marine Park. This may well change, however, due to the legislation limiting the number of dive boats which can enter the Bloody Bay Marine Park.

Above: *Red hind grouper, Epinephelus guttatus, can grow to 130cm (4ft).*

49 DIVERS' DELIGHT
★★★★

Location: Deep dive. Single pin mooring buoy. See map page 129.
Access: Boat.
Conditions: Moderate current, more exposed on surface, very good light for photographs.
Minimum depth: 20m (66ft)
Maximum depth: Beyond 30m (100ft)
Similar to Site 51.

50 HOWARD'S HOLE (HAROLD'S HOLE)
★★★★

Location: Deep dive. Single pin mooring buoy. See map page 129.
Access: Boat.
Conditions: Moderate current, more exposed on surface, very good light for photographs.
Minimum depth: 20m (66ft)
Maximum depth: Beyond 30m (100ft)
Similar to Site 51.

51 THE EDGE
★★★★

Location: Deep dive. Southeast of Kingston Bight Lodge. Single pin mooring buoy. See map page 129.
Access: Boat.
Conditions: Moderate current, more exposed on surface, very good light for photographs.
Minimum depth: 20m (66ft)
Maximum depth: Beyond 30m (100ft)
This vertical wall on the corner of the reef is spectacular and deeply cut with chutes and canyons, lovely colourful rope sponges and many species of wrasse and butterflyfish. Cowfish, filefish, triggerfish, trumpetfish, angelfish as well as many species of wrasse and parrotfish also abound. The pudding wife (*Halichoeres radiatus*) is one of the larger wrasse species on the reef with distinctive marbled markings around the eye. Good chance to see sharks and turtles here.

52 HOORAY REEF
★★★★

Location: Deep dive. Single pin mooring buoy. See map page 129.
Access: Boat.
Conditions: Little or no current on inner reef, moderate and more exposed on outer reef. Visibility over 25m (80ft).
Minimum depth: 15m (50ft)
Maximum depth: Beyond 30m (100ft)
Similar to Site 56.

53 LUCAS'S LEDGES
★★★★

Location: Deep dive. Single pin mooring buoy. See map page 129.
Access: Boat.
Conditions: Little or no current on inner reef, moderate and more exposed on outer reef. Visibility over 25m (80ft).
Minimum depth: 15m (50ft)
Maximum depth: Beyond 30m (100ft)
Similar to Site 56.

54 ROCKHOUSE WALL
★★★★

Location: Deep dive. Single pin mooring buoy. See map page 129.
Access: Boat.
Conditions: Little or no current on inner reef, moderate and more exposed on outer reef. Visibility over 25m (80ft).
Minimum depth: 15m (50ft)
Maximum depth: Beyond 30m (100ft)
Similar to Site 56.

55 SPLITSVILLE
★★★★

Location: Deep dive. Single pin mooring buoy. See map page 129.
Access: Boat.
Conditions: Little or no current on inner reef, moderate and more exposed on outer reef. Visibility over 25m (80ft).
Minimum depth: 15m (50ft)
Maximum depth: Beyond 30m (100ft)
Similar to Site 56.

56 CORAL CITY
★★★★

Location: Shallow dive. Between Kingston Bight Lodge and Diggary's Point. Single pin mooring buoy. See map page 129.

Access: Boat.
Conditions: Little or no current on inner reef, moderate and more exposed on outer reef. Visibility over 25m (80ft).
Minimum depth: 15m (50ft)
Maximum depth: Beyond 30m (100ft)
The southern reef along to Sandy Point in the east is very similar in structure with large coral crests and sandy canyons. The wall further out slopes more gently than Bloody Bay Wall, but is also completely covered in marine life including some very large barrel sponges and inquisitive fish – which are good for photographers. The blue variety of the lettuce leaf nudibranch can be found on this fairly typical spur and groove reef.

> **BARREL SPONGES**
>
> The barrel sponge is among the largest marine organisms in the Cayman Islands, growing to over 2m (6ft) across. Resist the temptation to climb inside – even though you may feel it would make a good photograph!
>
> Although the barrel sponges look strong they are in fact quite delicate and can be damaged very easily.

The mooring buoy line is attached to the mooring pin on the reef. The day boats attach their lines onto the mooring buoy to avoid dropping their own anchors.

HOW TO GET THERE

By air: At the Edward Bodden Field airport at the west end of Little Cayman, you land on a grass strip runway of 1,000m (3,300ft). There are no Customs or Immigration facilities, so international flights are not allowed. The airfield is privately owned and most of the resorts help to keep the grass cut. There are regular flights each day from Grand Cayman and Cayman Brac by Island Air. The aeroplane which lands at Little Cayman Island is always en route to or from the Brac, so those travelling further actually get twice the opportunity to look at the splendid aerial view of the reefs around both islands.

Island Air, PO Box 1991G, Island Air Hangar, Owen Roberts, International Airport, George Town, Grand Cayman, tel 949–0241/6027/fax 949–7044, res: 949–5152/5252.

Little Cayman Air Terminal; tel 948–0021

Pilot Reservation: Little Cayman; tel 948–0041

Baggage allowance
See page 122.

Flights
Grand Cayman to Little Cayman
Each day leave Grand Cayman:
    dep 8:00   arr 8:45
    dep 15:50   arr 16:35

Little Cayman to Grand Cayman
Each day leave Little Cayman:
    dep 9:55   arr 10:40
    dep 17:45   arr 18:30

Cayman Brac to Little Cayman
Each day leave Cayman Brac:
    dep 9:30   arr 9:45
    dep 17:20   arr 17:35

Little Cayman to Cayman Brac
Each day leave Little Cayman:
    dep 8:55   arr 9:10
    dep 16:45   arr 17:00

WHERE TO STAY

Hotels and condominiums are similarly priced, although the styles vary. The older properties, such as Pirates Point, McCoy's Lodge and Southern Cross, house their guests in a type of prefabricated bungalow; Little Cayman Beach Resort has a Florida feel to it, being on two floors, fully air-conditioned, with a poolside bar, etc; and the more modern cottages and villas feature the traditional style of Cayman house, but are excellently equipped with full services.

Each of the resorts has its own restaurant, and meals are generally served buffet- or family-style. Pirates Point is world famous for the cuisine prepared by the celebrated Gladys Howard.

Conch Club Condos, PO Box 51, Blossom Village, tel toll-free 800–327–3835, tel/fax 1–813–323–8727. New development of pastel-yellow apartments.

Lighthouse Point Condominiums, Sea View Villas, Sunset Cottage, c/o McLaughlin Enterprises Ltd., Blossom Village; tel 948–1000/fax 948–1000. Well-appointed but lacking in atmosphere unless you come in a group.

Little Cayman Beach Resort, Blossom Village, tel toll free: 800–327–3835, tel 948–1033/fax 948–1040. Modern club feel with pool and poolside bar. Rooms on two floors of a U-shaped structure. Several fast day boats, excellent equipment rentals and fully stocked shop. Regular instruction courses to all levels of expertise.

Paradise Divers, PO Box 26, tel toll free: 800–450–2084; tel 948–0004/fax 948–0004. Modern rental equipment, well-stocked shop. Instruction available. Next to airport.

Paradise Villas, PO Box 30, Blossom Village; tel 948–0001, fax 948–0002. Modern, traditional, Cayman-style buildings overlooking the sea. Small pool. Self-catering units, but restaurant attached.

Pirates Point Resort Ltd, Preston Bay, tel toll free 800–327–8777; tel 948–1010/fax 948–1011. Older property, exterior looks a bit ramshackle, but chalet accommodation of an excellent standard. Friendly family atmosphere in bar, emphasis on food. Only two dives per day. Those who want more frequent diving are recommended to stay elsewhere.

Sam McCoy's Fishing and Diving Lodge, Chip McCoy's Little Cayman Adventures, North Side, tel toll free 800–626–0496, tel 948–0026/fax 948–6821. Older property, looks a bit run-down. Not much atmosphere unless you are in your own group. Meals served family style. Chalet accommodation.

Southern Cross Club, 1340 E. Merchants Plaza, Indianapolis, IN 46204, USA; tel 1–317–636–9501/fax 1–317–636–9503; South Hole Sound, tel toll free 800–899–2582; tel 948–1099/fax 948–1099. Recently refurbished and well spaced out. Small pool and sun deck next to the beach, good fishing facilities. Laid-back atmosphere.

Suzy's Cottage, c/o Cayman Villas, PO Box 681, Grand Cayman Island, tel toll free 800–235–5888, tel 945–4144, fax: 949–7471. Typical Cayman-style wooden cottage with verandah, in excellent position with great views.

The Village Inn, Blossom Village; tel 948–1069/fax 948–0069. Cayman-style villas, modern, clean and well-appointed.

WHERE TO EAT

There is only one restaurant as such on Little Cayman Island: The Hungry Iguana, part of the Paradise Villas complex adjacent to the airport and situated behind 'main street' overlooking the sea. However, the other resorts all have in-house restaurants and you can eat at these if you book in advance. Pirates Point has an excellent reputation among gourmets.

The Hungry Iguana, Blossom Village; tel 948–0007.

DIVE FACILITIES

Live-aboard boats
Little Cayman Diver II, PO Box 280058, Tampa, FL, 33682–0058, USA, tel toll free: 800–458–BRAC; tel 1–813–932–1993/fax 1–813–935–2250. Has an excellent reputation among live-aboard dive boats in the Caribbean.

    Cabins are all en suite and most have proper beds and not bunks. Centre of operations is on Cayman Brac, but all diving is done along the popular Bloody Bay Marine Park.

Cayman Aggressor, PO Drawer K, Morgan City, LA 70381, tel toll free 800–348–2628; tel 1–504–385–2416/fax 1–504–384–0817; PO Box 1882, George Town, Grand Cayman; tel 949–5551/fax 949–8729. Large live-aboard operating each week out of Grand Cayman.

    First dives are designed to check your buoyancy before the boat travels overnight to arrive in Little Cayman along Bloody Bay for the rest of the week's diving. Boat sleeps 18 passengers with five crew.

    You are allowed unlimited diving (within reason). The boat has an excellent reputation and the safety-conscious organization is second to none.

FILM PROCESSING

Little Cayman Beach Resort, Blossom Village; tel 948–0099/fax 948–0099. Full E-6 processing plus video editing suite. Slide shows take place regularly. Well-equipped rental stock of the highest quality.

    Photographic instruction is available and you can even have a video of your dive vacation made for you.

HOSPITAL & RECOMPRESSION CHAMBER

There is no hospital on Little Cayman, but there is a weekly clinic each Wednesday. All emergencies are referred to Grand Cayman. There is an emergency air service available to the hospital or recompression chamber.

Recompression Chamber, PO Box 1551G, George Town, Grand Cayman; tel 949–2989, emergency tel: 555. The chamber also operates a medical alert flight with Island Air if there are any problems on the Island. DAN – the Divers Alert Network – also consulted, when necessary, for additional help.

Air Ambulances
Aero Care, tel toll free: 800–627–2376; tel 1–806–747–8923. Operated by Aero Care based in Lubbock, Texas, this jet service will take you back to the USA if necessary.

Island Air, tel toll free: 800–922–9626; tel 949–5252. Island Air offer a 30 minute response time with a full 24 hour learjet service with professional medical care.

Executive Air Services; tel 949–7775/fax 945–5732, transport patients from George Town Hospital and offers a full 24 hour service with registered doctors and nurses.

National Air Ambulance; tel 1–305–358–9900/fax 1–305–359–0039. Operating out of Fort Lauderdale in Florida, offer a worldwide capability with a bedside to bedside service.

LOCAL HIGHLIGHTS

Owen Island is a nature reserve with no human habitation. To get there, set off anywhere along the beach, depending on how far you want to swim! It is a delightful snorkel swim out to this island over a beautiful blue lagoon which is clear, shallow and protected. At **Tarpon Lake**, fishing and nature trails are available from the newly opened jetty. The lake was flooded during Hurricane Gilbert and the tarpon now in the lake are a sub-species of those found out on the reef. The edges of the lake are very rough scrub and during the dry season there is a rather distinct smell of rotten eggs.

The Nature Preserve **Booby Pond** is owned by the National Trust and permanent protection is now available for the island's 3500 nesting pairs of red-footed boobies (one of the largest breeding colonies in the western hemisphere). There are also 100 pairs of the magnificent frigate bird. Boobies mate for life and nest from February through to July in the branches of mangrove trees.

Only one chick is hatched per pair and both parents share in the rearing and feeding of the chick.

Car Hire
During your holiday, you will tend to stay in and around your resort; however, if you do want to explore the Island, then a rental car is a necessity, because there are no taxis on the island. It will only take you a half day at the most to explore Little Cayman but it is well worth the effort. Costs are similar to those on Grand Cayman, at around $50 per day, depending on the style and size of vehicle. Depending on the time of year, a car is also useful for visiting some of the further snorkelling areas.

McLaughlin Enterprises Ltd, Blossom Village; tel 948–1000, fax: 948–1000. Sixteen vehicles, including jeeps, etc. Situated next to the airport building, just two minutes walk from the plane.

Bank
A branch of **Barclays Bank** is open on Wednesdays, 10:00–12:00 and 13:00–16:00.

The idyllic Paradise Villas in Blossom Village, adjacent to the airport, Little Cayman.

Parasitism is the relationship between two plants or animals in which one benefits at the expense of the other, without actually killing the host. A relationship where the host is specifically killed is called parasitoidism.

In the Cayman Islands it is quite common to find the isopod *Anilocra laticaudata* on the blackbar soldierfish (*Myripristis jacobus*). These crustaceans attach themselves to the head or gill openings of the fish and dine at leisure on the tissue. Similar species of the animal can be found on a few angelfish and butterflyfish.

Commensalism is the mutual association between two or more individuals in the common interests of nutrition, shelter, support, locomotion or transportation. In general terms, one of the species involved is able to benefit from the association and the other is unaffected. The commensal (the species which derives the benefits) may be external, such as the remora, or internal such as the micro-organisms found in the digestive tracts of animals.

In the Cayman Islands, commensalism is evident in a number of different ways. The remora or suckerfish (*Echeneis naucrates*) can be found 'hitching a lift' from the manta ray off Little Cayman or on a number of nurse sharks. They have also been seen on turtles. The remora attaches itself by means of a suction disc and travels with its host with the opportune intention of stealing food. The diamond-backed blenny (*Malacoctenus boehlkei*) lives under the protective embrace of the giant anemone (*Condylactis gigantea*). This distinctive small blenny lives around the bases of reef columns and when threatened, immediately hides within the anemone's tentacles, seemingly unaffected by the stinging cells.

Mutualism is the association between two different species of animals in which each is benefited. Although equated with the much broader concept of symbiosis, mutualistic arrangements are most likely to occur between species with very different living requirements.

Bar jacks (*Caranx ruber*) form a close association with the southern stingray (*Dasyatis americana*) and can be seen shadowing the ray as it searches for food. When the ray disturbs the marine organism, the much faster moving jack will eat the food species which move too fast for the ray.

Symbiosis can be any of several living arrangements between numbers of two different species including mutualism, commensalism and parasitism from both a beneficial or harmful point of view. Members are called symbionts. The terms symbiosis and mutualism are often equated and this can lead to confusion when describing an animal's habits and habitat. In a very broad sense, any animal which has an association with a different species is symbiotic.

Classic case studies in the Cayman Islands include the Pederson's cleaning shrimp (*Periclemenes pedersoni*) and the giant anemone. These tiny shrimp live with immunity amongst the anemone's stinging tentacles. In return for this protection, the shrimp keeps the anemone clean of parasites and waste products and will also clean any number of passing fish. Perhaps the most surprising symbiosis is that of an algae which produces the colour pigmentation in the lining of the coral animal's tissue. These interesting shades of green, orange, blue and brown are all the result of an algae.

Giant anemone, Condylactis gigantea.

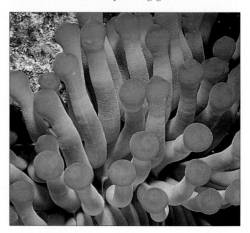

Above: *Southern stingray, Dasyatis americana, and barjack, Caranx ruber.*
Below left: *Diamond Blenny, Malacoctenus boehlkei.*
Below right: *Periclemines pedersoni, Pederson's cleaning shrimp.*

The Marine Environment

THE CORAL REEFS OF THE CAYMAN ISLANDS

The Cayman Islands are the tips of submarine mountains, surrounded by clear, clean, deep water. Because there are no rivers on the islands, and no sewage is pumped into the sea, there is no sediment in the water. What planktonic sediment there is rapidly sinks into the depths. The Cayman Islands' major barrier reefs, such as North Wall, are located far from the shore, but much of the coastline lies within the protection of a fringing reef. This sheltered lagoon environment is not only a safe haven for swimming and snorkelling, it is also the major breeding area for many species of fish and invertebrates.

Coral reefs everywhere in the world are fragile living communities made up of many thousands of individuals and the reefs of the Cayman Islands are no exception. The sub-littoral region can be divided into a number of different areas or habitats. Directly from the shore you will encounter a fringing reef. In most cases this is fairly flat and sandy on the top from the constant battering it has received over the centuries by tide, weather and man, although there is the occasional knob of hard coral or sea fan. In the open sand areas you will generally find turtle grass and this will drop down to an outer fringing reef on the other side of the lagoon or will form a much larger barrier reef consisting of elkhorn and staghorn corals. Barrier reefs grow parallel to the coastline.

Beyond this shallower drop you will encounter a steeply inclined sand stage interspersed with large clumps of hard coral and sea fans, sometimes known as 'bommies', but generally referred to as a patch reef system. The patch reef is generally where you will find the highest proportion of marine life during your diving and any night diving you do will probably be in this environment.

The 'silverside' shoals are found in the patch reef, for example at The Meadows along Bloody Bay Wall on Little Cayman. These types of coral formations gradually take on the characteristics of a spur and groove reef, which is very typical of the Caymans, and especially of the exposed nature of that particular region of the islands. The physical characteristics indicate that the spur and groove reef is the most susceptible to adverse weather conditions. The spur is a finger of coral and the groove is a sand chute: both lead over the edge of the wall in many cases.

Spur and groove reefs always run perpendicular to the shore, so it is always easy to find your way back up into shallower water. The North Wall on Grand Cayman in particular quite often has rough sea conditions, but once underwater, there is no doubt that this is one of the most spectacular dives in the world.

In deeper locations, this spur and groove reef merges into the start of the wall or drop-off. In other areas, the reef systems merge into one and the wall may start very close to the shore. Large coral heads or pinnacles form the ceiling of the wall and mark where the reef plunges into the depths. The outer reef drop-offs are also interspersed with gullies, canyons, tunnels, caves, chimneys and sand chutes.

Shear Wall, sometimes known as Great Wall West, off Bloody Bay in Little Cayman (Site 25) is one such location. There are a number of coral pinnacles and small gullies, but the reef's major claim to fame is the vertical wall which drops from around 7m (21ft) into the depths. It was here I came across my first sea horse in the Cayman Islands.

The corals themselves come in many different shapes and sizes. Remember that what you are actually seeing of the coral reef is only the outer layer - a thin crust of living organisms building over the ancient skeletons of past coral reefs, changing in shape and structure as the environment changes around it.

The largest of the hard or stony corals (the major reef builders) is the great star coral (*Monastrea cavernosa*). Each individual colony can grow up to 3m (10ft) and the boulder star coral (*Monastrea annularis*) which also grows to the same dimensions, has a more knobbly effect.

Brain corals such as *Colpophyllia natans* can grow up to 2m (7ft). Of these brain corals, the species which perhaps most resembles the convolutions of the human brain is *Diploria labyrinthiformis*. Graham's sheet coral (*Agaricia grahamae*) can be found on the outer edges of the wall and Lettuce coral (*Agaricia tenuifolia*) is more often found on the reef top.

Gorgonian sea fans also come in many different varieties and the central location of the Cayman Islands in the Caribbean means there is a higher than average representation of species to be found. Sea plumes and fans are also very much in evidence. Always be careful when approaching these corals because they bend and sway in the current and it is very easy to misjudge your dis-

Opposite: *The yellow tube sponges at Joy's Joy (dive site 29, page 139) are one of the many fascinating species to be found in and around Cayman waters.*

tance underwater and bump into them. Fan corals are also home to a vast number of invertebrates such as nudibranchs, shrimps and filefish.

The Cayman Islands are regarded by many as the third greatest diving destination in the world, only after the Great Barrier Reef off Queensland, Australia, and the northern reefs of the Red Sea. In the Caribbean, the wall diving of the Cayman Islands is second-to-none. This is undoubtedly the mecca for scuba divers in this hemisphere.

A GUIDE TO THE COMMON FISH OF THE CAYMAN ISLANDS

The following is a brief description of several of the more flamboyant or colourful characters on the reef. Please note that a number of species are indeed poisonous or may sting or bite: wild animals (and fish are no exception) must be approached carefully and sympathetically. Any creature which does not move when approached by a diver will definitely have some other means of defence, so PLEASE BE CAREFUL.

Stingray
The Cayman Islands are world renowned for the southern stingrays (*Dasyatis americana*) which inhabit the shallows at Stingray City and the Sandbar on Grand Cayman. These fish can be approached readily, but do be careful of the stinger in the tail. Never grab hold of the tail. The best observations to be made are after their regular feeding frenzy, when the animals quickly revert back to their normal foraging behaviour.

Southern stingray *Dasyatis americana*

Grouper
The grouper family comprises some 16 species. One of the most common groupers is the Nassau grouper (*Epinephelus striatus*), which can grow to 130cm (4ft). The largest of the family group is the jewfish (*Epinephelus itajara*), which can reach 2m (7ft) long but are now sadly rare due to predation by man over the centuries. One of the most common of the smaller groupers is the coney (*Cephalopholis fulvus*). This fish, which can grow to 40cm (16in), appears to be always standing guard on a coral head waiting for a tasty morsel to swim by. They come in various colour variations from a dark reddish-brown to bright yellow.

Nassau Grouper *Epinephelus striatus*

Creole fish
The Creole fish (*Paranthias furcifer*) can be found on the deeper slopes off the wall, they inhabit large vase sponges and are often found drifting in small shoals. Sand perch are also common and inhabit the coral rubble areas of the inner reef and eel grass beds. They build burrows and are often seen 'perched' close by. The fairy basslet (*Gramma loreto*) is one of the reef's most colourful inhabitants - at only 7.5cm (3in) this bi-coloured fish, with its purple to violet front and yellow-gold tail, is a real eye-catcher. They flit about around small recesses and near the mouths of smaller caves.

Creole fish *Paranthias furcifer*

Snapper
Snappers such as the schoolmaster (*Lutjanus apodus*) are often seen around the various wrecks in Cayman waters, and the blue striped grunt (*Haemulon sciurus*) can be found with them. Size 45cm (18in). Perhaps the most common of the snapper family is the yellowtail snapper (*Ocyurus chrysurus*). These inquisitive fish can congregate in fairly large schools and are forever following the divers about looking for tasty morsels. In fact they tend to get in the way of photographers!

Schoolmaster snapper *Lutjanus apodus*

White margate
The white margate (*Haemulon album*) can be seen stacking up on the outer edges of the reef along with the White Grunt (*Haemulon plumieri*). The latter has blue stripes to its head compared to the higher backed pearl grey-blue appearance of the white margate.

White margate *Haemulon album*

Parrotfish
The smaller striped family groups and juveniles of the princess parrotfish (*Scarus taeniopterus*) only grow to 10-18cm (4-7in) while the supermale grows to 32cm (13in). One of the larger parrotfish to be found regularly is the spotlight parrotfish (*Sparisoma viride*). These fish change through several colour phases before they reach the supermale size of 60cm (2ft).

Spotlight parrotfish *Sparisoma viride*

Hogfish
The common hogfish (*Lachnolaimus maximus*) and the Spanish hogfish (*Bodianus rufus*) are both represented in the Cayman Islands. The common hogfish can reach 1m (3ft) in length and is an active forager amongst the sand flats of the mid reef. They are quite often found near feeding stingrays. The larger adults develop a pronounced snout and the first three spines of the dorsal fin are long. They are constantly swimming. The smaller species (*Bodianus rufus*) is much more brightly coloured with a purple upper band fore-body changing to a yellow-gold belly and tail.

Spanish hogfish *Bodianus rufus*

Blenny
Gobies and blennies spend their lives living on the coral heads. They do not have swim bladders so consequently when they do swim, it is only in short bursts of speed. The peppermint goby (*Coryphopterus lipernes*) is one such fish and is generally perched on the hard stony corals. The cleaning goby (*Gobiosoma genie*) congregate in 'cleaning' stations where they wait in groups for fish requiring their services.

Arrow blenny *Lucayablennius zingaro*

Squirrelfish

Squirrelfish and soldierfish are fairly common around the reef and several of the species will congregate together in small numbers in caves and recesses. The common squirrelfish (*Holocentrus adscensionis*) has white triangular markings on the tips of its dorsal spines and is overall reddish in colour with light silvery stripes running horizontally along the body. The bigeye (*Priacanthus arenatus*) is a close relative and is usually a uniform dark red colour. They drift in small groups over the edge of deeper reefs and are commonly seen at night.

Longjaw squirrelfish *Neoniphon marianus*

Bar jack

Bar jacks (*Caranx ruber*) are very common on the sand flats amongst the compact coral heads. They are often in mating pairs and while one stays silvery blue, the mate turns almost completely black and looks and acts like the other's shadow. They are also closely associated with the southern stingray and are seen feeding alongside them. Several species of jack, including the bar jack, can be seen darting into the schools of silverside minnows picking off fish at random. They appear to work together in a pack. Amongst the other silvery fish are the saucer eye porgy (*Calamus calamus*), which can be quite curious about scuba divers, and the Bermuda chub (*Kyphosus sectatrix*) which are often seen in fairly large schools.

Bar jack *Caranx ruber* with Southern stingray

Barracuda

The largest of the silvery predators on the reef is the great barracuda (*Sphyraena barracuda*). This aggressive looking fish is usually on its own and may be found close to the mooring buoys where it will lay in wait under the shadow of a tied up dive boat. Barracuda can grow to 1.8m (6ft).

Silversides

The smallest of the silverfish most likely to attract your attention is the school of silversides. These small fish only growing as large as 8cm (3in) and comprise several species of fish such as anchovies, herring and scad (members of the families). During their juvenile stage Silversides are at their most vulnerable and group together for protection in huge shoals amongst the gullies and caves of the patch reef. They are incredible to witness when they move as one entity.

Great barracuda *Sphyraena barracuda*

Silversides *Atherinidae, Clupeidae, Engraulidae, Carangidae*

Butterflyfish

There are six species of butterflyfish recorded in Cayman waters and two of the prettiest are the spotfin butterflyfish (*Chaetodon ocellatus*) and the four eye butterflyfish (*Chaetodon capistratus*). The spotfin has a white body with a yellow trim and a black vertical band through the face and eye. The four eye has a large eye 'painted' near the tail and is marked with numerous dark thin lines and a darker bar through the eye.

Foureye butterflyfish *Chaetodon capistratus*

Trumpetfish

Trumpetfish are also a fairly common sight around Cayman reefs, as is their close relative the cornetfish. The trumpetfish (*Aulostomus maculatus*) can grow to 1.8m (6ft) and have many different colour variations from yellow to an almost Scottish tartan colour. Its trumpet-shaped mouth is distinctive. The Cornetfish (*Fistularia tabacaria*) grows up to 1.8m (6ft), has a long tail filament and blue dashes or spots on the body.

Trumpetfish *Aulostomus maculatus*

Scorpionfish

The excellent camouflage techniques of Scorpionfish ensure they are found only rarely in Cayman waters. They are more visible at night, when the divers' torches will pick up the brightly coloured pectoral fins as they move off rapidly when disturbed. Be careful where you put your hands - they sting. Better still, stay clear of reef.

Juvenile scorpionfish *Scopaena plumieri*

OTHER FISH TO LOOK OUT FOR

Rays

In addition to the southern sting ray, four other species of ray can be seen in Cayman waters. A manta ray (*Manta birostris*) could once be seen nightly off The Meadows along Bloody Bay Wall in Little Cayman. Here the manta (nicknamed Molly) would perform swoops and rolls in front of divers as she scooped up plankton and krill, attracted by the lights of the divers' torches (see feature page 134). Look closely at manta rays as they swim past you: they may have a couple of remora or sucker-fish attached to their flanks. The remora (*Echeneis naucrates*) hitches a ride on mantas, sharks and turtles and eats any leftover scraps.

The spotted eagle ray (*Aetobatus narinari*) is also found regularly off Bloody Bay Wall. This large ray has a snout something like that of a pig's which it uses to dig and forage beneath the sand for crustaceans and molluscs.

The electric or torpedo ray (*Torpedo nobiliana*) is much smaller in size and grows up to a length of about 1.5m (5ft). The rounded body has two organs which it uses to stun its prey with an electrical charge of between 14 and 37 volts. They should be treated with respect. There is a smaller species, *Narcine brasiliensis*, but this is very rare.

The last ray species to be found around the islands is the yellow sting ray (*Urolophus jamaicensis*). This ray grows to a maximum of only 50cm (15in) and is circular in shape with a venomous spine near the end of its strong tail.

Eels

Moray eels are common around the Caymans and there are two species of conger and snake eels. The green moray (*Gymnothorax funebris*) is the largest of all the eels found in the Caymans. There is a resident beast on the wreck of the Oro Verde (see site 30, page 50) which is about 1.8m (6ft) long. The spotted moray (*Gymnothorax moringa*) at only 60cm (2ft) long is perhaps the most common around all three islands. They hide during the day in recesses in the reef and are active predators by night. They are quite easily approached and have the habit of opening and closing their mouth, which looks threatening, but is actually just an aid to respiration.

The goldentail moray (*Gymnothoraxmiliaris*) is brown with small yellow spots and is the smallest of the Cayman morays at under 60cm (2ft) in length. Its head often protrudes from the reef. The much rarer chain moray (*Echidna catenata*) is slightly larger with a large dark brown to black body with irregular yellow bars and yellow eyes.

Snake eels have a fin which travels along the length of the back and they live under the sand during the day. They are active foragers at night and there are only two species recorded in Cayman waters.

The sharptail eel (*Myrichthys breviceps*) and the gold spotted eel (*Myrichthys ocellatus*). Both are extremely rare, but can be approached fairly easily by divers.

The garden eel (*Heteroconger halis*) lives in vertical burrows in the softer sand areas and quite often large numbers of them can be seen swaying gently in the current, picking off plankton as it drifts past. They can be found near the wreck of the Oro Verde, off Cayman Brac and Little Cayman, but they are extremely shy and withdraw into their burrows long before you reach them.

Wrasse

In the wrasse family, the largest is probably the pudding wife (*Halichoeres radiatus*). It has greenish blue scrolls on its head and is blue to green overall and grows up to 50 cm (18in). There are many smaller species such as the yellowhead wrasse (*Halichoeres garnoti*) and the bluehead wrasse (*Thalassoma bifasciatum*). Both species also go through several colour changes before reaching maturity and the young are often seen in small social groups flitting amongst the coral heads.

Tarpon

The Cayman Islands are well known for their schools of tarpon (*Megalops atlanticus*) and, several dive sites have been named after this aggressive hunter. Tarpon can grow to a maximum of 2.4m (8ft), although they are usually around the 1m (3ft) range. They are unafraid of scuba divers.

Jawfish

A curious fish found amidst the coral rubble is the jawfish (*Opstognathus aurifrons*). It has a yellowish head and a pale body and can be seen hovering above their burrows. The male jawfish incubate the eggs inside the mouth!

Angelfish

The queen angelfish (*Holacanthus ciliariaris*) can reach 45cm (18in) and is particularly striking in colour, with an electric blue body running to gold fins, tail and face. There is also a very distinctive 'crown' on the forehead. Queen angelfish are slow moving amongst the coral sea fans and plumes and can be approached by divers with caution.

Damselfish

One of the most common species of the damselfish and chromis is the sergeant major (*Abudefduf saxatilis*). This is one of those species which lives in the upper water areas and is always there when food is introduced. They have five vertical black body bars and grow to 17cm (7in). They can be very aggressive when protecting their eggs, as can the yellowtail damselfish (*Microspathodon chtysurus*). This small oval-shaped fish has a dark body with iridescent blue spots along the back and a yellow tail.

Pufferfish

Pufferfish and porcupine fish are quite common, as are their close relatives the boxfish. Neither the balloonfish (*Diodon holocanthus*), nor any other species, should be handled, since there is a possibility that their skin might become diseased. The smooth trunkfish (*Lactophrys triqueter*) is another reef dweller and they are seen regularly.

Sharks

Sharks are not common in Cayman waters but the most frequently sighted is the nurse shark (*Ginglymostoma cirratum*). Distinguishable by the two barbells on the top of its lip and small mouth, it is a fairly docile creature unless disturbed.

A GUIDE TO THE COMMON INVERTEBRATES OF THE CAYMAN ISLANDS

Eighty-eight per cent of all living creatures in the sea are invertebrates and the Cayman Islands, due to their central location in the Caribbean, have a very high proportion of all the species found in the Americas. There are sponges, jellyfish, hydroids, anemones, corals, tube worms, flat worms, segmented worms, crustaceans, molluscs, echinoderms, bryozoans and tunicates.

Sponges

There are several species of sponge in Cayman waters and they can be found in large numbers. There is the yellow tube sponge (*Aplysina fistularis*) and the pink vase sponge (*Niphates digitalis*). On the deeper reefs off the wall, you will encounter the rope sponges (*Aplysina cauliformis* and *Aplysina fulva*), but perhaps the most dramatic of all is the giant barrel sponge (*Xestospongia muta*). Please be careful with all sponges as they are extremely delicate.

Jellyfish and hydroids

Jellyfish and hydroids are closely related. In essence, although free-swimming, the jellyfish is a stage of the same type of creature as the hydroid. Anemones are another relative and all are armed with stinging cells with which to paralyse their prey. The moon jellyfish (*Aurelia aurita*) is one of the few animals which is found in every ocean of the world; the Portuguese man-of-war is well known for its long string of tentacles which can trail over 10m (33ft). The more common hydroid is the stinging hydroid (*Aglaophynia latecarinata*). The feather-like plumes may inflict a rather nasty sting on the softer areas of your skin if you brush up against them.

Anemones

The anemones of the Cayman Islands come in many different shapes and sizes. The giant anemone (*Condylactis gigantea*) is perhaps the most common on the outer reef and has quite long tentacles tipped with a purple knob. In association with this anemone, you may find the diamond-backed blenny and several species of shrimp and crab. The corkscrew anemone (*Bartholomea annulata*) is more commonly found in shallower water amongst the coral rubble and it is often in association with the red snapping shrimp.

Bearded fireworm

The bearded fireworm (*Hermodice carunculata*) is another animal to look out for. It can grow to 15cm (6in) and is particularly exotic. However, the fine hairs or bristles along its body can easily penetrate the skin and cause a painful skin irritation.

Worms

There are a number of segmented or tube worms around the reefs, the most colourful being the social featherduster worm (*Bispira brunnea*) and the magnificent featherduster worm (*Sabellastartia magnifica*). Both can be found in abundance. The most beautiful of the species is the aptly named Christmas Treeworm (*Spirobranchus giganteus*). Only 3cm (2.5in) high, this worm comes in a multitude of different colours and is mostly noticed when disappearing rapidly down into the tubes in the coral when a diver approaches.

Shrimps

The coral banded shrimp (*Stenopus hispidus*) is also one of those species which is found in all the tropical oceans. It is the waving of the antennae which first attracts divers to this colourful small shrimp with its long pincers. The peppermint shrimp (*Lysmata wurdemanni*) can be found regularly at night in and around a number of species of sponge. The red night shrimp (*Rhynchocinetes rigens*) is usually spotted at night by its bright green reflective eyes.

Lobsters

Slipper lobsters and spiny lobsters inhabit the reef ledges but perhaps the most charismatic of all the crustaceans are the hermit crabs. The red reef hermit (*Paguristes cadenati*) can be quite wary of divers and retreat into its mobile home. The white speckled hermit (*Paguristes punticeps*) is much larger and can grow to 12cm (5in). The arrow crab (*Stenorhynchus seticornis*) can also be found on the reef edges at night.

Molluscs

The mollusc family is well represented. There are of course the shells: the queen conch (*Strombus gigas*) is the species most favoured for harvest, and the meat is offered in a number of Cayman Island restaurants. The Atlantic deer cowrie (*Cyprae cervus*) is very attractive and can be found browsing on algae during night dives. One of the more brightly coloured of the Cayman shells is the flamingo tongue (*Cyphoma gibbosum*). Its speckled mantle folds up around the body of the shell and it can be found feeding on sea fans.

Nudibranchs

Nudibranchs or sea-slugs are of course very attractive and it is always a rare pleasure when you find them and are able to photograph them. They feed on a number of different animals and algae and are invariably brightly coloured. The Lettuce Sea Slug (*Tridachia crispata*) can be camouflaged by the surrounding algae and is quite difficult to find.

Octopus and squid

Octopus and squid are often found prowling the Cayman reefs at night. The squid in particular appear fascinated by the divers' lights and the inevitable food which these lights attract. Crinoids or featherstars crawl out onto the coral surface as night falls and brittlestars curl around the sea fans and whips. Basket starfish extend their multi-jointed arms into the current and sea urchins vie for space amidst the sponges and corals. Sea cucumbers are a relative of the starfish and you can find a number of species around the Caymans, including the three-rowed sea cucumber (*Isostichopus badionotus*).

Tunicates

Tunicates or sea squirts are fairly common and you can be sure to spot the light bulb tunicate (*Clavelina picta*). This tiny tunicate is found in clumps from a few to several hundred individuals and is generally attached to gorgonian fan corals and black coral. Invertebrates perhaps have the most to yield to the inquisitive diver and underwater photographer. The colours of the animals are invariably bright, many of the creatures are comical in appearance and actions and, overall, they are a delight to study.

CONSERVATION IN THE CAYMAN ISLANDS

Department of the Environment

The Protection and Conservation Unit of the Department of the Environment based on Grand Cayman maintain the islands 'Marine Park Zones'. Formerly known as Natural Resources, it was originally established in 1984 and became the Department of the Environment on 1 April 1993. The Department, which has now merged with the Environmental Health Section, the Natural Resources Unit and the Mosquito Research Control Unit, falls under the ministry of Agriculture, Environment, Communications and Works (AECW).

The Protection and Conservation Unit's overall mission is the protection and conservation of the natural environment, as well as the research and monitoring of the stocks of conch, lobsters and grouper as part of a continuing resource programme. There is also a full monitoring programme on the coral reefs.

The Department is also particularly proud of the introduction of 203 permanent mooring buoys around the islands. The single pin moorings are changed every year to allow for coral regeneration and to spread the load of diver damage. There are 22 double pin mooring buoys for larger live-aboard dive boats and plans are afoot to increase this number. They are already committed to installing an additional number over the next five years in Grand Cayman alone.

The Protection and Conservation Unit is also responsible for publicising and promoting the conservation message to everyone visiting the islands. They use the news media; print and distribute leaflets and posters; and educate the dive guides and instructors.

For further information you can contact the Department of Environment; tel 949-2557/fax 949-8912

Diver Damage and Conservation

Remember that the reefs around the Cayman Islands are protected by law (see Summary of Marine Conservation Laws, pages 159-162).

When approaching marine life, you must do so sensitively and with empathy. Try and understand that what you are looking at is just one small link in the most complex ecosystem on Earth.

It is imperative that you always have full control over your buoyancy because a misplaced fin or equipment console can seriously wound or kill the coral. The average yearly growth of coral is incredibly small so take care at all times.

Turtles are fascinating and graceful creatures, but please do not try to hold onto them. If you find one sleeping at night, stay well clear because to grab hold of it could give the creature such a shock that it may blunder into a cave and be drowned or seriously damage itself and the corals around it.

Pufferfish should also be left untouched. They have a natural defence mechanism of sucking in water very rapidly until they are balloon-sized with all their defensive spines jutting out. Yes, they look comical when inflated and unable to swim properly, but continual handling of these fish will remove the protective mucus membrane over the skin, infection can set in and the fish will die.

The long-spined black sea urchins should also be treated with similar caution. Apart from the very obvious danger of having the spines embedded in soft parts of your flesh, it is also illegal to cut up these creatures to feed other animals on the reef. It may look good on the photograph, but it is wrong to do so. Barrel sponges are another target for visiting divers. Some of the larger species can grow to over 2 metres (7ft) and to climb inside one for fun, or as a photo opportunity, may actually kill these fragile organisms.

There are over 1000 different species of animals and plants found in the near-shore waters of the Cayman Islands. Nearly all of the animals are interdependent and they exist only due to the very fragile balance between them.

The major inhabitants are the corals and algae. All corals are animals and are in fact a cousin of the common anemone. Sea fans, sea plumes and sea whips, although they look like plants, are also animals. Sponges are the next largest group of animals of which there are many fragile species.

Algae grows much faster than coral, (the fastest growing living thing is actually a marine algae). If a coral is accidentally damaged, algae takes a very fast grip on the damaged area and can very soon smother and kill the coral. These two groups are in constant competition with each other.

Some varieties of coral such as staghorn and elkhorn coral are particularly fragile and if an area of coral is damaged (which is part of the marine habitat) you can easily break off a piece accidentally with your fin. The living tissue found in almost all corals is found on and just below the surface of the coral. Destroying this outer layer whether through accident or design, will kill the entire organism. Even your hand on the coral can remove the protective mucus and expose the coral to stress and damage. Brain coral grows about 1cm (1/2in) each year and elkhorn coral can grow up to 10cm (4in) each year.

Most of the fish are also slow in their growth patterns and if an area of coral is damaged which is part of the marine habitat associated with particular fish and invertebrates, the spin-off on the rest of the reef's population can be catastrophic. A 2 per cent reduction in the coral community will not only make the reef look less inviting or 'pretty' to the visiting diver, it will also drastically reduce the fish stocks and the number of other creatures such as shrimp, lobster and octopus.

SUMMARY OF MARINE CONSERVATION LAWS IN THE CAYMAN ISLANDS

Protection of Certain Species
Lobster
- Closed season 1 February-31 July inclusive.
- 15cm (6in) tail length minimum size.
- Catch limit: 5 per person or 15 per boat, per day, whichever is less.
- Only spiny lobster (*Panulirus argus*) may be taken.

Conch
- Pronounced 'konk' (*Strombus gigas*).
- Catch limit: 15 per person or 20 per boat per day, whichever is less.
- No one may purchase or receive more than 20 conch from Cayman waters per day.

Grouper
- Certain areas off the east end of the three islands are protected for grouper spawning: Coxwain Bank off East End, Grand Cayman; Grouper Hole, Little Cayman and an area off the northeast point of Cayman Brac. (A grouper 75cm (2 1/2 ft) long may be 25 years old).
- Only residents of the Cayman Islands may enter these waters.
- Within these areas, fishing by spear gun, fish trap and any kind of net is prohibited. Line fishing only permitted.

Turtle
- No one may injure, molest or take a turtle in Cayman waters without a licence from the Cayman Marine Conservation Board.
- Possession of turtle eggs is prohibited.
- For licensed fishermen, the closed season is 1 May–31 October inclusive.
- Turtles may be taken only with a licence - licences given only to those who have traditionally taken turtles in Cayman waters, subject to the following conditions - Limit: six per licensed fisherman per season; no use of spear guns or harpoons; minimum size 54kg (120lbs) for green turtles; 36kg (80lbs) for hawksbill and logger head; must be tagged and approved by fisheries officer before slaughter.

Other Species
- No taking of any coral, algae, sponges or turtle eggs.
- No taking of hermit crabs except in reasonable quantities for fish bait or human consumption.

Control of Fishing Methods
- No taking of any kind of marine life while on SCUBA.
- Fishing with poison or noxious substances prohibited.
- No one may use a spear gun in Cayman waters unless licensed by the Cayman Marine Conservation Board.
- Spear guns may not be used in any Marine Park area; Replenishment Zone; Marine Park Zone or Environmental Zone.
- Catch limit: six fish per day, of which no more than three may be of the same species.
- Importation of spear guns and parts prohibited.
- Gill nets prohibited.
- Seine nets must be licensed by the Cayman Marine Conservation Board.
- Seine nets cannot be used on Little Cayman or in any Replenishment, Marine Park or Environmental Zone.

General Rules
- Damaging coral by anchor, chains or any other means anywhere in Cayman waters prohibited.
- Export of live fish or other marine life prohibited.
- No effluent or raw sewage may be dumped into Cayman waters.

Conservation Law Enforcement
Violations of any of these laws is an offence carrying a maximum penalty of a CI$5000 (US$6250) fine and one year in jail. Upon conviction, forfeiture of the vessel or other equipment may also be ordered. In June 1993, the Government amended the Marine Conservation Act raising the fine for any vessel polluting the Caymans' territorial waters to international standards (CI$500,000 or US$625,000).

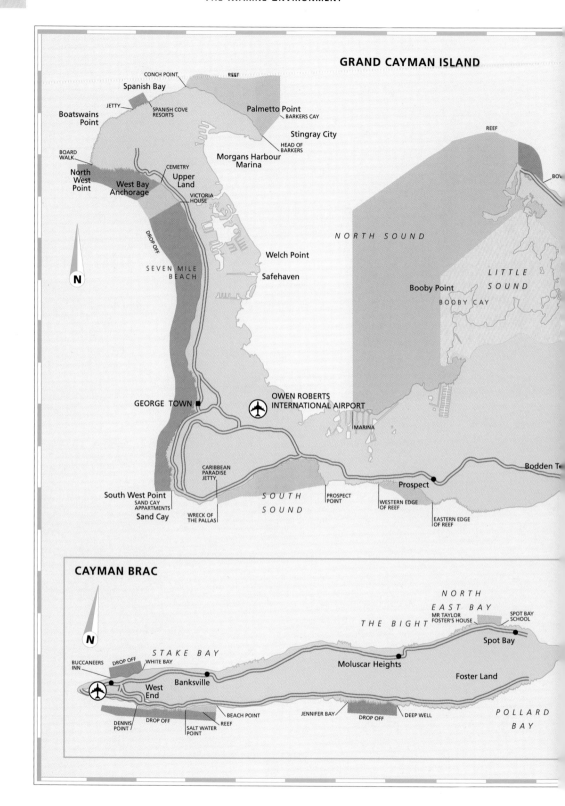

GRAND CAYMAN ISLAND

CONCH POINT
REEF
Spanish Bay
JETTY
SPANISH COVE
RESORTS
Palmetto Point
Boatswains
Point
BARKERS CAY
Stingray City
BOARD
WALK
Morgans Harbour
Marina
HEAD OF
BARKERS
REEF
North
West
Point
CEMETRY
Upper
Land
West Bay
Anchorage
VICTORIA
HOUSE
BOV
DROP OFF
N O R T H   S O U N D
Welch Point
L I T T L E
S O U N D
S E V E N   M I L E
B E A C H
Safehaven
Booby Point
B O O B Y   C A Y

GEORGE TOWN
OWEN ROBERTS
INTERNATIONAL AIRPORT

MARINA

Bodden T

CARIBBEAN
PARADISE
JETTY
Prospect
South West Point
SAND CAY
APPARTMENTS
Sand Cay
WRECK OF
THE PALLAS
S O U T H
S O U N D
PROSPECT
POINT
WESTERN EDGE
OF REEF
EASTERN EDGE
OF REEF

CAYMAN BRAC

N O R T H
E A S T   B A Y
MR TAYLOR
FOSTER'S HOUSE
SPOT BAY
SCHOOL
T H E   B I G H T
Spot Bay
S T A K E   B A Y
BUCCANEERS
INN
DROP OFF
WHITE BAY
Moluscar Heights
Foster Land
Banksville
West
End
DENNIS
POINT
DROP OFF
BEACH POINT
REEF
SALT WATER
POINT
JENNIFER BAY
DROP OFF
DEEP WELL
P O L L A R D
B A Y

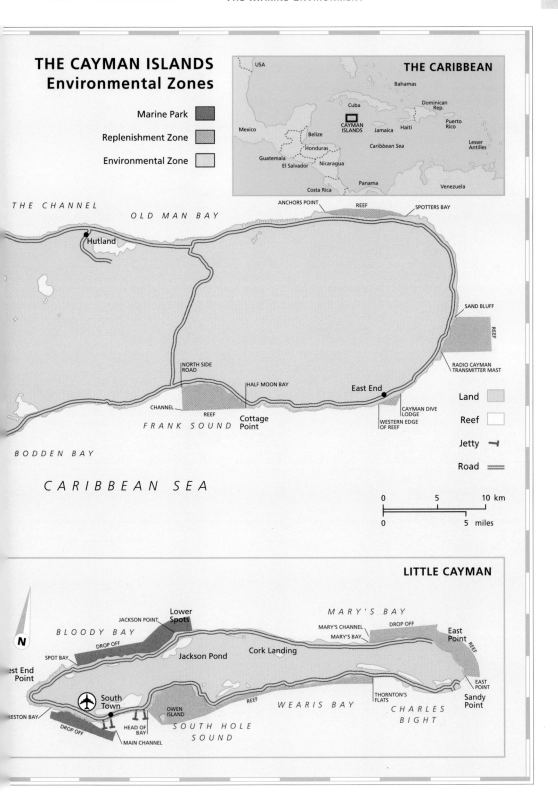

THE CAYMAN ISLANDS
Environmental Zones

Marine Park
Replenishment Zone
Environmental Zone

THE CARIBBEAN

USA

Bahamas

Cuba

Dominican Rep.

Mexico

Belize

CAYMAN ISLANDS

Jamaica Haiti

Puerto Rico

Lesser Antilles

Guatemala

Honduras

Caribbean Sea

El Salvador Nicaragua

Costa Rica

Panama

Venezuela

THE CHANNEL

OLD MAN BAY

ANCHORS POINT

REEF

SPOTTERS BAY

Hutland

SAND BLUFF

REEF

RADIO CAYMAN TRANSMITTER MAST

NORTH SIDE ROAD

HALF MOON BAY

East End

CHANNEL

REEF

Cottage Point

FRANK SOUND

CAYMAN DIVE LODGE

WESTERN EDGE OF REEF

BODDEN BAY

CARIBBEAN SEA

Land
Reef
Jetty
Road

0   5   10 km

0   5 miles

LITTLE CAYMAN

MARY'S BAY

Lower Spots

JACKSON POINT

BLOODY BAY

DROP OFF

MARY'S CHANNEL

DROP OFF

East Point

MARY'S BAY

REEF

SPOT BAY

N

Jackson Pond

Cork Landing

est End Point

EAST POINT

THORNTON'S FLATS

Sandy Point

RESTON BAY

South Town

REEF

WEARIS BAY

CHARLES BIGHT

OWEN ISLAND

DROP OFF

HEAD OF BAY

SOUTH HOLE SOUND

MAIN CHANNEL

Rules for Cayman Islands Marine Parks

There are four registered Zones within the boundaries of all three Cayman Islands. The Marine Park Zone; Replenishment Zone; Environmental Zone and Animal Santuary/RAMSAR Zone.

Marine Park Zone:
- No taking of any marine life alive or dead, except:
- Line fishing from shore is permitted.
- Line fishing at and beyond the drop-off is permitted.
- Taking fry and sprat with a fry or caste net is permitted.

NOTE: Fish traps, spear guns, pole spears, seine nets are totally prohibited.

- No anchoring - use of fixed moorings only, except:
- Boats of 18m (60ft) or less may anchor in sand, so long as no grappling hook is used and neither the anchor nor the rope or chain lies on coral.
- Anchoring permitted in designated Port anchorage areas.
- Anchoring prohibitions suspended during emergencies and by permission of Port Director.
- Bloody Bay, Little Cayman - Special restrictions have been placed on the use of the Bloody Bay Marine Park: no commercial operators may use the park without prior permission from the Marine Conservation Board.

Vessels must use one of the fixed moorings in Marine Park Zones, except that anchoring is allowed in designated Port anchorage areas, and vessels up to 18m (60ft) long may anchor in sand as long as rope, chain and anchor do not lie on coral. There is a mooring system for use in the islands' waters and it is an offence for any vessel to cause reef damage with anchors or chains in Cayman waters, whether or not the vessel is in a protected area.

Replenishment Zone:
- No taking of conch or lobster by any means.
- Line fishing and anchoring are permitted.
- Spear guns, pole spears, fish traps and nets prohibited, except that fry and sprat may be taken by a fry or cast net.

Environmental Zone:
- No taking of any marine life, alive or dead, with no exceptions.
- Public may access only at speeds of 5 knots or less.
- No anchoring of any boat.
- No in-water activity.

NOTE: Line fishing, fish traps, seine nets, spear guns and pole spears are totally prohibited.

Animal Sanctary/RAMSAR Zone:
- No hunting.
- No collecting of any species.
- No littering.
- No exceptions.

For additional information, a detailed synopsis of all Marine Conservation Laws and other regulations governing Cayman's territorial waters is in a 15-page booklet prepared by Government Information Services, Marine Parks Rules and Sea Code in the Cayman Islands; available from Broadcasting House behind the Government Administration Building in George Town; tel 949-8092, and in a section of the Cayman Islands Handbook published by Cayman Free Press. tel 949-5111.

UNDERWATER PHOTOGRAPHY

Underwater photography is the answer for those who want to record their dives more accurately than can be remembered in a log-book or diary. From my earliest days of diving, I could never completely remember every single detail of the dive or be able to describe the intricacies of the colour markings on a species of fish to try and identify it properly. In fact, there were very few identification books available at that time either. In the past 30 years, however, all that has changed dramatically. The world's first amphibious camera for the mass market was designed by Jean de Wouters d'Oplinter and developed by Jacques Yves Cousteau. From there, the industry has evolved to include specialised lenses, flash, and waterproof housings, built to fit the world's most advanced camera systems and technology.

On my introduction to underwater photography, I quickly discovered that not only did I have a recording tool, but I was able to bring the wonders of our underwater world to the attention of a much wider audience. My interest in the underwater world has never been the same since.

For the beginner, perhaps the best way to start is with one of the 'instant' disposable cameras. They are inexpensive and you will be able to get 'instant' results. These cameras are only good for about 2m (6ft) of depth and others are effective to about 8m (30ft), but you can rent a waterproof box from a number of locations and this will allow you to use the camera down to 30m (100ft).

To take photographs underwater, think ahead regarding your choice of camera. You must be certain that as your ability progresses, your camera can evolve into a fully operational system, compatible with as great a variety of equipment as possible. This will include the camera, a choice of lenses, flash and the means to connect it to the camera. If you are unsure of which system to buy, then perhaps the best option would be to rent the outfit from one or other of the two main photo retailers in the Cayman Islands and attend an instruction course to acquaint yourself with the intricacies and pitfalls of each type of camera system.

When choosing equipment, submersible waterproof housings are always an option for your land camera, bearing in mind that you already know how your camera works. They can be bulky, but are strong and reliable and work out cheaper than the Nikonos RS-AF. Lighting is always with a waterproof flash of some type and most are compatible with whichever camera or housing you choose. Again, a specialist photographic shop will supply the necessary advice.

No matter which type of system you plan to choose, whether it be the amphibious type such as the Nikonos or Sea & Sea system, or a housed land SLR camera in a waterproof box, you must always treat it with the greatest respect and care. Before any trip, you must ensure that all of the connections are clean and that all 'O' rings are free of dust and are given a fresh light coat of silicone grease. Also check for any nicks or cuts in the seals. Ensure that the flash fires correctly with the camera shutter and that you have sufficient power to operate. For those with rechargeable flash, make certain that the recharger works and also that it is compatible with the electrical supply on the islands.

Film stock used is generally of slide or transparency variety with film speeds of between 50—100 ISO. This allows for better quality of sharpness and colour reproduction.

For the more instant type of cameras, print film is more usually used to produce those instant 'happy snappies' of your holidays and this film speed is around 200—400 ISO.

As always remember to make sure of your buoyancy in the water as a misplaced fin can knock against the coral and cause unnecessary damage.

Wide Angle Photography

The sight of a diver surrounded by huge sponges against the deep blue background gives a real feel for the great view underwater and this is one of the reasons why wide angle is without doubt the most popular for perspective photographs of the Cayman Walls. Wide angle photographs are also the most published by magazines and, if you were to ask any professional underwater photographer what their preferred lens would be, the choice would almost certainly be a wide angle lens.

Wide Angle Application
- Cliff and reef drop-off panoramas
- Exterior of shipwrecks
- Interiors of shipwrecks and caves
- Divers in action
- Divers and fish/animal interaction
- Wide angle flash and flash fill techniques
- Large Fish
- Close focus attention
- Available light and silhouettes

Macro Photography

Macro photography is a specialised form of underwater photography, where the camera lens is positioned very close to a subject in order to record, at high magnification, a relatively large image of the original subject. I would personally recommend that you start underwater photography with a macro system - it is undoubtedly the easiest form of underwater photography. Frustrations common to many other types of photography are minimised and very soon you will be amazed by the sharp images and vibrant colours that only macro photography produces. You can achieve very good pictures very quickly and steadily improve your techniques as you learn more about composition.

The different perspective that macro photography gives opens up a whole new world of tiny animals and plants not normally seen during average diving conditions. Your eyes get trained very quickly into finding creatures small enough to fit into the format you are using and what were once rather boring dives on gravel beds, sandy bottoms, or under jetties now yield a wealth of life.

Benefits of Macro Photography
* A different perspective
* High magnification
* Maximum colour saturation
* Sharp focus
* Ease of learning and execution
* Can be done anywhere, under almost an conditions
* Easiest to use on night dives
* Greatest return for the least investment

Before embarking on this new underwater adventure, it is advisable to attend an underwater photography work shop. There are a number of centres offering this type of instruction from beginners upwards (see regional directories). Specific classes are scheduled throughout the year: on a one-off basis, both Sunset and Fisheye will provide individual instruction as necessary. Even non-photographer 'buddies' will benefit from the classes, because modelling, composition and buoyancy are very important.

The Beginners Guide To Obtaining Successful Underwater Photographs

1. Approach one photographic technique or problem at a time. Do not try to do everything at once.
2. Record the technical details of each photograph as you take them to find out which settings get the best results (aperture, speed, distance etc).
3. Keep your flash or strobe well away from the camera (unless working in a macro situation). Position it to the top left of the camera so that the light beam makes an angle of 45° along the camera to subject axis.
4. Pre-aim your flash out of the water at first, to

obtain the correct reading to counter the effects of light refraction.
5. Find the aperture that produces the most consistent results for you. Next time you take photographs at that setting take an extra photograph, one either side of that aperture (one stop lower and one stop higher). This is called 'bracketing' and will take care of subjects with different brightness.
6. Get as close as you can to your subject. Close ups have the most impact and better colour saturation.
7. Note the position of the sun when you enter the water. Use the sun to create back-lit shots to add depth and interest.
8. Never take a picture below you, always shoot horizontally or upwards.
9. Pre-set your focus and allow the subject and yourself to approach each other gently and sympathetically.
10. Take your photographs in clear water and bright sunlight if you can.
11. Never use the flash when the camera to subject distance is greater than one-fifth of the underwater visibility - if the visibility is 5m (16.5ft), focus and use the flash at only 1m (3ft), that will cut down the reflection back or 'back scatter' of particles in suspension in the water.
12. Set your camera to the fastest aperture that the flash will synchronise to (unless using an automatic housed system).
13. Attend an underwater photography instruction course.
14. Be ruthless. Really, the only way you learn is by self criticism - it is important to put as much film through the camera as possible and learn by your mistakes.

UNDERWATER VIDEO

They say a picture is worth a thousand words, well what better place than the Cayman Islands to tell that story. Stills photography is all very well in recording that tiny moment in time of a marine subject. But when you are faced with a group of stingrays zooming in to envelop you at Stingray City or watching the underwater ballet of the manta ray or even swimming through a hole in the wall surrounded by millions of silversides, then video is what you need. We are transfixed by the moving image and nothing tells this story of our marine wonders better.

It is extremely difficult to keep up with the progress in the technology of underwater video. Ostensibly, virtually all of the videos are designed for the terrestrial holiday market and the sophistication arises from the various waterproof housings. The quality of the image has improved by leaps and bounds as has the miniaturisation of the systems. The cameras are becoming smaller and lighter with no loss of quality whatsoever. The image produced is now of broadcast quality and there is an even chance that if you are able to be in the right place at the right time to record some spectacular underwater event, it could be used in that evening's television news!

Another advantage is that there is no waste with video. You can re-use the tape at any time. The greatest problem you may come up against is the use of the rechargeable power packs. Change each pack before you dive to be certain that you have enough power to catch that magic moment.

A number of the dive stores have underwater video equipment for rent and you can soon see for yourself exactly which system it is that you prefer. The only drawback is that the format is changing constantly and your modern state-of-the-art video and housing may soon be obsolete.

Both Fisheye and Cathy Church on Grand Cayman offer a full editing suite to include music and titles for your rental video. Instruction is also available through a pre-recorded video and by a book from Jim Church. Jim also offers courses for a number of students on one of the live-aboard dive boats.

Health and Safety for Divers

The information in this section is intended as a guide only, it is no substitute for thorough training or professional medical advice. The information is based on currently accepted health and safety information but it is certainly not meant to be a substitute for a comprehensive manual on the subject. We strongly advise that the reader obtains a recognised manual on diving safety and medicine before embarking on a trip.

- Divers who have suffered any injury or symptom of an injury, no matter how minor, related to diving, should consult a doctor, preferably a specialist in diving medicine, as soon as possible after the symptom or injury occurs.
- No matter how confident you are in formulating your own diagnosis remember that you remain an amateur diver and an amateur doctor.
- If you yourself are the victim of a diving injury do not be shy to reveal your symptoms at the expense of ridicule. Mild symptoms can later develop into a major illness with life threatening consequences. It is better to be honest with yourself and live to dive another day.
- Always err on the conservative side when considering your ailment, if you discover you only have a minor illness both you and the doctor will be relieved.

GENERAL PRINCIPLES OF FIRST AID

The basic principles of first aid are:
- doing no harm
- sustaining life
- preventing deterioration
- promoting recovery

In the event of any illness or injury a simple sequence of patient assessment and management can be followed. The sequence first involves assessment and definition of any life threatening conditions followed by management of the problems found.

The first thing to do is to ensure both the patient's and your own safety by removing yourselves from the threatening environment (the water). Make sure that whatever your actions, they in no way further endanger the patient or yourself.

Then the first things to check are:
- A: for AIRWAY (with care of the neck)
- B : for BREATHING
- C: for CIRCULATION
- D: for DECREASED level of consciousness
- E: for EXPOSURE (the patient must be adequately exposed in order to examine them properly)

- **Airway (with attention to the neck):** - is there a neck injury? Is the mouth and nose free of obstruction? Noisy breathing is a sign of airway obstruction.
- **Breathing:** Look at the chest to see if it is rising and falling. Listen for air movement at the nose and mouth. Feel for the movement of air against your cheek.
- **Circulation:** Feel for a pulse next to the win pipe (carotid artery)
- **Decreased level of consciousness:** Does the patient respond in any of the following ways:
  - A - Awake, Aware, Spontaneous speech
  - V - Verbal Stimuli, does he answer to 'Wake up!'
  - P - Painful Stimuli, does he respond to a pinch
  - U - Unresponsive
- **Exposure:** Preserve the dignity of the patient as far as possible but remove clothes as necessary to adequately effect your treatment.

Now, send for help

If you think the condition of the patient is serious following your assessment, you need to send or call for help from the emergency services (ambulance, paramedics). Whoever you send for help must come back and tell you that help is on its way.

Recovery Position

If the patient is unconscious but breathing normally there is a risk of vomiting and subsequent choking on their own vomit. It is therefore critical that the patient be turned onto his side in the recovery position. If you suspect a spinal or neck injury, be sure to immobilize the patient in a straight line before you turn him on his side.

Cardiopulmonary Resuscitation (CPR)

Cardiopulmonary Resuscitation is required when the patient is found to have no pulse. It consists of techniques to:
- ventilate the patient's lungs - expired air resuscitation
- pump the patient's heart - external cardiac compression.

Once you have checked the ABC's you need to do the following:

Airway

Open the airway by gently extending the head (head tilt) and lifting the chin with two fingers (chin lift). This will life the tongue away from the back of the throat and open the airway. If you suspect a foreign body in the airway sweep your finger across the back of the tongue from one side to the other. If one is found, remove it. Do not attempt this is in a conscious or semi-conscious patient as they will either bite your finger off or vomit.

Breathing
- If the patient is not breathing you need to give expired air resuscitation, in other words you need to breath air into their lungs.
- Pinch the patient's nose closed
- Place your mouth, open, fully over the patient's mouth, making as good a seal as possible.
- Exhale into the patient's mouth hard enough to cause the patient's chest to rise and fall.
- If the patient's chest fails to rise you need to adjust the position of the airway.
- The 16% of oxygen in your expired air is adequate to sustain life.
- Initially you need to give two full slow breaths.
- If the patient is found to have a pulse, in the next step continue breathing for the patient once every five seconds, checking for a pulse after every ten breaths.
- If the patient begins breathing on his own you can turn him into the recovery position.

Circulation

After giving the two breaths as above you now need to give external cardiac compression.
- Kneel next to the patient's chest
- Measure two finger breadths above the notch where the ribs meet the lower end of the breast bone.
- Place the heel of your left hand just above your two fingers in the centre of the breast bone
- Place the heel of your right hand on your left hand
- Straighten your elbows
- Place your shoulders perpendicularly above the patient's breast bone
- Compress the breast bone 4 to 5cm to a rhythm of 'one, two, three . . .'
- Give fifteen compressions

Continue giving cycles of two breaths and fifteen compressions checking for a pulse after every five cycles. The aim of CPR is to keep the patient alive until more sophisticated help arrives in the form of paramedics or a doctor with the necessary equipment. Make sure that you and your buddy are trained in CPR. It could mean the difference between life and death.

TRAVELLING MEDICINE

Many doctors decline to issue drugs, particularly antibiotics, to people who want them 'just in case'; but a diving holiday can be ruined by an otherwise trivial ear or sinus infection, especially in a remote area or on a live-aboard boat where the nearest doctor or pharmacy is a long and difficult journey away.

Many travelling divers therefore carry with them medical kits that could lead the uninitiated to think they were hypochondriacs! Nasal sprays, eardrops, antihistamine creams, anti-diarrhoea medicines, antibiotics, sea-sickness remedies ... Forearmed, such divers can take immediate action as soon as they realize something is wrong. At the very least, this may minimize their loss of diving time. Remember that most decongestants and sea-sickness remedies can make you drowsy and therefore should not be taken before diving.

DIVING DISEASES AND ILLNESS

Acute Decompression Illness

Acute decompression illness means any illness arising out of the decompression of a diver, in other words, by the diver moving from an area of high ambient pressure to an area of low pressure. It is divided into two groups:
- Decompression Sickness
- Barotrauma with Arterial Gas Embolism

It is not important for the diver or first aider to differentiate between the two conditions because both are serious and both require the same emergency treatment. The important thing is to recognise Acute Decompression Illness and to initiate emergency treatment. For reasons of recognition and completeness a brief discussion on each condition follows:

Decompression Sickness

Decompression sickness or 'the bends' arises following inadequate decompression by the diver. Exposure to higher ambient pressure underwater causes nitrogen to dissolve in increasing amounts in the body tissues. If this pressure is released gradually during correct and adequate decompression procedures the nitrogen escapes naturally into the blood and is exhaled through the lungs. If this release of pressure is too rapid the nitrogen cannot escape quickly enough and physical nitrogen bubbles form in the tissues.

The symptoms and signs of the disease are related to the tissues in which these bubbles form and the disease is described by the tissues affected, e.g. joint bend.

Symptoms and signs include:
- Nausea and vomiting
- Dizziness
- Malaise
- Weakness
- Joint pains
- Paralysis
- Numbness
- Itching of skin
- Incontinence

Barotrauma with Arterial Gas Embolism

Barotrauma refers to the damage that occurs when the tissue surrounding a gaseous space is injured followed a change in the volume or air in that space. An arterial gas embolism refers to a gas bubble that moves in a blood vessel usually leading to obstruction of that blood vessel or a vessel further downstream.

Barotrauma can therefore occur to any tissue that surrounds a gas filled space, most commonly the:
- Ears • middle ear squeeze • burst/ear drum
- Sinuses • sinus squeeze • sinus pain, nose bleeds
- Lungs • lung squeeze • burst lung
- Face • mask squeeze • swollen, bloodshot eyes
- Teeth • tooth squeeze • toothache

Burst lung is the most serious of these and can result in arterial gas embolism. It occurs following a rapid ascent during which the diver does not exhale adequately. The rising pressure of expanding air in the lungs bursts the delicate alveoli of lung sacs and forces air into the blood vessels that carry blood back to the heart and ultimately the brain. In the brain these bubbles of air black blood vessels and obstruct the supply of blood and oxygen to the brain, resulting in brain damage. The symptoms and signs of lung barotrauma and arterial gas embolism include: Shortness of breath, chest pain, unconsciousness

Treatment of Acute Decompression Illness
- ABC's and CPR as necessary
- Position the patient in the recovery position with no tilt or raising of the legs
- Administer 100% Oxygen by mask (or demand valve)

- Keep the patient warm
- Remove to the nearest hospital as soon a possible
- The hospital or emergency services will arrange the recompression treatment required

Carbon Dioxide or Monoxide Poisoning Carbon dioxide poisoning can occur as a result of skip breathing (diver holds his breath on SCUBA); heavy exercise on SCUBA or malfunctioning rebreather systems. Carbon monoxide poisoning occurs as a result of: exhaust gases being pumped into cylinders; hookah systems; air intake too close to exhaust fumes. Symptoms and signs would be: Blue colour of the skin; shortness of breath; loss of consciousness.

Treatment: Safety, ABC's as necessary; CPR if required;100% oxygen through a mask or demand valve; remove to nearest hospital

Head Injury All head injuries should be regarded as potentially serious.

Treatment: The diver should come to the surface, and wound should be disinfected, and there should be no more diving until a doctor has been consulted. If the diver is unconscious, of course the emergency services should be contacted; if breathing and/or pulse has stopped, CPR (page 169) should be administered. If the diver is breathing and has a pulse, check for bleeding and other injuries and treat for shock; if wounds permit, put sufferer into recovery position and administer 100% oxygen (if possible). Keep him or her warm and comfortable, and monitor pulse and respiration constantly. **DO NOT** administer fluids to unconscious or semi-conscious divers.

Hyperthermia (increased body temperature) A rise in body temperature results form a combination of overheating, normally due to exercise, and inadequate fluid intake. The diver will progress through heat exhaustion to heat stroke with eventual collapse. Heat stroke is an emergency and if the diver is not cooled and rehydrated he will die.

Treatment: Remove the diver from the hot environment and remove all clothes. Sponge with a damp cloth and fan either manually or with an electric fan. Conscious divers can be given oral fluids. If unconscious, place the patient in the recovery position and monitor the ABC's. Always seek advanced medical help.

Hypothermia Normal internal body temperature is just under 37°C (98.4°F). If for any reason it is pushed much below this – usually, in diving, through inadequate protective clothing – progressively more serious symptoms may occur, with death as the ultimate endpoint. A drop of 1C° (2F°) leads to shivering and discomfort. A 2C° (3°F) drop induces the body's self-heating mechanisms to react: blood flow to the peripheries is reduced and shivering becomes extreme. A 3C° (5°F) drop leads to amnesia, confusion, disorientation, heartbeat and breathing

A Does the diver know:
  who he or she is?
  where he or she is?
  what the time is?

B Can the diver see and count the number of fingers you hold up?
Place your hand 50cm (20in) in front of the diver's face and ask him/her to follow your hand with his/her eyes as you move it from side to side and up and down. Be sure that both eyes follow in each direction, and look out for any rapid oscillation or jerky movements of the eyeballs.

C Ask the diver to smile, and check that both sides of the face bear the same expression. Run the back of a finger across each side of the diver's forehead, cheeks and chin, and confirm that the diver feels it.

D Check that the diver can hear you whisper when his/her eyes are closed.

E Ask the diver to shrug his/her shoulders. Both sides should move equally.

F Ask the diver to swallow. Check the Adam's apple moves up and down.

G Ask the diver to stick out the tongue at the centre of the mouth — deviation to either side indicates a problem.

H Check there is equal muscle strength on both sides of the body. You do this by pulling/pushing each of the diver's arms and legs away from and back towards the body, asking him/her to resist you.

I Run your finger lightly across the diver's shoulders, down the back, across the chest and abdomen, and along the arms and legs, both upper and lower and inside and out, and check the diver can feel this all the time.

J On firm ground (not on a boat) check the diver can walk in a straight line and, with eyes closed, stand upright with his/her feet together and arms outstretched.

If the results of any of these checks do not appear normal, the diver may be suffering from decompression sickness, so take appropriate action (see previous page).

irregularities, and possibly rigor.

Treatment: Take the sufferer to sheltered warmth or otherwise prevent further heat-loss: use an exposure bag, surround the diver with buddies' bodies, and cover the diver's head and neck with a woolly hat, warm towels or anything else suitable. In sheltered warmth, re-dress the diver in warm, dry clothing and then put him/her in an exposure bag; in the open the diver is best left in existing garments. If the diver is conscious and coherent, a warm shower or bath and a warm, sweet drink should be enough; otherwise call the emergency services and meanwhile treat for shock, while deploying the other warming measures noted.

Near Drowning Near drowning refers to a situation where the diver has inhaled some water. He or she may be conscious or unconscious. Water in the lungs inter-feres with the normal transport of oxygen from the lungs into the blood.

Treatment: Remove the diver from the water and check the ABC's. Depending on your findings commence EAR or CPR where appropriate. If possible, administer oxygen by mask or demand valve. All near drowning victims may later develop secondary drowning, a condition where fluid oozes into the lungs causing the diver to drown in his own secretions, therefore all near drowning victims should be observed for 24 hours in a hospital.

Nitrogen Narcosis The air we breathe is about 80% nitrogen; breathing the standard mixture under compression, as divers do, can lead to symptoms very much like those of drunkenness - the condition is popularly called 'rapture of the deep'. Some divers experience nitrogen narcosis at depths of 30-40m (100-130ft). Up to a depth of about 60m (200ft) - that is, beyond the legal maximum depth for sport diving in both the UK and USA - the symptoms need not (but may) be serious; beyond about 80m (260ft) the diver may become unconscious. The onset of symptoms can be sudden and unheralded. The condition itself is not actually harmful: dangers arise through the diver doing something foolish.

Treatment: The sole treatment required is to return immediately to a shallower depth.

Shock Shock refers not to the emotional trauma of a frightening experience but to a physiological state in the body resulting from poor blood and oxygen delivery to the tissues. As a result of oxygen and blood deprivation the tissues cannot perform their functions. There are many causes , the most common being the loss of blood.

Treatment: Treatment is directed as restoring blood and oxygen delivery to the tissues, therefore maintain the ABC's and administer 100% oxygen. Control all external bleeding by direct pressure, pressure on pressure points and elevation of the affected limb. Tourniquet should only be used as a last resort and only then on the arms and legs. Conscious victims should be laid on their backs with their legs raised and head to one side. Unconscious, shocked victims should be placed on their left side in the recovery position.

GENERAL MARINE RELATED AILMENTS

Apart from the specific diving related illnesses, the commonest divers' ailments include sunburn, coral cuts, fire-coral stings, swimmers' ear, sea sickness and various biting insects.

Cuts and Abrasions

Divers should wear appropriate abrasive protection for the environment. Hands, knees, elbows and feet are the commonest areas affected. The danger with abrasions is that they become infected so all wounds should be thoroughly rinsed with water and an antiseptic as soon as possible. Infection may progress to a stage where antibiotics are necessary. Spreading inflamed areas should prompt the diver to seek medical advice.

Swimmer's Ear

Swimmer's ear is an infection of the external ear canal resulting from constantly wet ears. The infection is often a combination of a fungal and bacterial one. To prevent this condition, always dry the ears thoroughly after diving and, if you are susceptible to the condition, insert alcohol drops after diving. Once infected, the best possible treatment is to stop diving or swimming for a few days and apply ear drops such as:
- 5% acetic acid in isopropyl alcohol *or*
- aluminium acetate/acetic acid solution

Sea or Motion Sickness

Motion sickness can be an annoying complication on a diving holiday involving boat dives. If you are susceptible to motion sickness, get medical advice prior to boarding the boat. A cautionary note must be made that the antihistamine in some preventative drugs may make you drowsy and impair your ability to think while diving.

Biting Insects

Some areas are notorious for biting insects. Take a good insect repellent and some antihistamine cream to relieve the effects.

Sunburn

Take precautions against sunburn and use high protection factor creams.

Tropical diseases

Visit the doctor before your trip and make sure you have the appropriate vaccinations for the specific countries you are visiting.

Fish that Bite
- **Barracudas**
  Barracudas very rarely bite divers, although this has been known to happen in turbid or murky shallow water, where sunlight flashing on a knife blade, camera lens or jewellery has confused the fish into thinking they are attacking their normal prey, such as sardines.
  Treatment: Thoroughly clean the wounds and use antiseptic or antibiotic cream. Bad bites will also need antibiotic and anti-tetanus treatment.

- **Moray Eels**
  Probably more divers are bitten by morays than by all other sea creatures added together – usually through putting their hands into holes to collect shells or lobsters, remove anchors or hide baitfish. Often a moray refuses to let go, so, unless you can persuade it to do so with your knife, you can make the wound worse by tearing your flesh as you pull the fish off.

Treatment: Thorough cleaning and usually stitching. The bites always go septic, so have antibiotics and anti-tetanus available.

- **Sharks**
  Sharks rarely attack divers, but should always be treated with respect. More bits from sharks in the Caribbean have been attributed to divers who have handled an otherwise docile creature. **Do not handle sharks**. One of the most common species around the Cayman Islands is the nurse shark, often found "sleeping" under a coral ledge. Other species to be encountered are the lemon shark and the Caribbean reef shark. None of these species is considered harmful to divers.
  Treatment: Victims of shark bites usually have severe injuries and shock. Where possible, stop the bleeding with tourniquets or pressure bandages and stabilize the sufferer with blood or plasma transfusions before transporting to hospital. Even minor wounds are likely to become infected, requiring antibiotic and anti-tetanus treatment.

- **Triggerfish** Large triggerfish – usually males guarding eggs in 'nests' – are particularly aggressive, and will attack divers who get too close. Their teeth are very strong, and can go through rubber fins and draw blood through a 4mm (1/6 in) wetsuit.
  Treatment: Clean the wound and treat it with antiseptic cream.

Venomous Sea Creatures

Many venomous sea creatures are bottom-dwellers, hiding among coral or resting on or burrowing into sand. If you need to move along the sea bottom, do so in a shuffle, so that you push such creatures out of the way and minimize your risk of stepping directly onto sharp venomous spines, many of which can pierce rubber fins. Antivenins require specialist medical supervision, do not work for all species and need refrigerated storage, so they are rarely available when required. Most of the venoms are high-molecular-weight proteins that break down under heat. Apply a broad ligature between the limb and the body — remember to release it every 15 minutes. Immerse the limb in hot water (e.g., the cooling water from an outboard motor, if no other supply is available) at 50°C (120°F) for 2 hours, until the pain stops. Several injections around the wound of local anaesthetic (e.g., procaine hydrochloride), if available, will ease the pain. Younger or weaker victims may need CPR (page 166). Remember that venoms may still be active in fish that have been dead for 48 hours.
- **Cone Shells** Live cone shells should never be handled without gloves: the animal has a mobile tube-like organ that shoots a poison dart. The result is initial numbness followed by local

muscular paralysis, which may extend to respiratory paralysis and heart failure. *You should not be collecting shells anyway!*
Treatment: Apply a broad ligature between the wound and the body. CPR may be necessary.

- **Fire Coral** Fire corals (*Millepora* spp) are not true corals but members of the class Hydrozoa – i.e., they are more closely related to the stinging hydroids. Many people react violently from the slightest brush with them, and the resulting blisters may be 15cm (6in) across.
Treatment: As for stinging hydroids .

- **Fire Worms** These attractive small worms with their clumps of white hairs along their sides display bristles when touched. These bristles easily break off in the skin causing a painful burning feeling and intense irritation. Treatment: Hot water and vinegar.

- **Jellyfish** Most jellyfish sting, but few are dangerous. However, when seasonal changes are in their favour you can encounter the Portuguese man-of-war (*Physalia physalis*): These are highly toxic and continued exposure to the stinging cells may require hospital treatment.

- **Scorpionfish** These are not considered dangerous in Cayman waters, but care, as always should be taken with the spines on the top of the dorsal fin. If you are stung, the pain can be eased by placing the affected into very hot water.
Treatment: Apply a broad ligature between the injury and the body and wash the wound. CPR may be necessary. Antivenins are available but need skilled medical supervision.

- **Sea Urchins** The spines of sea urchins can be poisonous. Even if not, they can puncture the skin – even through gloves – and break off, leaving painful wounds that often go septic.
Treatment: For bad cases give the hot-water treatment; this also softens the spines, helping the body reject them. Soothing creams or a magnesium-sulphate compress will help reduce the pain, as will the application of the flesh of papaya fruit. Septic wounds require antibiotics.

- **Sea Wasps** (*Carybdea alata*) can be found in shallow warm water at night and are attracted to light. These creatures often swarm and stings can be severe, causing muscle cramps, nausea and breathing difficulties. Whenever the conditions are favourable for thimble jellyfish (*Linuche unguiculata*), there is always the chance of much smaller and almost invisible microorganisms in the water column. You should wear protection such as a wet suit or a Lycra skin suit. There are local remedies available for stings, but acetic acid or vinegar is as good as anything. In cases of severe stinging, medical attention will be required.

- **Stinging Hydroids** Stinging hydroids often go unnoticed on wrecks, old anchor ropes and chains until you put your hand on them, when their nematocysts are fired into your skin. The wounds are not serious but are very painful, and large blisters can be raised on sensitive skin.
Treatment: Bathe the affected part in methylated spirit or vinegar (acetic acid). Local anaesthetic may be required to ease the pain, though antihistamine cream is usually enough.

- **Stinging Plankton** You cannot see stinging plankton, and so cannot take evasive measures. If there are reports of any in the area keep as much of your body covered as possible.
Treatment: As for stinging hydroids.

- **Sting Rays** Sting rays vary from a few centimetres to several metres across. The sting consists of one or more spines on top of the tail; though these point backwards they can sting in any direction. The rays thrash out and sting when trodden on or caught. Wounds may be large and severely lacerated.
Treatment: Clean the wound and remove any spines. Give the hot-water treatment and local anaesthetic if available; follow up with antibiotics and anti-tetanus.

- **Others** Venoms occur also in soft corals, the anemones associated with Clownfish and the nudibranchs that feed on stinging hydroids; if you have sensitive skin, do not touch any of them. Electric (torpedo) rays can give a severe electric shock (200–2000 volts); the main problem here is that the victim may be knocked unconscious in the water and drown.

Cuts

Underwater cuts and scrapes – especially from coral, barnacles or sharp metal – will usually, if not cleaned out and treated quickly, go septic; absorption of the resulting poisons into the body can cause bigger problems.

After every dive, clean and disinfect any wounds, no matter how small. Larger wounds often refuse to heal unless you stay out of seawater for a couple of days. Surgeonfish have sharp fins on each side of the caudal peduncle, which they use against other fish, lashing out at them with a sweep of the tail. They occasionally do likewise when defending their territory against a trespassing diver. Their 'scalpels' are often covered in toxic mucus, so wounds from surgeonfish should be cleaned and treated with antibiotic cream.

As a preventive measure against cuts in general, the golden rule is: do not touch. Learn good buoyancy control so that you can avoid touching anything unnecessarily: never forget that every area of the coral you touch will be killed as a result of your contact.

Fish-feeding

You should never feed fish anything other than their natural foods. It is not advisable to feed fish at any time, since it can upset the natural balance of the reef community by leading to an increase in the population of species which accept food against those that do not. It can also create expectations which may have unpleasant consequences for divers who follow, if they are unaware that fish are normally fed at a particular site.

Berg, Daniel & Denise : *Tropical Shipwrecks* (1989), Aqua Explorers Inc., New York

Cohen, Shlomo & Roni : *Cayman Divers Guide* (2nd edn 1991), Seapen, Israel

Colin, Dr Patrick I. : *Caribbean Reef Invertebrates and Plants* (1978), T.F.H. Publications Ltd

Humann, Paul : *Reef Coral Identification* (1993), New World Publications, Florida

Humann, Paul : *Reef Creature Identification* (1993), New World Publications, Florida

Loggins, R.M. : *A Diver's Guide to Little Cayman Island* (1993), Recondite Publishing, Grand Cayman

Roessler, Carl : *The Cayman Islands* (2nd edn 1993), Gulf Publishing Co., Texas

Sefton, Nancy : *Dive Cayman* (1981), Franklin Press, Miami, Florida

Sefton, Nancy & Webster, Steven K. : *Caribbean Reef Invertibrates* (1986), Sea Challengers, California

Vine, Peter : *Caribbean Divers' Guide* (1991), Immel Publishing, London

Caribbean Islands Handbook (1992), Trade & Travel Publications Ltd., Bath

Cayman Islands Annual Report 1993, published by the Government of the Cayman Islands

Cayman Islands Yearbook 1994, published annually by Cayman Free Press

Diving in the Cayman Islands: Economic Impact Study by Madigan Pratt & Associates (1995)

Encyclopaedia Britannica (15th edition), Encyclopaedia Britannica Inc.

Marine Park Rules and Sea Code in the Cayman Islands (1994), Cayman Islands Government Information Services

What To Do Cayman (Volume 13, 1995), Tourist Publications (Cayman) Ltd.

Index